P9-BYV-919

CERRO COSO
COMMUNITY COLLEGE
LIBRARY

Colleges of Choice

CERRO COSO
COMMUNITY COLLEGE
LIBRARY

Colleges of Choice

The Enabling Impact of the Community College

Edited by
JUDITH S. EATON

American Council on Education • Macmillan Publishing Company
NEW YORK
Collier Macmillan Publishers
LONDON

CERRO COSO
COMMUNITY COLLEGE
LIBRARY

Copyright © 1988 by American Council on Education and
Macmillan Publishing Company,
A Division of Macmillan, Inc.

The American Council on Education/Macmillan Series in Higher Education

All rights reserved. No part of this book may be reproduced or transmitted in any form or by any means, electronic or mechanical, including photocopying, recording, or by any information storage and retrieval system, without permission in writing from the Publisher.

Macmillan Publishing Company
866 Third Avenue, New York, N.Y. 10022

Collier Macmillan Canada, Inc.

Library of Congress Catalog Card Number: 87-17188

Printed in the United States of America

printing number
1 2 3 4 5 6 7 8 9 10

Library of Congress Cataloging in Publication Data

Colleges of choice : the enabling impact of the community college/
  [edited by] Judith S. Eaton.
      p.   cm.—(The American Council on Education/Macmillan series
  in higher education)
  Includes index.
  ISBN 0-02-908790-2
  1. Community colleges—United States. 2. Community colleges—
  United States—Administration.   I. Eaton, Judith S.   II. Series.
  LB2328. C578   1987
  378'.052—dc19   87-17188
                                             CIP

Contents

Contributors

Richard L. Alfred is associate professor of higher education, director of the Community College Program in the Center for the Study of Higher Education, and chair of the Program in Higher and Adult Continuing Education at the University of Michigan.

Alison R. Bernstein is program officer, Education and Culture Program, The Ford Foundation. She is co-author (with Virginia Smith) of *The Impersonal Campus: Options for Reorganizing Colleges to Increase Student Involvement, Learning, and Development* (1979).

Robert Birnbaum is professor of higher and adult education, Teachers College, Columbia University, and associate director, National Center for Postsecondary Governance and Finance. He is the author of *Creative Academic Bargaining* (1980) and *Maintaining Diversity in Higher Education* (1983).

David W. Breneman is president of Kalamazoo College, coauthor of *Financing Community Colleges* (1981), and former Senior Fellow, Economics Studies Program, The Brookings Institution.

James L. Fisher is author of *The Power of the Presidency* (1984), former president of the Council for the Advancement and Support of Education, former president of Towson State University and founder & chief executive of James L. Fisher, Ltd.

Richard K. Greenfield is executive director, College Consortium for International Studies, and former chancellor, St. Louis Community College District.

Eileen Kuhns is coordinator and associate professor, Education Administration, The Catholic University of America. She has served as dean, executive dean, and academic vice-president at two- and four-year colleges.

David Macarov is professor at the Paul Baerwald School of Social Work, The Hebrew University, Jerusalem. He is the author of *Incentives to Work* (1970), *The Design of Social Welfare* (1978), *Work and Welfare: The Unholy Alliance* (1980), *Worker Productivity: Myths and Reality* (1980), and numerous scholarly articles.

S. V. Martorana is professor of education, College of Education, and senior research associate, Center for the Study of Higher Education of the Pennsylvania State University. He has published extensively on community college finance, governance, and planning.

Robert H. McCabe is president of Miami Dade Community College in Florida. He was 1986–87 president of the League for Innovation, vice-chair of the College Board, and holds seats on the Southern Regional Education Board and the Council of Financial Aid to Education.

Charlene Nunley is vice-president for planning and advancement of Montgomery College in Maryland. Her background includes work in institutional research, planning, and management.

Leonard P. Oliver directs Oliver Associates, a public policy consulting firm in Washington, D.C. He is also an associate of the Kettering Foundation and executive director of the League for the Humanities.

Richard C. Richardson, Jr., is professor of higher education at Arizona State University and associate director of the Center for Postsecondary Governance and Finance. He is the author of many publications, including *Literacy in the Open Access College* (1983) and *Students in Urban Settings: Achieving the Baccalaureate* (1985).

Preface

Good judgment about change in higher education is not easy to exercise. The varied dimensions of the enterprise are demanding—calling for the courage to be conservative about change, the character to act on change where needed, and the good sense to distinguish between these circumstances. The words which describe the intent of the higher education enterprise have not varied greatly over the years, but the education to which these words refer has altered significantly. An "educated person" in 1900 is different from that person in 1987. Phrases such as "career education" or "civic education" now have referents distinct from those of an earlier era.

There are other dilemmas as well. The higher education enterprise guards traditional values yet assumes responsibility for leadership in innovation. We are the repository of what is treasured from the past yet in charge of thoughtful presentation of values for the future. Two- and four-year colleges and universities, public and private, operate among conflicting societal expectations.

The focus of this book is community colleges. Will the unique qualities that produced the remarkable growth in community college education in mid-century be adequate to sustain the future effectiveness of these institutions? Or, will community colleges undergo radical changes during the next twenty years? What are thoughtful hypotheses about community college survival and success? Will community colleges insist upon retaining now-traditional community college values in their approach to the future? Is this wise?

Consider our present need for talented and thoughtful leadership. Consider our present need to gauge our intellectual depth and substance as institutions of higher learning. Consider the early orientation of community colleges—"outside of," "other than"—the newcomer to higher education. The early days are gone. Although accepted with some reluctance, we have become central to genuine realization of educational opportunity. Consider the implications of this crucial change in position for the values that undergird our vision and for our commitment as a learning community.

The contributors to this volume have attempted to address the important issues of community college values, collegiate commitment, and leadership. They address a sense of the future. They do not always agree and have varying visions of the community college. On the other hand, they sometimes come to strikingly similar conclusions from their varying points of departure. Their differences are enlightening. Their similarities are thought-provoking. Above all, the contributors are clear that we are undergoing an important shift in values and thinking about community college education—an enterprise about which we all deeply care.

Colleges of Choice

Overview: Colleges of Choice

JUDITH S. EATON

*It seems clear now, however, that our public, our stu-
dents, and our faculty value access—but they also value
collegiate identification.*

This is a book about change. It is concerned to further establish
community colleges as institutions of choice rather than colleges of
convenience—some would say colleges of last resort. This calls for
some reorientation of community colleges in order that they are
central participants in the higher-education enterprise of the future.

This work also attempts to respond to a sense of urgency reflected in fundamental questioning of effectiveness, mission, and

1

purpose on the part of virtually all colleges and universities.
Higher-education institutions are evaluating their delivery of services and setting of standards. They are considering the clientele
directly involved in attempting to benefit from these services and
the general society that is significantly affected by the successes
and failures of higher education. Our important questions include:

- Should the extent and scope of higher education services to
  which we committed ourselves in the 1960s remain a *public-
  policy priority* for the future?

- What are the *purposes of higher education* for the future? Do
  they differ from higher-education purposes of the past? Is
  what we have traditionally meant by "education" radically
  changing?

- Can we preserve an egalitarian commitment to educational
  opportunity and preserve *defensible standards of excellence* in
  higher education?

This is a chapter about differences. We will examine important
community-college values of the past and suggest that alternative
values be emphasized for the future. We will consider roles and
responses for community colleges in relation to the values for which
we argue. We will offer some observations about the higher-
education community and especially community colleges in relation to the questions raised above.

A Framework of Values

Within higher education, community colleges emerged in the 1960s
as alternatives to the more traditional higher-education options
available in the society. They were in many ways intentionally
peripheral to the educational enterprise as carried out by four-year
colleges and universities. The organizing principles of these colleges were (1) commitment to be different from traditional higher
education through emphasis on access, convenience, low cost, and
location of services; (2) emphasis on two-year paraprofessional

training; (3) reliance on quantitative growth as adequate to measure success; (4) commitment to personalized education through emphasis on teaching as the primary institutional activity; and (5) commitment to civic education as reflected in efforts to diminish the institutional barriers between these colleges and the communities they served through community-based education.

The community colleges responded to the need for training of paraprofessionals in a growing economy through "terminal" occupational education. They responded to the demand for transfer education through emphasis on the associate of arts degree. At that time, it made sense to identify the associate of arts or applied science degrees as points of critical student accomplishment, "end" points. We did not talk about multiple-career lives and intermittent education and the need for an ongoing, student–school partnership. We envisioned education as a preparatory activity. Transfer students without degrees were viewed with some suspicion as compared to those who obtained degrees and transferred. We saw institutional relationships at the two- and four-year level as controlled by obstacles and did not envision a flow of educational experience over many years between and among our colleges and universities.

It is interesting to note what these early organizing principles did not stress. The intellectual foundation of the community-college enterprise was not a subject of special attention. Community colleges either assumed that this was understood by the population interested in higher education or did not require emphasis. Community colleges explicitly rejected selective admission requirements. The collegiate function was discussed almost exclusively as a transfer activity. These colleges sought to go beyond accessibility to availability and thus did not rely heavily on traditional campus life and traditional campus facilities.

Even through the first half of the 1980s, community colleges have not varied in practice from these organizing principles. The American Association of Community and Junior Colleges identifies 1,221 community colleges as serving a predominantly occupationally oriented clientele. Stress is placed upon access, service, convenience, and low cost (AACJC, 1986). While there is discussion of quality and excellence, the AACJC language reflects little attention paid to the collegiate function, to intellectual inquiry, and to the notion of a generally educated population. Its members are struggling in their use of "older" tools for "newer" problems such as (1) part-time, nondegree students for whom degree programs are not meaningful forms of educational direction; (2) minority enrollments that call for reassessment of the appropriateness of presently structured educational experiences; (3) an era of quality in which there appears to be consensus in the higher-education community that access without educational equity is not educational opportunity; and (4) a growing acknowledgment that individual effectiveness in our society requires conceptual skills that go beyond the training dimension of many occupational programs and beyond the skills we are able to impart through developmental and literacy programs.

All of this leads one to suggest that the organizing principles upon which an emerging community-college profile will be based should be at some variance with the prevailing traditions reflective of our origins and our past success. This does not involve a dramatic restructuring of community college mission and operation. It does require the establishment of a contemporary framework of values by which the future "work" of the community college will be organized, understood, and sanctioned. If adopted, it will provide coherence and meaning for future community-college efforts.

Three forms of valuing define this framework for the emerging community college:

- Valuing an expanded collegiate identity;

- Valuing context-defined, quality leadership;

- Valuing an institutional attitude incorporating a future orientation.

Collegiate identity speaks to our valuing the intellectual enterprise and reflecting that valuing in all we do. It speaks to the centrality of teaching and learning in our institutions. More narrowly, this collegiate dimension is the informing principle by which we can give structure and meaning to our instructional function. *More broadly, it describes a climate of opinion, a context for sanc-*

tioning all other efforts. It is important to realize that which the renewed emphasis on the collegiate is *not:* We are not calling once again for assertion of the primacy of the transfer function and ascendancy of the liberal-arts curriculum at the price of diminishing other programs and services.

Our second valuing, leadership, refers to the skills and abilities we need from the individuals charged with intellectual and organizational responsibility for students. It is important that leadership effectiveness be described not through the identification of desirable and timeless traits or behaviors, but in language that reflects the strengths and characteristics needed for institutional effectiveness in these times.

The third and final element of the framework is an orientation to the future while attending to present needs. This speaks to the prevailing approach of an institution in its internal and external relationships. It has to do with the attitudes toward change within organizations. Thus, the framework of values for the emerging community-college profile urges a special commitment to the central role of intellectual inquiry (the teaching and learning experience), to the quality and style of the people needed for our efforts (the leadership experience), and to the prevailing institutional climate in which our efforts are undertaken (the culture experience).

Why these values and not others? The consideration of these values is essential to the further establishment of our institutions as colleges of choice. In an effort to meaningfully respond to the present-day challenges to higher education, community colleges face issues of institutional identity, quality, and effectiveness which undergird our concerns about scope and adequacy of service and mission. Identity, quality, and effectiveness require attention in order that intelligent decisions are made about curriculum, faculty, and facilities. Identification of these values is an effort to emphasize those responsibilities of greatest importance at this juncture in the life of community colleges. This does not mean that other values are dismissed as unimportant or unacknowledged. It does mean that values that attract our attention as important are context dependent and time related. In the 1960s and 1970s, greater importance was placed on the valuing of access, valuing our differences from traditional education, valuing growth as a mode of ensuring democratic education, and valuing entrepreneurial leadership to meet these needs. This did not mean that all other values were explicitly rejected. These other values were simply not the focus of the same significant attention at that time.

Institutions and organizations can sustain change in a variety of ways. One method is to assume the viability of past assumptions and past practice and to create change through variation on that which has been effective in the past. An alternative is to realize that however valuable past thinking and action have been, there can be changes in circumstances facing organizations that diminish the benefit of these same approaches for the future. As a higher-education enterprise of major importance, we are at a point where a fresh approach to first principles is essential. We need guiding principles for a differently perceived and valued higher-education enterprise.

Commitment to the Collegiate Enterprise, Leadership and the Future

The Collegiate Enterprise

The collegiate identity of our institutions has frequently been the subject of controversy among community-college leaders and the cause of frustration among faculty. When we speak of collegiate identity, we are talking primarily about campus-based, classroom-oriented, professional teaching and learning with an intellectually defensible foundation. The collegiate purpose of the community college has historically been identified with its academic function: the humanities; the social sciences; the natural sciences; and the arts. Controversy emerges between those who perceive the academic function as education with an avowed practical purpose and those who disagree. Debate continues between those who see the liberal arts as vocationally important and those who do not. This is the case in spite of the vocational role historically enjoyed by the liberal arts.

In advocating an expanded collegiate identity for community colleges, we are going beyond the traditional dilemma surrounding academic focus and even beyond concern for the traditional transfer function. The expanded collegiate commitment is more comprehensive: It intends that (1) we fully recognize our comprehensive *intellectual responsibility* within higher education; (2) we purposefully encourage an institutional image reflecting *the central role of higher learning* in order that the public values and understands what we are; and (3) we set requirements for educational content in all programs that reflect any of many defensible approaches to general education. Expanded collegiate identity calls for an institutional image in which intellectual activity is viewed as primary in relation to other activities such as training, service, and support. These take on meaning and worth in relation to institutional commitment to intellectual activity.

These other functions of our colleges including remedial and literacy efforts, public-private training efforts, and community-service commitments are strengthened as a result of strengthening community-college collegiate identity. Why? It is because the public expects colleges to be collegiate and fails to respect those that are not; because community-college student pride is related to collegiate identification; because faculty pride is strongly dependent on a sense of the collegiate; and because the higher-education community fails to respect higher-education efforts that ignore this basic valuing. An expanded collegiate identity will strengthen historically atypical and nontraditional community-college commitments to access and availability. In the past, we have operated from an unstated assumption that we should signal our desirable differences through institutional behaviors that were not standard for collegiate behavior. This, in our view, reinforced the notion of access. It seems clear now, however, that our public, our students, and our faculty value access—but they also value collegiate identification. An expanded collegiate identity is a potentially powerful friend to the community-college mission—not its enemy.

To expand the collegiate identity of our institutions in this new context means:

- That associate-degree programs *of all kinds* need to be evaluated in the context of their potential for *achieving the baccalaureate;*

- That the "terminal" role of community-college occupational education is *less* important, and that the concept of "career-transfer" education, whether through obtaining additional degrees or recurring education opportunities, is *more* important;

- That lifetime education needs a *valued intellectual context* in order to be respected by the anticipated large numbers of returning, educated adults;

- That students require identification with a respected community of learning in order that they value their community-college education and themselves as students;

- That services that support direct instruction derive their meaning in relation to intellectual inquiry as fundamental to institutional purpose.

Without valuing high standards of cognitive activity, conceptual skill, intellectual curiosity, and academic tradition, we fail to bring coherence to our purpose and activity. The centrality of a self-conscious approach to cognitive and affective learning defines higher education and its hope. A college is a college only if it is a community of learning. A community of learning values a tradition of enabling enlightenment. Personal-support services, social services, community activity, and technical training all relate to the core of the community of learning, but they are not truly at the heart of the enterprise.

The Leadership Responsibility

The leadership responsibility in community colleges had been effectively carried out through meaningful management of growth: enrollments, facilities, budgets, and staff. This lasted until the early 1980s. Growth brought its unique set of problems: a diversified student population; increased costs; community criticism concerning institutional availability and institutional effectiveness; and growing reliance on part-time staff. Growth produced pressure for more and more commitments to the service area of a college.

Community-college administrators felt that they were providing leadership when

- they effectively nurtured growth;
- they tried to assist faculty in dealing with student diversification;
- they created partnerships of all kinds: local, regional, and national partnerships particularly emphasizing education for work;
- they frequently and vigorously spoke to the notion of America's community colleges as "Democracy's College"—fulfillment of the American dream of educational opportunity.

They were successful.

Today, however, we are managing stabilization and even decline of enrollment and resources. Student diversification has its negative dimensions as reflected in burned-out faculty, high attrition rates, and differential student-success rates that, unfortunately, can be correlated with racial and socioeconomic background. Partnerships abound; their success is far from confirmed. With more and more colleges providing for open admission for at least some of their student populations, a case can be made that opportunity for higher education is no longer the monopoly of the community college. If leadership calls for responsiveness to the circumstances in which it is exercised, then leadership in community colleges will undergo change.

Leadership in developing the future of community colleges requires attention to the three fundamental questions raised at the beginning of this chapter. It is expected to be activist in nature; it should have an agenda. It requires the capacity to value the past, but to go beyond it. It calls for creative solutions to persistent problems. It calls for courageous envisioning of that which is untried. It calls for the ability to develop direction, articulate values, and to sustain hope. This means concern with quality as well as access, the perception of education as an enabling activity, education for work *and* education for life. This means advocacy for colleges of choice. The activities of the past and their justification require reconsideration. It is leadership that is responsible for this reflective activity.

Leadership is essential to making important things happen; it is indicative of strength and integrity. We can value autonomy and collegiality and, at the same time, value decisive and forceful leadership. There is no need to apologize for the value of sensitive, enlightened authority. There are variants of democracy that have limited benefits.

It is also time that community colleges realize that higher-education leadership has an intellectual dimension. Many community-college presidents and senior officers lack any background in quality general education or an academic discipline. Rightly or wrongly, this can produce a significant cognitive gap between faculty and administrators that undermines the intellectual vitality of the institution, and lack of regard from the other sectors of higher education. Chief executive officers and senior officers carry a tremendous obligation for institutional image. The public values that which it respects. We limit respect by limiting the intellectual dimension of institutional image.

We are calling here for goal-influenced, result-focused, vigorous executive activity. We are seeking leaders who are willing to think differently, who are sensitive to the value of demanding professional standards in their environments, and who realize their personal and professional responsibility to the intellectual dimension of their organizations.

A Future Orientation

There is a sense in which we create the future. We do this by allowing others to describe it and agreeing with them that certain events or circumstances will occur. We then act *as if* these occurrences will take place. In addition to providing leadership in valuing flexibility and openness concerning the future, it is important that we reorient our institutions, that we focus institutional energy on the challenges of the future rather than the problems of the past or the annoyances of the present. This requires an interest in describing the conditions of the future, the valuing of forecasting and analysis of future trends, and the developing of techniques and strategies that would enable professionals to constructively and creatively meet the needs of students and society. Commitment to the future has to do with the *psychological* orientation of an institution toward what it learns about the future. It has to do with institutional climate. Information about the future that is ignored and unused is of little assistance to the students of ten years from now.

A future orientation can include futurist thinking and a preoccupation with electronic technology, but will need to go beyond these interests. Strategic or other forms of planning alone will likely be less than adequate as the primary vehicle for this orientation to tomorrow. Frequently and unfortunately, planning is not viewed as central to meaning and commitment in an institution. Focus on the future also means cognizance of institutional needs and creativity concerning institutional vision as well as coherent planning efforts. Any community college embraces a variety of competing visions from diversified sources (faculty, trustees, community, administrators, students). Meaningful *institutional identity* requires the courage of *institutional leadership* to articulate, defend, and guard an *institutional vision* among many competing visions. A future orientation requires a sense of institutional purpose that has acceptance as well as a coherent view of that which is likely to occur.

A future orientation puts community colleges in charge of our destinies. It enables us to stop wasting energy on arguments of the present whose solutions will not help the future. It suggests that intelligent awareness of the future is essential to institutional effectiveness, to academic commitment and to meaningful leadership.

Public Priority, Educational Purpose, and Academic Standards

Higher Education: A Public Priority?

Several factors combined to produce a national public-policy commitment to higher education between 1960 and 1970. These included the baby boomers beginning to go to college, a growing economy, the liberal–populist political tradition of John Kennedy and Lyndon Johnson, and the civil-rights movement. Growth, opportunity, and the perception of a "right to education" dominated the literature and thinking of these years. Not so coincidentally, these were years of enormous growth for community colleges. There were 704 institutions in 1963 and 1,141 in 1973; there were 914,494 community-college students in 1963 and 3,100,951 in 1973 (Cohen and Brawer, 1982). Community colleges fit the thinking and the preferences of the times. The times could also afford the expansion of higher education. Educational entitlement was fashionable.

In the decade of the 1980s, we are seeking to preserve the commitments made to the higher-education enterprise during the 1960s. Yet, the circumstances are very different. This is an era of conservative presidents if not conservative thinking (Ferguson and Rogers, 1986); there is more limited economic growth; the moral imperative accompanying the civil rights era has not been adequately sustained; and the baby boomers are forty.

The major sectors of public and private higher education have, over the years, managed to retain their special identities while creating an overlapping, patchwork approach to educational services. There are many examples. Private colleges and universities receive substantial public funding. Liberal arts colleges have expanded their commitment to occupational education. Research universities also place major emphasis on their public-service activities. Urban universities provide special open-admission programs and continuing education.

Public-policy support for higher education will likely continue. We will not, however, be able to take growth in fiscal support for granted. We will experience greater accountability. With more limited funding and fewer students, some sectors will be increasingly forced to make difficult decisions about important priorities. Stable-to-declining enrollments and modestly increasing costs will characterize virtually all of the 3,300 colleges and universities in the country.

Given these conditions, it is reasonable to maintain that community colleges will become the colleges of choice in providing lower-division educational services in the future. Why? Community colleges will be even more affordable (when compared to other institutions) then they have been in the past. They will be increasingly important to those four-year colleges and universities already paying greater attention to upper division and graduate programs as part of their finding it necessary to choose among competing priorities. They will increasingly meet the need for education for greater numbers of minorities. They are located in population centers. Because their tuition is low, they have some flexibility in accommodating legislative efforts to contain tuition costs. They can better withstand a reduced national commitment to financing higher education through student-aid programs—again, because tuition costs are comparatively low.

This means that the perceived role of the community college will change. Instead of being viewed as an intellectually compromised alternative for the educationally least prepared, community colleges will be viewed as necessary to those seeking meaningful points of entry to higher education—a cost effective, quality activity for college freshmen and sophomores. Community colleges will move from an option without glamour and sanction to a more central and critical role in relation to other higher-education sectors. This will enable these sectors to carry out their respective educational agendas more efficiently and effectively. Community colleges will be sanctioned as a result of the self-interest of other colleges and universities. But—all of this is less likely to occur if community colleges fail to take their collegiate commitment more seriously. An alternative scenario might be described as well.

Community colleges may be pushed from the educational stage as a result of increased competition for students among sectors. The decrease in the number of high-school graduates attending college, fewer numbers of people in the 18–24-year-old age cohort, declining minority enrollments in higher education, and fewer full-time students may result in a reduction of community-college attendees. Part-time, recurring-education adults may not make up the difference. Student financial aid will maintain itself at an adequate level to sustain enrollments at least at public state colleges and universities—eclipsing the attractiveness of the cost-effectiveness of community colleges for students.

Four-year colleges and universities have successfully incorporated a number of the convenience–and accessibility features of community colleges such as evening and weekend programs, continuing-education programs, and special efforts with business and industry. Four-year colleges and universities offer associate degrees. They hold the promise of greater prestige and sense of pride for the students who identify with these institutions. All of this could mean that community colleges would be perceived as valuable only to the extent that they provide vocational training, community-based education, and literacy-education services.

Enrollments and economics alone will not determine which (if either) scenario will prevail. The perceived collegiate value of the community college will be a factor as well. This is not to say that collegiate identity will determine the future of community-college education. It is to point out that this issue may seriously compromise educational access and educational equity in the future. The latter scenario and its role for community colleges is not without benefit, but it may well mean a significant diminishing of educational options for many. Institutions without clearly perceived collegiate responsibility are not viewed as fully enfranchised colleges. If community colleges are limited to vocational training and literacy efforts and are precluded from collegiate activity, it will be more difficult for community-college students to pursue baccalaureate education. The collegiate connection will be lost. Community colleges would not be viewed as key points of educational entry. Under either scenario higher education remains a public priority. Community-college leaders have decisions to make concerning their place and importance in the future educational enterprise.

What Are the Purposes of Education?

Peter Drucker (1982) pointed out that organizations in American society were taking on an increasing number of public and private roles that were essentially unrelated to their fundamental organizational reason for existing. He reminded us of the social-responsibility role, the educator role, and the community-leadership role of private manufacturing and service companies.

This same phenomenon has occurred within the higher-education community. We, to varying extents, fill various community-service needs such as health care, day care, and neighborhood renewal. Colleges and universities assist in economic development through the maintenance of programs that could not be carried out in the absence of such institutional support. We are bankers, land developers, and lobbyists.

There is much of value in all of these roles and—to some extent—they all relate to the higher-education enterprise. The issue here is not that we do these things, but that continuing to do them can lead to major alterations in the activity of our institutions. These college functions appear to have a somewhat distant relationship from the teaching, learning, and research fundamental to our institutions. As colleges and universities take on more and more responsibilities that are important but not central to our primary cognitive educational charge, we may question whether or not we are, indeed, altering what is meant by "education" in this country. We may question the purpose of our enterprise.

There are also persuasive social arguments that the avowed and actual purposes of higher education in this country differ. The rhetoric accompanying the activities of colleges and universities reflects valuing education as essential to opportunity and success. One is led to believe that education is a significant, meaningful alternative to the path of privilege associated with affluence, and that education overcomes the limitations of poverty (Astin, 1985; Rossides, 1984). While it is the case that we are the most educationally active nation in the world (*New York Times*, 1985), it is also important to note who goes to certain kinds of colleges and universities and who does not. A case can be made that there is tracking in higher education based on wealth and birth that limits the credibility one can associate with the rhetoric of opportunity. There are those who argue that this tracking is intentional and that community colleges are important participants in this phenomenon (Zwerling, 1976).

What of community-college education in relation to these tendencies toward tracking and toward diversity of purpose? Consider its past and present purposes:

1. Education for work (occupational programs);

2. Education for more education (transfer activity);

3. Education for elimination of skill deficiencies (remedial, developmental, and literacy programs).

If community colleges increasingly become the primary point of entry for much of higher education, these purposes will likely undergo a shift in emphasis and scope, a broadening—not radical alteration:

1. Education for work will refer to (a) the attainment of technical skills *accompanied by* (b) information and conceptual skills, and (c) lifetime education skills;

2. Education for more education will encompass (a) transfer education, (b) "recurring education," (c) occupationally related degree education, and (d) occupationally related continuing education;

3. Education for elimination of deficiencies will be evaluated in terms of the extent to which it is forward looking: assisting people with life success as distinct from focusing only on remediating the inadequacies of earlier educational experiences.

On one level, we are talking about diminishing the rigidity of present curricular design through new curricular structures that do not rely on assumptions such as the necessity to distinguish occupational education from academic education and the liberal arts from technology. We are suggesting that curriculum development be based on a positive response to four questions: Is the curricular substance comprehensive? Does it make adequate theoretical and applied intellectual demands? Does it assist in the development of productive habits of learning? Is it enabling—developing capacities for life success?

On another level, we are identifying the purposes of education with the development of literacies:

- *Critical literacy* provides a high level of independent thinking, capacity for critical analysis and interpretation of substantive material: it provides for active, creative thinking through manipulation of qualitative and quantitative theoretical constructs (Richardson, 1983);

- *Information literacy* provides the needed capacity to find information, read it, analyze it, interpert it, apply it, and communicate it (McCabe, 1985);

- *Civic literacy* provides for development of effective citizen and political skills;

- *Cultural literacy* provides for intellectual, artistic, historical, and linguistic awareness;

- *Social literacy* provides for knowledge and sensitivity toward others, of self, and of groups;

- *Scientific literacy* provides for understanding of quantitative theoretical constructs including math, logic, and computers.

We are talking here about determining educational purpose based upon its future conceptual usefulness for students in any life endeavor they may choose. This will diminish the potential for multiple levels of quality and therefore an inequitable distribution of opportunity within higher education. This can discourage tracking. This approach to purpose can also be protected from undue emphasis on diversity of institutional roles. This is a matter of institutional choice.

It is, however, perhaps naive to believe that the prestige hierarchy identified with higher-education institutions will disappear. But there is hope that the impact of hierarchy can be modified through efforts to ensure educational equity. The hierarchy is likely to remain with us as a manifestation of socioeconomic and cultural preference. Perhaps it should. Our society can sustain elite education such as our fine private liberal-arts colleges and outstanding historically black colleges—provided that the higher-education community continues to strengthen its commitment to educational equity. Community colleges, through clarification of purpose and insistence upon meaningful standards of quality, provide a clear agenda of intent for their higher-education effort: education for competence, mobility, and success. It is appropriate to be elitest about the quality fo the community-college educational agenda provided that one preserves an egalitarian commitment to the availability of that education.

How Do We Deal with Standards?

The National Center for Educational Statistics estimates that, in 1983–1984, 82 percent of all colleges and universities in the country were offering some work in either remedial math, reading, or writing (U.S. Department of Education, 1985). Few question the desirability of access to education as reflected in policies of entrance and the opportunity to improve basic skills reflected by varied support programs. Many are concerned that goals associated with education such as education for a quality life, education as an enabling activity, and education for work cannot be realized unless such freedom of admission is accompanied by demanding standards for accomplishment following admission. There is evidence that those who were promised the most as a result of emphasis on access in higher education have received the least (Astin, 1982). Consider the impact of time devoted to educational pursuit that does not result in development of talent and resourcefulness needed for life success. Consider whether societal obstacles facing the less-than-fortunate should also result in educational underpreparedness for achievement and autonomy.

If Harlan Cleveland is correct in stating that ". . . Colleges and universities, especially public colleges and universities, are the egalitarian means for making an aristocracy of achievement acceptable in a democratic society" (1985), then one would expect schools to reenforce the notions of talent development and merit as fundamental to opportunity, equity, and equality in the society. Yet, we are faced with a avalanche of illiteracy out of proportion to those who have access to education and actually participate in its activity. The illiteracy goes beyond the incapacity to read and write. It includes civic, cultural, and cognitive illiteracy—all resulting in a fundamental incapacity to function privately, personally, or publicly in our society in a meaningful manner (Kozol, 1985). We seem to ignore the relationship between the quality of education and the quality of our society.

Access has been an appropriate response of community colleges to the ongoing challenge of available education in a democratic society; dilution of standards and reduction in quality are not. When confronted with admission of the underprepared, some in higher education have been willing to substitute mediocrity for excellence to appear to achieve the laudable purpose of education for life success. It has been less than effective—as many commission reports tell us, as corporate spokespersons tell us, as the thoughtful among us tell us. Have we had the courage to listen carefully?

But reaffirmation of standards in the face of open admission does not adequately deal with the impact of societal neglect, imbalance, and unfairness. If schools are to remain predicated on behavior such as discipline, cognitive acuity, and motivation for student success, societal structures such as the traditional family, religious institutions, and personal life ties will need to be reaffirmed or replaced. The current state of life of many lower-income whites and especially minorities in urban areas clearly does not contribute to the likelihood of educational success for life success—given our present approach to the educational enterprise.

The growing body of literature dealing with impact of ongoing poverty on values and social orientation reflects concern regarding the dissonance between the world of the persistently poor and the world of the nonpoor (Kaus, 1986; Wilson, 1985). The persistently poor cannot be expected to make effective use of elementary, secondary, and postsecondary education until and unless conditions of health, income, family, and social structure are simultaneously addressed. We do not fully understand the impact of these life conditions on differential academic performance of varying racial and ethnic minorities. One point, however, is clear. No single issue is more serious for the future of our society. There is no social issue to which community colleges could more profitably devote themselves.

Community colleges can carefully examine the structure and content of their educational services and ensure that educational efforts reflect cognizance of the life conditions that impede learning for this increasingly large group of people who persist in poverty. In addition, community colleges can take responsibility for influencing of community opinion. We can encourage major change in educational services that are not effective for these groups. Mandatory public education (K–12) has been rendered marginally effective in some places as a result of structural and value dissonance between educators and those they purport to educate. Higher education faces similar problems.

There is a civic-education role of major importance to be carried out at the institutional level by community colleges, especially our urban institutions: It calls for leadership in focusing public attention on meeting the needs of those who are part of the environment of poverty. This is distinct from continuing to maintain that our present institutions are of value to these individuals and groups—if only the world of the poor could be modified. It is we who need to change.

Community colleges have a series of obligations that go beyond commitment to equality as expressed through access to commitment to equity as reflected in talent development of our students. Institutions with our unique, simultaneous commitment to access and standards can play a powerful role in dealing with the culture of poverty.

The Future

Consider, then, the following hypotheses concerning effective education in the community college of the future:

1. Community colleges are increasingly the crucial points of entry to all of higher education for greater numbers of people; they will further dominate the lower-division market of the baccalaureate. They will be the primary institutional providers meeting the public demand for accessible, quality education;

2. The collegiate identity of community colleges will become stronger—but not at the price of traditional occupational education and not at the price of commitment to developmental and literacy education. Rather, this collegiate focus will become the vehicle whereby (a) heretofore more narrowly defined occupational education adapts to the need for education for multiple-career lives and whereby (b) literacy education is a genuine access point to

education and life success. Traditional vocational education for paraprofessionals is giving way to career-transfer education. Traditional academic transfer and articulation efforts are expanding to encompass the more broadly conceived "pursuit of the baccalaureate." Literacy and developmental efforts are focusing on future life success—some are genuine precollegiate activities and others are increasingly accepted forms of skill improvement for those not seeking collegiate activity.

3. The egalitarian features of community-college education which result in skepticism concerning community-college effectiveness and quality will undergo a shift in perception and value. Accessibility and low cost will no longer imply undesirability and disdain for educational service. The forms of racism that further discourage a positive perception of community colleges will diminish as larger and larger numbers of minorities make their way to our colleges and universities and as their demands for quality, comprehensive education are articulated and acknowledged.

We are talking about differences—alternative attitudes toward our students, ourselves, and our communities. We are talking about ways in which community colleges can contribute to the priority, purposes, and quality of higher education in the future. We are talking about more than our survival—our integrity is at stake. Consider the community college as a college of choice. Consider the consequences of *not* changing.

References

AMERICAN ASSOCIATION OF COMMUNITY AND JUNIOR COLLEGES. "Some Telling Facts About Community Colleges." Washington, D.C.: American Association of Community and Junior Colleges, 1986.

"AMERICANS FOUND MOST EDUCATED IN WORLD." *New York Times* (October 20, 1985):39.

ASTIN, ALEXANDER W. *Achieving Educational Excellence.* San Francisco: Jossey-Bass, 1985.

———. *Minorities in Higher Education.* San Francisco, Jossey-Bass, 1982.

BASTIAN, ANN, FRUCHTER, NORM, GITTEL, MARILYN, GREER, COLIN, and HASKINS, KENNETH. "Choosing Equality: The Case for Democratic Schooling." *Social Policy* 15(4) (Spring, 1985):34–51.

CLEVELAND, HARLAN. *"The Knowledge Executive: Leadership In an Information Society."* New York: Truman Talley Books, 1985.

COHEN, ARTHUR M. "What Do Our Students Know?" *Community College Review* 13(4) (1986):6–11.

Cohen Arthur M., and Brawer, Florence. *The American Community College.* San Francisco: Jossey-Bass, 1982.

DRUCKER, PETER F. *The Changing World of the Executive.* New York: Truman Talley Books, 1982.

FERGUSON, THOMAS, and ROGERS, JOEL. "The Myth of America's Turn to the Right." *The Atlantic Monthly* 257(5) (May, 1986):43–53.

FINN, CHESTER E. JR., RAVITCH, DIANE, and FRANCHER, ROBERT T. *Against Mediocrity: The Humanities in America's High Schools.* New York: Holmes and Meier, 1984.

KAUS, MICKEY. "The Work Ethic State" *The New Republic* 195(1) (July 7, 1986):22–33.

KOZOL, JONATHAN. *Illiterate America.* New York: Andover Press, 1985.

RICHARDSON, R.C., JR., FISK, E.C., and OKUN, M.A. *Literacy in the Open Access College.* San Francisco: Jossey-Bass, 1983.

ROSSIDES, DANIEL W. "What Is The Purpose of Education? The Worthless Debate Continues." *Change* 16(3) (April, 1984):14–20 and 44–46.

U.S. Department of Education. National Center for Educational Statistics *Bulletin.* Washington, D.C.: September, 1985.

WILSON, William JULIUS. "Cycle of Deprivation and the Underclass Debate." *Social Science Review.* 59(4) (December, 1985):541–559.

ZWERLING, L. S. *Second Best: The Crisis of the Community College.* New York: McGraw-Hill, 1976.

PART
ONE

Collegiate Identity

"For despite all the subordinate roles for community colleges, as educational institutions, they are of necessity judged by the value they add to their students' intellectual capabilities and moral qualities."
Arthur M. Cohen

"Even though some community college spokespersons are inclined to downplay the transfer functions these days, the community college's piece of the action in educating

*aspirants to the bachelor's degree is just as important as it
has ever been."*

Alexander Astin

*"As long as intelligence is better than stupidity, knowl-
edge than ignorance, and virtue than vice, no university
can be run except on an elitist basis."*

John Silbur

*". . . if you redefine excellence recklessly enough, there
will be no shortage of excellence."*

George F. Will

1

The Presence of Access and the Pursuit of Achievement

RICHARD C. RICHARDSON, JR.

The effort to shift the discussion from access to achievement has suffered from accusations that those who raise questions about quality are opposed to access.

The concept of access is central to understanding the contribution of community colleges to American higher education from the 1960s to the 1980s. It is equally important in any analysis of the issues confronting community colleges in the future. The achievements of these 20 years are a familiar story to community-college

25

professionals. In 1963, 375 public two-year colleges enrolled 735,000 students. Less than 20 years later, the number of colleges had almost tripled and enrollments had multiplied by a factor of 6. But the enrollment growths were only part of the story.

In 1963, 63 percent of the students attending two-year colleges were men. Twenty years later, 55 percent were women. Within two-year colleges, growth was not so much a function of increases in the percentage of traditional age students as it was a consequence of significant growth in the proportions attending from all segments of American society. Women, working adults and minorities all made significant strides in increasing their participation rates. In fact, by the early 1980s, the participation rates for women and minorities had either reached parity or were closely approaching that status for all groups except Hispanics. The central role of the community college in producing these statistics is apparent from the extent to which women and minorities tend to be overrepresented in two-year institutions and underrepresented in other sectors of postsecondary education (Grant and Snyder, 1984).

The 1960s and the 1970s were decades when access was the magic word. Community colleges were successful if they enrolled more students each succeeding year regardless of why those students came or what happened to them after they enrolled. But the 1980s are different. The emphasis has shifted from measuring access in terms of participation to a concern with equality of opportunity measured by accomplishment or the extent to which students achieve defined educational objectives by participating in postsecondary education. Even the American Association of Community and Junior Colleges, which as recently as two years ago was "thumping the tub" for job-training partnerships and high technology, has now decided that one of its top priorities for the remainder of this decade must be doubling the number of associate degrees awarded (AACJC, 1985).

The success story of the past two decades also has its down side. In some communities, two-year institutions are viewed increasingly as centers for leisure-time activity, social-welfare institutions, or places for underprepared learners, but not as educational institutions providing opportunities with excellence in the terms of the model of their national organization. Clearly, community colleges have been much more successful in providing access measured by rates of participation than they have been in producing solid evidence about outcomes related to student achievement. It is only necessary to compare the increase in the number of degrees and certificates awarded with increases in participation rates to become fully aware of just how great the gap has become.

A tendency to rely upon a modern day parable of the Good Shepherd has not been helpful in relations with legislators and other external groups that control scarce resources. Whenever anyone questions current practice, they are told in great detail about how the lost sheep was saved. What they really want to know, of course, is what happened to the other 99. But by the time they are told for the tenth time about all the places searched and the obstacles overcome, and how grateful the lost sheep was when finally found, their eyes have glazed over. Community-college administrators believe they have been persuasive only to discover, to their dismay, that when their listeners return to the feed store, they send only enough grain to feed about 60 of the sheep.

The effort to shift the discussion from access to achievement has suffered from accusations that those who raise questions about quality are opposed to access. Just as patriotism is the last refuge of a scoundrel, so is access the last refuge of those who believe that the idea of "all things to all people" is so powerful that it is unnecessary to examine outcomes. But two-year colleges need not respond to concerns about quality and standards by closing the open door. Neither should they equate such concerns with the desire to limit access. There are alternatives for preserving access without giving up standards, but pursuing them will require more emphasis on achievement and less concern with body counts.

This chapter provides a brief history of how community colleges became impaled on the horns of the access/quality dilemma. Following this summary account, a series of issues central to any effort to resolve the dilemma are considered. Finally, the chapter identifies some of the key variables that community colleges will need to address to deal with the demands of the excellence movement with the same degree of success they achieved in promoting access.

Access and the Community College

In the early 1960s, when community colleges accepted responsibility for spearheading the effort to address traditional inequities in access to higher education, open admissions was defined as the "right to fail." In that era, few community colleges offered well-developed programs for remediation. Instead, colleges followed the practice of permitting students to enroll in courses regardless of whether their reading, writing and math skills were equal to coping with course requirements. Emphasis on the right to fail contributed to an extremely high failure rate among students. Public reaction to the failure rates, particularly as educational opportunity became interwoven with the civil-rights movement, led to a number of practices that now interfere with the ability of community colleges to address issues related to achievement.

In the late 1960s and early 1970s, open admissions as the right to fail was replaced with the right of students to expect some program where they could succeed, and success was defined as staying in school. Students could succeed according to this definition regardless of previous preparation, motivation, or effort.

Unfortunately, deficiencies accumulated over 12 or more years of public schooling could not be overcome in a single semester or a single year. Only the mildly remedial (and that number was no larger than 10 to 15 percent of those enrolling in developmental programs in many colleges) were able to move into regular degree programs within the expected time. So the purposes of developmental programs were enlarged to include self-actualization, and more students stayed enrolled for longer periods of time. Such enrollments became increasingly important to fiscal stability as the growth years of the 1960s and early 1970s came to an end.

Because many programs remained open to students who were unqualified to do the work required, other policy changes became necessary, especially during the era of Vietnam veterans and the introduction of need-based financial aid. Students required financial assistance to remain enrolled and financial assistance was predicated on maintaining satisfactory progress. So failing grades were eliminated and withdrawal without penalty was permitted in many colleges through the last day of the semester. It became common to award degree credit for remedial work so that students could earn the 12 credits required each semester to keep them eligible for financial aid. Many colleges introduced the general-studies degree for students who earned 64 hours of credit without taking a coherent sequence. In some colleges at present, students may still earn this degree without ever taking any course for which another course is a prerequisite.

The policies developed to help underprepared students stay in school also affected better prepared students, especially since many community colleges interpreted open admissions as giving everyone the right to try anything as long as the additional sections generated revenues that exceeded the costs of offering them. Growing numbers of part-time students taught largely by a part-time faculty contributed to loss of coherence in the curriculum. Most recently, the growing numbers of students interested in career education has caused many to conclude that the career preparation ought to be the primary purpose of community colleges.

Throughout the 1970s and during the first two years of the current decade, two-year college enrollments continued to increase, but the growth in absolute numbers was accompanied by danger signals. Many colleges experienced losses in full-time equivalent enrollments on which they were reimbursed as the number of full-time students declined more rapidly than they could be replaced by part-time students whose numbers continued to grow. Then, in 1983 and 1984, for the first time in their history, community colleges across the country experienced back-to-back losses in total attendees as well as full-time equivalent enrollments (AACJC, 1984).

The danger signals were not confined to enrollment figures. Cohen and Brawer (1982) documented the deterioration of the collegiate function by pointing out that in terms in liberal arts offerings, community colleges were becoming one-year institutions. Astin's study of minorities in American higher education (1982) warned that for some of these students, the open door led to a dead end. Breneman and Nelson (1981) found the dominant administrative strategy on most campuses they visited was to maximize enrollments without concern for setting educational priorities. Kissler (1982) reported that fewer students were transferring from

California community colleges to the University of California and the academic performance of those who did transfer was declining. And a study of literacy in an open-access community college (Richardson, Fisk, and Okun, 1983), found that a college established to level up disadvantaged students was in fact leveling down the academic demands of the education being offered. Whatever else one concludes from these studies, it is difficult to see them as indicators of opportunity with excellence.

The facts are clear. Community colleges have tried to do more for a larger number of people with less money than any other segment of American postsecondary education. In the process, they have recorded many triumphs, but there have also been failures. Is it possible? Can two-year colleges serve the same number of students without additional dollars, and improve the quality of what they are doing—perhaps even aspire to excellence? At present, there is no answer to these questions because a concern about quality among comprehensive community colleges, as an alternative to the pursuit of numbers, is such a new phenomenon. As long as success could be measured by comparing the number who enrolled for classes during the current semester with the number enrolled a year ago, there was little incentive to consider in any systematic fashion the changes to policies and practices necessary to doing better rather than doing more. But now two-year colleges have both the opportunity and the necessity of examining the issue of access as it relates to the new priority of achievement. The presence of achievement in the equation suggests the need to reconsider some old questions.

Pursuing Excellence with Scarce Resources

Advocates of strategic planning suggest that before determining institutional priorities, planners should consider threats and opportunities in the external environment as well as institutional strengths and weaknesses. The following may help to focus this process for community colleges as it relates to the pursuit of excellence. There are four major questions that need to be addressed.

Access to What?

Does access mean providing everyone with the right to participate in: (a) the first two years of a baccalaureate degree program; (b) one- or two-year vocational and technical programs designed to prepare individuals for immediate employment or to upgrade those already employed; (c) short-term training or retraining to meet the needs of business, industry, government, or unemployed workers; (d) unlimited remediation in writing, math, reading, and English as a Second Language; (e) individual credit courses for personal enrichment; (f) recreation and leisure-time activities; (g) credit-free courses in poodle grooming and cake baking on a self-supporting basis; or (h) all of the above?

Access under What Conditions?

If resources are constrained, what priorities should be established among the functions noted above, all of which have been defended at one time or another by some community-college educator? Should everyone, for example, be admitted to everything regardless of their level of preparation? Should students be guaranteed their right to fail by permitting them to disregard the evidence provided by test scores and previous performance as well as the advice of counselors, and permitted to enroll in any course for which there is no prerequisite? Should colleges focus on the 18–22-year-old population, the working population, the out-of-employment population, the aging population, or all of the above? What about the special case of minorities who depend upon community colleges for their access to a much greater extent than their nonminority counterparts? If community colleges do not assess the skills of entering students or require placement according to demonstrated skills, how can they avoid providing separate and unequal opportunities for those who have no alternative to attending colleges where course standards must be adapted to reflect the underprepared students exercising their right to fail?

What Message Should Accompany Access?

Should access be offered to all who take the trouble to seek it, or should it be a consumer good, hawked in the shopping malls alongside sale-priced clothing and the latest hit recordings? Many educators have emphasized the importance of marketing to achieve the true democratization of higher education. Others less high-minded see it as a response to the importance of maintaining enrollments to preserve the college funding base.

And what is the message that two-year colleges send to high schools as a consequence of their recruiting and admissions practices? Why should students spend time taking tough subjects in high school if they are guaranteed admission to a community college and their right to fail? Or, why should they even bother graduating from high school if they can count upon being pursued in shopping centers regardless of previous preparation?

What Are Reasonable Expectations Concerning the Amount and Duration of State Subsidies?

For how many years should the student be given the right to fail? Should there be any expectations for progress during that period of time or any requirements that community colleges track students and account for the number of classes successfully completed or the student competencies achieved? Should states provide financial assistance to part-time students as well as full-time students? Or perhaps this question should be rephrased since no state has yet been able to fully fund both its part-time and full-time students: Should the state devote part of its available financial aid to part-time rather than full-time students?

Should states subsidize as college students those who are engaged in basic literacy training, who will never earn a degree or certificate because their deficiencies will cause them to run out of financial aid long before they qualify for a regular program? If a state decides that the community college is the appropriate place to provide English as a second language for recent immigrants and basic literacy training for those whose skills are below the sixth-grade level, should community colleges be required to treat such instruction as if it were college-level training in terms of calculating the basis for reimbursement? Should students who attend such training be required to enter into some sort of subterfuge with the institution in order to remain eligible for student financial assistance?

These are not easy questions that lend themselves to simple answers. Many of them involve tenets that have been viewed as sacred to the concept of an open-door college. But all have implications for quality and achievement. If resources are held constant, the greater the number served, the lower the quality of the experience for each. Most of us have no difficulty understanding that traveling first class represents a better experience than occupying one of the economy seats, but we do not seem as ready to accept the notion that serving 10 percent more students with the same number of dollars diminishes the quality of the services they receive. At least in an airplane, everyone gets to the same place at the same time. In a community college, available evidence suggests that students with comparable objectives do not achieve the same outcomes through attending a community college that they might achieve by going to a different type of institution.

Responding to access issues in the achievement-oriented environment of the next decade will require reexamination of three policy areas where past practices have emphasized participation rather than measurable student outcomes. These policy areas include the external environment, the college environment, and the classroom.

The External Environment

In the external environment, the most obvious variables that need to be considered are those related to student demographics. At present, most students who study full time attend public four-year colleges—71 percent. By contrast, students attending community colleges are likely to study part time—63 percent (ACE, 1984). And minority students, the population that will grow most rapidly during the next two decades, disproportionately attend two-year colleges. According to the *Fourth Annual Status Report on Achievement of Minorities*, during the 1982 academic year, 56 percent of all Hispanics and 44 percent of all blacks enrolled in colleges and universities attended two-year institutions. The comparable figure for whites was 37 percent (ACE, 1984).

During the next decade, two-year colleges will serve a higher proportion of students who are minority, underprepared, and economically disadvantaged. More will be women, many the single heads of households with dependent children. In addition, there will be a major increase in the older part-time student in the 35–44-year age range as the baby boomers enter middle age.

Concurrent with these demographic changes are tightening admission standards among four-year institutions and a stronger focus on academic preparation in the K–12 sector. Unless two-year colleges can find some way to maintain a reasonable share of prepared high-school graduates, the college parallel function already threatened will become increasingly endangered as small enrollments make advanced courses uneconomical and student underpreparation continues to erode course standards. There is evidence that this is happening already, especially in smaller institutions. In a study recently completed for the Ford Foundation (Richardson and Bender, 1986), urban community colleges with significant enrollments of minority students were found to concentrate primarily on remediation and vocational–technical offerings with little emphasis on providing a convenient and complete schedule of college-parallel offerings.

Of course, vocational–technical offerings represent the predominant function of most two-year colleges at present, but there is a danger when such offerings become the exclusive function of institutions serving high proportions of students who have no alternative for access to postsecondary education. Many opportunities in an information society require possession of the baccalaureate degree. Limiting opportunities for baccalaureate study in colleges serving large minority populations opens the system to the criticism of class-based tracking where less advantaged segments of the population are systematically channeled into lower-level occupations because of the educational opportunities made available to them. Vulnerability to this criticism is further enhanced by the admission standards employed by many two-year colleges in screening applicants for high-demand, high-cost programs in areas such as nursing and dental hygiene. In many two-year colleges, minorities are as underrepresented in these high-demand fields as they are among the baccalaureate graduates of four-year institutions. Taking their positions are reverse transfers from four-year colleges, many holding the bachelor's degree at the time they enter an associate-degree program. Reverse transfers are, of course, much safer prospects in terms of performance on state licensing exams by which programs in the allied health areas are frequently judged.

Underlying all other issues related to demographics and access is the challenge of remediation. Strengthening student skills in reading, writing, and mathematics is no longer a minor part of most two-year college programs. In urban areas, it has become the predominant function with 85 percent or more of all students requiring remediation in one or more of the three areas (McCabe, 1982–83). The increased emphasis on academic skills in the K–12 sector may represent the long-term solution, but it will not alter conditions in most two-year colleges in the next decade. Four-year institutions will be waiting anxiously to skim off each year's crop of prepared seniors. The prospect for community colleges in terms of student preparation will, if anything, worsen as states in pursuit of excellence implement their versions of the student screening arrangements long in use in Western European countries and Japan where the college-going rates have been only a fraction of those achieved in the United States.

At the same time that students are being more carefully sorted following high school, there looms on the horizon the possibility of "rising junior" exams. These tests are already administered in Florida and Georgia to determine student eligibility for moving into upper-division status in a four-year institution and are under consideration in at least eight additional states. Increasingly, community colleges will face pressures to demonstrate that students unprepared for baccalaureate work when they left high school have corrected deficiencies and are ready to engage in head-to-head competition for grades with their university counterparts who were prepared.

The remedial function, while a significant challenge during the next decade, may also be an important factor in maintaining two-year college enrollments as returning adults join recent high-school graduates who are underprepared in seeking assistance in strengthening academic skills to meet the emerging demands of an achievement-oriented society.

Responding appropriately to the challenges and opportunities posed by the growing importance of the remedial function will require better understanding of the two-year college mission by those agencies that provide resources including local communities and state legislators. Remediation in the recent past has frequently been viewed as paying for the same education twice, or as a function that should gradually wither away as standards are improved in the K–12 sector. The distaste for remediation as a mission for postsecondary institutions has led to restrictive policies and inadequate funding. Altering attitudes about remediation among policy makers who control resources will require the same enthusiasm and genius that has in the past been demonstrated in promoting high technology and job preparation. It will also require hard evidence about the improvements in measurable competencies of those who enroll in remedial offerings.

The College Environment

Providing effective programs and services to a changing student clientele will require changes in the internal environments of most community colleges as well as changed attitudes in the external environment. One prominent barrier to change in many two-year colleges at present involves the absence of faculty commitment to administrative priorities accompanied by their growing alienation from the role of community-college faculty member as this has been institutionally defined by administrators.

At the root of the problem are the attitudes of administrators and faculty members. Most community-college administrators have been trained as managers through programs in educational administration rather than as academics through immersion in a teaching discipline. For many in leadership positions, the classroom represents a distant experience. As one result, administrators value efficiency and effective management techniques rather than the academic concerns of the faculty. Value differences between administrators and faculty members about the importance of knowledge, standards, and the academic experience contribute to misunderstanding and lack of communication.

In most two-year colleges, administrators occupy the top positions in a bureaucracy that diminishes the importance faculty members attach to their own role. Talented teachers must move from the classroom into administration in order to advance within their profession. Absent are the faculty rank structure and titles through which university faculty members receive recognition. Absent also is the expectation that administrators will return to the classroom after some period of service. Movement into administration is most commonly a one-way street from which incumbents exit if at all, kicking and screaming, or feet first unless, of course, they are earlier called to a more significant administrative position in a larger institution.

While the problems of faculty involvement and vitality are by no means limited to two-year institutions, there exists a growing body of evidence that these problems are most acute in two-year colleges because of heavy teaching loads, management-imposed accountability systems that have harmed trust, and an absence of opportunities for career advancement other than through entering administration.

The litany of faculty concerns is lengthy and increasingly well documented. A lack of student motivation, enthusiasm for learning, and willingness to work independently discourages faculty members who care about their disciplines (Hutton and Jobe, 1985; Diener, 1985). The increasing vocational emphasis produces student apathy in humanities classes where the approach to learning conflicts with techniques emphasized for short-term training (Seidman, 1985). The student centeredness of the institution along with heavy teaching loads leaves little time for leisure among committed faculty members and not infrequently produces role conflict (Hutton and Jobe, 1985; Seidman, 1985). The rapid growth and diffusion of the institutions' mission in the hands of entrepreneurial administrators leaves faculty with a sense of powerlessness (Seidman, 1985); conveys the impression that neither administrators nor boards give fair consideration to their ideas (Hutton and

Jobe, 1985); and leads to conclusions that faculty members do not have adequate opportunities to participate in decision making (Diener, 1985). The perceived characteristics of their working environment causes many faculty members to conclude that the institution does not value them or their services (Schuster and Bowen, 1985).

The extensive use of part-time faculty and the statements made by administrators in defending such use has caused full-time faculty members in particular to conclude they are not valued (Richardson, Fisk, and Okun, 1983). It is difficult to feel good about a job that can be done by part-time workers at a lower salary and with greater expertise and equal commitment. The sense of not being valued produces, in turn, isolation from other faculty members and ultimately from the institution as the major area in which to derive satisfaction. And so, faculty members turn to outside jobs or associations to furnish the satisfaction they cannot experience in the two-year college as their role has been defined. In consequence, they become unavailable for the pursuit of emerging priorities and resistant to changes that would cause them to take time and energy from their outside interests. Administrators alienated from the majority of their full-time faculty, who jointly absorb the largest single slice of institutional resources, must turn increasingly to part-time staff to initiate change. Part-time staff also have divided loyalties.

This picture is, of course, a "worst-case scenario." There remains in every two-year college a cadre of committed faculty who will spare no time or effort to carry out the activities they believe are important to the students they serve. But in one institution where the issue of faculty commitment was closely studied (Richardson, Fisk, and Okun, 1983), the committed faculty constituted a small and declining number who over time either became less involved or entered administration. Not only were committed faculty members required to assume the burden of their absent colleagues, but they had to do it in the absence of institutional arrangements for recognition and rewards. Many of their faculty colleagues belittled them for supporting administrative priorities.

The issue of renewing faculty vitality represents a key element in altering the college environment to make it more responsive to the emerging priorities of the next decade. In the final section of this chapter, the responsibility of administrators for the teaching and learning process is emphasized as a way of altering the college environment of the learning environment for which they have primary responsibility.

Effectiveness of the Learning Environment

Administrators and faculty members are not unaware of the problems described in the preceding section of this chapter. The most common response has involved professional development activities to alter faculty behavior within the classroom setting. Implicit in this approach has been the notion that if faculty members receive instruction from authorities in how to improve their teaching they will respond more effectively to the changing clientele they must teach. From an administrative perspective, this approach has the great advantage of not requiring any changes in the way administrators behave. Unfortunately, from the standpoint of creating change, most faculty members already know more about how to teach than they are using. As a result, new ideas are tried by a small group of committed faculty, but few if any changes in teaching approaches can be observed among the majority.

This chapter argues for a different approach. The decisions administrators make touch every facet of institutional experience and so they affect teaching and learning in fundamental ways because this is the core activity in which community colleges engage. But administrators do not always recognize their influence on instruction, nor are they uniformly enthusiastic about accepting the responsibility that accompanies that influence. The most effective way of altering classroom behavior is by changing administrative practice to improve the institutional environment rather than by increasing faculty knowledge about how to teach in an environment that often discourages their use of new knowledge.

Of the 20 recommendations contained in The National Institute for Education's *Involvement in Learning* (1984), the report of the study group on the conditions of excellence in American higher education, no less than 13 have primary implications for administrators. Beyond emphasizing the centrality of administrators to efforts aimed at improving the quality of the learning process, a number of these recommendations identify strategies of special promise. These include:

- Design learning technologies to increase, not reduce, interaction between faculty and students;

- Offer systematic programs of guidance and advisement that reach all students and involve as participants administrators, faculty, peer counselors, and student-affairs personnel;

- Provide fiscal support, space, and recognition to existing cocurricular activities to maximize student involvement;

- Consolidate as many part-time teaching lines as possible in full-time positions;

- Determine the knowledge, capacities, and skills students should have before graduation and make certain the content and delivery of the curriculum matches them;

- Assess the knowledge, capacities, and skills developed by students through a systematic program;

- Use reward systems to place particular emphasis on teaching effectiveness.

These recommendations are selected for emphasis because they coincide closely with some of the insights gained from research projects over the past six years.

A recent study of one urban community-college district in all of its phases of activity resulted in this conclusion: ". . . determined administrative leadership that knows where it wants to go . . . through control of the resource allocation process and a judicious blending of other strategies available to administrators, can make significant progress toward achieving change even in a limited period of time. . . ." (Richardson, Fisk, and Okun, 1983). But change is not neutral nor is it necessarily beneficial. And most of the decisions made by administrators in this study focused on activities ancillary to the teaching and learning process. Perhaps even more problematic, decisions in areas not perceived by administrators to be related to the educational program often had unforeseen and unintended impact in the classrooms. Over an 18-month period, only 2 percent of the decisions made by senior management and the chief executive officer were concerned with instruction or the curriculum. The senior decision-making body in this study did not perceive its responsibilities to be concerned centrally with the core learning activities of its constituent colleges. Yet, despite the absence of agenda items dealing with instruction, the decisions taken by this group had important consequences for teaching and learning. These consequences most commonly went unnoticed in the absence of direct involvement of administrators in the teaching and learning process. Fundamental in the study was the realization that administrators did not really understand the requirements for teaching the new clientele they had so zealously recruited.

Literacy in the Open Access College (Richardson, Fisk, and Okun, 1983) urges administrators to accept primary responsibility for the fact that an institution established to level up disadvantaged segments of the population has in practice experienced much of its success through lowering the standards expected from those who participate. This is a harsh judgment but one that appears supported by the classroom behavior and administrative decisions to which that behavior could be traced. This study observes that the decisions that contributed to deterioration in program quality include:

- permitting students to register for courses without insuring they had the prerequisite skills;

- keeping students eligible for financial aid through liberal interpretations of the federal regulations and easy withdrawal policies;

- refusing to set priorities within the educational program under conditions of fiscal constraint;

- equating a college education with consumer goods by promoting it in shopping centers and on billboards;

- labeling courses to maximize funding potential rather than to communicate educational intent and level of difficulty;

- dropping course prerequisites to increase class size;

- failing to evaluate outcomes other than the generation of reimbursable credit hours;

- excessive use of part-time faculty without making adequate provisions for student advisement and orientation;

- permitting students to register as late as the third week of classes to bolster enrollments for reimbursement purposes.

Have administrators generally supported these kinds of decisions in community college? Do they have detrimental effects on the quality of instruction? Administrators should seek the answer to this question themselves by convening some of their more concerned and outspoken faculty members to discuss the topic of quality in the teaching and learning process and how it can be most effectively promoted in community-college classrooms without jeopardizing access.

In another study, we examined progress to the bachelor's degree for minority students who attend urban community colleges (Richardson and Bender, 1986). In addition to talking to faculty members and administrators in community colleges, the design of the study called for similar conversations with their counterparts in adjacent public universities to which the majority of their students transfer. Faculty were asked whether equivalent demands were placed on students in university and community-college classes designed to meet the same objectives. With few exceptions, faculty members in both settings said there was less rigor in the community-college classes. A community-college chemistry instructor elaborated, "We use the same text book but we cover fewer topics and we cover them in less depth." A survey of students transferring from the urban community colleges to their adjacent universities, confirmed that students shared the perceptions of faculty members. While praising their community colleges for their supportive environments and concerned staff, student responses and attached comments made it clear that if you wanted courses pegged at an appropriate level of difficulty, the place to go was the university (Richardson and Bender, 1986).

Some Considerations for the Future

Two-year colleges clearly offer high quality vocational–technical programs and these programs will continue to flourish in the next decade. The challenge for such institutions centers on comprehensiveness and the remedial function. Already there have been suggestions in several states that the college parallel function can be adequately handled by four-year institutions. Many of these colleges are underenrolled at present and will become more so during the next decade. But this obvious solution overlooks the access part of the equation and the extent to which two-year institutions serve as the entry point for especially minority students who remain seriously underrepresented in the selective programs offered by two-year colleges and in the ranks of graduates from four-year institutions. *Access broadly defined must include the baccalaureate degree if two-year colleges are to avoid contributing to the creation of a permanent underclass.*

In the fall of 1984, the number of full-time students attending public two-year colleges declined by 7.3 percent. (AACJC, 1984). The loss in full-time enrollments can be attributed in part to the community colleges' love affair with the mythical average student—29 years of age, enrolled in a single class, and not interested in earning a degree. The emphasis on part-time students without degree aspirations, however justified by changing demographics, has resulted in a widening gap between the credibility of university and community-college academic efforts. Concurrently, the traditional community-college advantages of location and cost have been seriously eroded by need-based financial aid. If administrators and faculty members do not confront quality issues squarely, their institutions run the risk of losing the critical mass necessary for offering credible transfer programs, and with the loss of these programs may go as many as half of the remaining full-time students.

What insights are available from these studies for administrators and faculty members looking for planning implications? First, it is clear that many of the practices described as contributing to public concerns about quality have been adopted in the name of preserving open access, even where the primary motivation has been to continue enrollment growth to preserve revenues. The first step, then, is to move beyond defensive rhetoric to a serious study of how community colleges can provide open access and quality, for it is clear that the former without the latter is an empty promise.

Beyond opening institutions to a serious discussion aimed at defining quality in teaching and learning, administrators and faculty members must make the attainment of quality a major priority. They can do this by:

- emphasizing assessment and mandatory placement as strategies for insuring that a majority of the students in degree-credit classes possess the skills necessary to allow the instructor to insist on appropriate standards of performance without causing unacceptable levels of attrition;

- finding out why students are attending before first registration and insuring that those with degree or transfer objectives receive high-quality advising from their first contact with the institution;

- defining exit competencies for such core areas as reading, mathematics, and writing, and assessing students to insure they have acquired those competencies by the time they are certified as having met their general-education requirements;

- labeling courses designed to transfer appropriately and limiting admission to students with appropriate preparation and objectives;

- insuring that information sent to secondary schools does not mislead the naive into believing that attending a community college can compensate for poor high-school preparation.

Educational leadership in community colleges is firmly in the hands of administrators. They will discharge this responsibility more intelligently if they reassert their role as teachers. We are familiar with all of the arguments about why administrators cannot or should not teach. Administrators can best confront their own biases and the results of their daily decisions by performing in the crucible of the classroom for at least one class each year. Administrators cannot possibly retain some of the assumptions they hold about the learning experiences they are able to provide to their new clientele if they spend some of their time trying to teach them.

In the final analysis, teaching and learning are what community colleges are all about. Effective management, according to Keller (1983), is at least as much a matter of doing the right things as doing things right. Community colleges have largely solved the access problem. Now the "right thing" involves making certain that the quality of teaching and learning fulfills the promise of access by altering in significant ways the life opportunities of those who enter two-year colleges. One important way for administrators to prepare for this challenge is to renew their knowledge of student needs, capabilities, and aspirations by returning to the classroom periodically. Current lack of communication between administrators and faculty, and problems of faculty disengagement might be substantially addressed, if administrators, for even a brief time, saw themselves as teachers first and managers second.

References

AMERICAN ASSOCIATION OF COMMUNITY AND JUNIOR COLLEGES. "AACJC Public Policy Agenda." Washington, D.C.: American Association of Community and Junior Colleges, 1985.

———. *Community, Technical, and Junior College Directory.* Washington, D.C.: American Association of Community and Junior Colleges, 1984.

AMERICAN COUNCIL ON EDUCATION. *1984–85 Fact Book on Higher Education.* New York: Macmillan, 1984.

ASTIN, A. W. *Minorities in American Higher Education.* San Francisco: Jossey-Bass, 1982.

BRENEMAN, D. W., and NELSON, S. C. *Financing Community Colleges: An Economic Perspective.* Washington, D.C.: The Brookings Institution, 1981.

COHEN, A. M., and BRAWER, F. B. *The American Community College.* San Francisco: Jossey-Bass, 1982.

DIENER, T. "Community College Faculty Job Satisfaction." *Community/Junior College Quarterly of Research and Practice* 9(4)(1985):347–358.

GRANT, W. V., and SNYDER, T. D. *Digest of Education Statistics.* Washington, D.C.: National Center for Education Statistics, 1983–84.

HUTTON, J. B., and JOBE, M. E. "Job Satisfaction of Community College Faculty." *Community/Junior College Quarterly of Research and Practice* 9(4)(1985):317–324.

KELLER, G. *Academic Strategy.* Baltimore: Johns Hopkins University Press, 1983.

KISSLER, G. R. The Decline of the Transfer Function: Threats or Challenges?" In Kintzer, F. (ed.), *New Directions for Community Colleges: Improving Articulation and Transfer Relationships* (39). San Francisco: Jossey-Bass, 1982, 19–29.

McCABE, R. A. "Quality and the Open Door Community College." In Cross, K. P. (ed.), *Current Issues in Higher Education* 1(1982–83): ED. 233 636.

NATIONAL INSTITUTE OF EDUCATION. *Involvement in Learning: Realizing the Potential of American Higher Education.* Washington, D.C.: U.S. Government Printing Office, 1984.

RICHARDSON, R. C., JR., and BENDER, L. W. "Helping Minorities Achieve Degrees: The Urban Connection." A Report to the Ford Foundation, 1986.

RICHARDSON, R. C., JR., FISK, E. C., and OKUN, M. A. *Literacy in the Open Access College.* San Francisco: Jossey-Bass, 1983.

SCHUSTER, J. H., and BOWEN, H. R. "The Faculty At Risk." *Change* 17(4)(1985):12–21.

SEIDMAN, E. *In the Words of the Faculty: Perspectives on Improving Teaching and Educational Quality in Community Colleges.* San Francisco: Jossey-Bass, 1985.

WESTERN INTERSTATE COMMISSION FOR HIGHER EDUCATION. *High School Graduates: Projections for the Fifty States.* Boulder: 1984.

WILSON, R., and MELENDEZ, S. E. *Fourth Annual Status Report Minorities in Higher Education.* Washington, D.C.: American Council on Education, 1985.

2

Urban Community Colleges and a Collegiate Education: Restoring the Connection

ALISON R. BERNSTEIN

. . . we must also begin to examine the practices which form the basis of college instruction. If they do not re-enforce college-level learning, we run the risk of disappointing and shortchanging millions of students.

A critic of community-college education recently wrote "By the early 1980s the community college had become increasingly cut off from the mainstream of higher education. Increasingly vocational in orientation, community colleges came to emphasize their college-parallel liberal arts programs less and less (Karabel, 1986). His analysis is based upon two seemingly related phenomena. The first focuses on public community colleges as predominantly vocational-training institutions. In the 1980s, more than two-thirds of matriculated students are enrolled in vocational programs and 71 percent of all associate degrees and certificates were awarded in vocational areas. Fifteen years ago, only 25 percent of enrollment and 45 percent of degrees were vocational (Pincus, 1986). The second phenomenon is the striking decline in transfer rates from two-year colleges to four-year colleges that has been observed over the last two decades. While no one knows precisely how many students nationwide begin in a community college and eventually transfer, various institutional and state studies indicated that between 25–35 percent of community-college students transferred in the 1960s. The percentage has dropped to 15 percent today (Cohen and Brawer, 1982).

Do these phenomena, the vocational character of community colleges and their limited transfer function, offer conclusive evidence that community colleges have cut themselves off from the mainstream of higher education? Our answer is "no." For example, the increasingly vocational nature of community-college education is paralleled at the senior-college level. In most four-year institutions, the number of business majors outstrips the traditional liberal-arts disciplines by as much as five to one. Moreover, as a recent study suggests, those community-college students who are successfully transferring to senior colleges are increasingly coming from the so-called terminal or two-year vocational programs (Richardson and Bender, 1986).

That community colleges are educating larger numbers of vocational or career-minded students may not necessarily undermine their function as collegiate institutions. Few would question whether Baruch College of the City University of New York or the Rhode Island School of Design, both vocational in their response orientations, had left the mainstream of higher education. Yet, many comprehensive community colleges have not managed to overcome the image that they are nothing more than "high schools with ashtrays" or vocational-training institutes. Where we assume that Baruch College offers collegiate-level business programs, we wonder whether a community college's business program is different from a course of study offered by a private-proprietary business institute. Certainly the former takes longer and it should include nonbusiness, general-education courses. Yet, we are uncertain about the collegiate quality of this degree.

A community college should be distinguishable from a trade or technical school because it requires collegiate-level performance of its students. It cannot hold its students to this level of achievement, however, unless it is prepared to offer them college-level work and a collegiate environment. The collegiate function of a community college is not automatically synonymous with any single variable such as the number of transfer students, or the number of earned doctorates on the campus—although these are often used as surrogates for interpreting the quality of higher education offered. Nor is it easy to measure, by some set of commonly agreed-upon criteria, the extent to which an institution is successfully performing its collegiate function. Nevertheless, there is a growing body of literature on community-college education that takes a critical look at teaching and higher learning in these institutions and finds considerable room for improvement. This chapter will first review the major criticisms of collegiate-level learning in some urban community colleges, offer some new findings on the validity of these criticisms, and finally, propose several practices that characterize collegiate-level learning in a large urban community-college setting.

Collegiate-Level Learning

Some Criticism

Criticisms of collegiate-level learning in community colleges are a relatively new phenomenon and generally fall into three broad categories. The first is that students' academic programs lack coherence. Students take a series of courses, usually one or two a semester, until they either complete the proscribed requirements or they drop out. For many students, there is little that distinguishes their experiences as degree candidates in a community college from part timers who have no set educational goals and are simply there to take a course or two. Their education takes on no particular pattern or shape. A second criticism of collegiate-level learning looks closely at classroom teaching itself, and suggests that instead of teaching higher-order literacy skills—conceptualization, problem solving, analytical reading and writing—community-college instructors teach by communicating bits of knowledge that students are expected to regurgitate in objective short-answer tests. This concept of "bitting" was first described by Richard Richardson in his thought-provoking study, *Literacy in the Open-Access College* (1983). Community colleges have also been criticized for the virtual absence of a sense of community and involvement in learning beyond the classroom. This criticism, which was embodied in the report of the Study Group on the Conditions of Excellence in American Higher Education, entitled *Involvement in Learning* (NIE, 1984), struck deeply at the notion of collegiality in community colleges. Because community colleges have largely part-time faculty and student bodies, the study group argues that they have not found ways to encourage students to think that they are part of an intellectual community whose engagement with learning continues after the end of class. Before examining the validity of each of these criticisms, it is important to understand why they have emerged at this time.

Background and Analysis

Before the early 1980s, few policymakers or researchers had questioned teaching and learning practices within community colleges. It was widely assumed that because there was no pressure to publish or perish, faculty members gave full attention to their teaching responsibilities. Also, it was assumed that the prevalence of smaller classroom size of community colleges provided the kind of close student–faculty contact that was lacking in larger, more impersonal settings. Indeed, that faculty members have greater teaching loads but smaller classes is common in community colleges. But these two aspects of undergraduate instruction at the community college do not necessarily translate into an effective teaching and learning environment. Too often administrators have used the primacy of teaching and smaller classes to justify their claims that community colleges are student-centered institutions without examining whether these factors actually lead to the creation of a collegiate environment.

In the past, community-college advocates coupled an emphasis on teaching in a small-classroom setting with the practice of open admissions to characterize the special nature of undergraduate education at the community-college level. Because they were open to all students regardless of their previous levels of academic preparation, community colleges could not be expected to adopt a four-year-college model of undergraduate instruction that included admissions standards, sequenced patterns of course instruction from introductory to advanced levels with required prerequisites for all liberal-arts undertakings, and more rigid policies governing academic progress. Because the community college was designed to give a second chance to those individuals whom traditional higher education had bypassed, it needed the freedom and flexibility to offer its own kind of undergraduate education.

While it is always difficult to generalize about so diverse a set of institutions, several common characteristics that distinguish undergraduate collegiate education in community colleges from four-year institutions have evolved over the last decade. These characteristics go beyond the differences in teaching loads or classroom size between two- and four-year institutions. To explore these characteristics, the Ford Foundation commissioned two reports that examined transfer education in a group of urban community and four-year colleges. The first report, entitled *Transfer Education in American Community Colleges,* was prepared in 1985 by the Center for the Study of Community Colleges. It involved surveys of faculty and student attitudes, practices, and behaviors regarding transfer education, and by extension, undergraduate collegiate-level learning in community colleges. The second report was prepared by Richard Richardson, Jr., and Louis Bender of Arizona State University and Florida State University, respectively. This study, *Helping Minorities Achieve Degrees: The Urban Connection* (1986), analyzed relationships between two- and four-year institutions in eight urban areas using interviews, questionnaires, and existing data bases. Taken together, these two efforts shed new light on teaching and learning practices in community colleges and how they differ from baccalaureate-degree-granting institutions.

The center's report involved a survey that was developed in 1984 and sent to a sample of 444 faculty members at two dozen urban community colleges nationwide. These faculty members primarily taught college and university-parallel courses, that is, the courses eligible for transfer credit at a senior institution. Of the 444 surveys distributed, usable responses were returned from 347 individuals for a total return rate of 78 percent. Faculty members were asked to indicate whether the course level they taught was remedial, introductory, or intermediate. Only 3 percent of the faculty members who completed the survey reported that they taught remedial courses, whereas over two-thirds of the courses taught by the sampled faculty fell into the introductory level. The remainder were classified as intermediate- or sophomore-level courses. Nearly 75 percent of the sampled faculty held full-time appointments at the colleges.

A larger student survey was also developed by the Center and mailed to over 2,900 students, of which 1,613 were returned. Like the faculty, these students were involved primarily in transfer and university-parallel courses. They were surveyed in those course sections identified as eligible for college credit. Minorities accounted for 64 percent of the total sample, and, of the total number of students, 56 percent were females.

In general, the responses of both students and faculty confirmed the conclusions of previous researchers who found that senior-college faculty are more likely to assign a greater quantity of reading assignments and use written assignments as a basis for evaluating student performance (Alba and Lavin, 1981; Smith, 1983). Specifically, the Center's report revealed that a majority of the faculty based at least 25 percent of a student's final grade on quick-score/objective tests. More alarming than this practice of relying on short-answer tests as the basis of the final grade, however, was the fact that 45 percent of the faculty surveyed reported not using essay exams as part of the final grade. Students also reported that they had few reading and writing assignments. The following data indicated that the average number of assigned text-books and written assignments for the majority of students is less than five a semester.

Reading and Writing Requirements Percent of Students

ASSIGNMENTS	NONE	LESS THAN 5	5–10	10 OR MORE
Required textbooks	3.0	45.5	39.1	12.4
Assigned termpapers/				
Reports	12.6	47.6	25.0	14.8
Essay Exams	11.4	38.0	33.7	16.8

Note: These data are only for students who indicated preparing for transfer as their primary reason for attending college. (Center for the study of Community Colleges, 1985, p. 129).

Students generally take detailed notes in class and, if they write, it is usually during the class in response to a specific question posed by the instructor.

The faculties' preference for short-answer exams, few writing and reading assignments and generally less conceptual work suggests that community colleges do not necessarily utilize the teaching and learning benefits that accompany smaller classes. Typically, larger lecture classes make it impossible for faculty to assign a great deal of written work or employ essay-based exams. But a smaller class should afford more opportunities for the faculty to encourage original written work from the students. Moreover, having fewer students should enable faculty to explore different pedagogies such as peer tutoring, group learning, and the examination of primary source material. The Center's report provides convincing evidence that community-college faculty rely too heavily on classroom lectures and rote regurgitation of material. This implies that there is little emphasis on requiring students to solve problems or deal with concepts rather than facts.

Another important finding from the Center's study relates to student–faculty interaction. Several questions in the faculty survey explored the type of information faculty have about their students on education and career aspirations, academic backgrounds, and employment. A majority did not have information on student transfer aspirations (67%), performance on basic-skills tests (81%), and employment status (80%). The faculties' lack of information regarding student characteristics seems to be a reflection of their lack of contact with students outside the classroom. Responses from both students and faculty indicated that only a small proportion of faculty interact with students in settings other than the classroom or the instructor's office. As the authors observe:

> Much of the literature on community colleges emphasizes that one of their strengths is a high level of concern for individual needs within a nurturing environment. An essential condition to a student-centered environment—faculty awareness of individual needs—is not demonstrated in the data reported. [Center for the Study of Community Colleges, 1985, p. 79]

To some extent, this finding contradicts the conclusions of Richardson's and Bender's 1986 analysis of two- and four-year college relationships in the urban setting. In surveying successful transfer students, these researchers found evidence for considerable differences between community college and university faculty in terms of openness to student ideas, availability, and helpfulness with career plans. They write "In the first two areas, community college instructors held more than a 3 to 1 advantage, reflecting the supportive environment of the community college" (Richardson and Bender, 1986). In marked contrast to responses about availability, however, were student reports that universities had courses more relevant to their educational goals and at more appropriate levels of difficulty.

Student data from the Richardson and Bender study corroborated faculty observations of greater rigor in university courses. It is significant that students endorsed the greater demands required by university courses. As one student wrote:

> Community colleges should better prepare their students for longer and more complex reading assignments. The exams should be more difficult and they should be structured for testing a student's knowledge of the materials instead of simply memorization and recall." [p. 172]

From comments of this type, Richardson and Bender draw important conclusions regarding the differences between the kind of collegiate education offered at community and four-year colleges.

Their report argues that the most fundamental difference between the two types of institutions involves faculty and administrators' attitudes about the importance of knowledge, standards, and the academic experience itself. As the authors observe:

> Course rigor and course grading standards clearly reflected the difference in values between universities and community colleges. In the community college, grading standards were said to be norm referenced (how the student performs in relation to others taking the same class) while in the university, faculty members believed that standards were criterion referenced (measured against a standard that does not change with variations in preparation or aptitude of those enrolled in the course). Both university and community college faculty agreed that rigor was greater in the university and offered evidence to support this belief. [p. 43]

Instead of reacting defensively to this claim that community colleges lack rigor, the majority of Richardson and Bender's respondents argued that they were proud of the supportive environment community colleges provided. "From their perspectives," the authors note, "the attitudes and practices of their university counterparts were deliberately elitist and subversive to the goals of equal access."

Research Recommendations

Neither Richardson nor Bender endorses one set of institutional values over the other. The difficulty lies, however, where students are caught between these conflicting institutional worlds in their pursuit of baccalaureate degrees. For example, the researchers argue that students should not have to choose between meeting the requirements for a community-college degree and fulfilling the lower-division program of studies specified for a baccalaureate degree. Currently, these two programs are rarely reconciled. Moreover, the authors believe that community colleges should increase the emphasis on program continuity and achievement without relinquishing the caring attitudes that have been their hallmark. This means that the community colleges should maintain a full range of transfer courses according to some preannounced and guaranteed timetable, and therefore reverse the frequent practice of cancelling sophomore-level courses because they are under-enrolled. In addition, Richardson and Bender recommend that community colleges strengthen course rigor by placing greater emphasis on reading for comprehension and writing to synthesize as contrasted with reading for recognition and multiple-choice examinations. In these ways, community colleges can continue to be student centered by making courses more comparable to those the students will experience after transferring. In summary, Richardson and Bender call upon community-college faculty and administrators to balance their emphasis on access and respon-siveness to students' developmental needs with an equal emphasis on effectiveness and quality control. The commitment to offer underprepared first-generation college students special supports should not diminish the college's responsibility to provide an en-vironment that stresses academic achievement. To do otherwise would be the equivalent of shortchanging many, if not most, stu-dents' collegiate goals.

Although the center's report and the Richardson and Bender study do not purport to offer the definitive statement on collegiate education in community colleges, they both examine several teaching and learning practices in two-year institutions that are at variance with those at senior colleges. For students who do not plan to pursue baccalaureate degrees, these differences in colle-giate-level learning do not appear to pose any immediate burden, since the students' only experience of college would be the courses they completed at the two-year institution. In practical terms, they will have no other frame of reference, and their level of satisfaction can be easily assessed by asking whether the community colleges meet their expectations. Of course, this kind of evaluation is highly individualistic and does not provide any sense of quality control. For the more than 60 percent of community-college students with baccalaureate aspirations, however, this kind of self-evaluation may be premature and insufficient. These students are entitled to assume that their community-college experience parallels the col-legiate experiences of students in four-year institutions. This does not mean that community colleges should imitate teaching and learning practices in research universities or even small liberal-arts colleges. It does mean that community colleges have an obligation to insure that students receive collegiate-level instruction. But what do we mean by collegiate-level instruction?

Suggested Practices

It is not easy to define the characteristics of college-level learning for any given institution. Naturally, one commonly agreed-upon characteristic is the expectation that students will comprehend material beyond twelfth-grade reading levels. As the Study Group on the Conditions of Excellence wrote in its report, "By urging the standard of a twelfth grade norm for completing remedial English classes, we are underscoring the fact that anything less—particularly in reading—leaves students wholly unprepared for the demands of college-level courses and does them a disservice" (NIE, 1984). In addition to proscribed reading levels, there are several practices that we associate with college-level learning that are not as evident in other postsecondary educational institutions. These practices do not in themselves insure that students are receiving collegiate instruction, but they do suggest that students are engaged in the process of higher learning. There are three general practices that should characterize collegiate-level learning in community colleges.

The first of these practices is frequent, increasingly complex writing assignments. College-level learning requires students to grapple with ideas, not just facts. These ideas must be communicated both orally and in written form. Nor is it enough to write one-page essays in a composition class. Students need to be challenged to express themselves in all their classes. This practice with writing should involve critical essays on assigned reading material, commentary on class discussions, term papers on a research topic, and essays responses for examination purposes. The ability to write a carefully crafted essay is undeniably one of the hallmarks of an educated person. As the late Mina Shaughnessy wrote, "Writing is not only a necessary skill in college and an advantageous skill in work but the most accessible way people have of exploring and perfecting their thoughts" (1977). Writing does not guarantee that the student is engaged in college-level learning. But it is virtually impossible for a student to demonstrate mastery over ideas and concepts without skill in writing.

The second practice that should characterize college-level learning in community colleges is perfecting the students' research and problem-solving skills. Unlike proficiency in learning a specific body of knowledge or technical field, college-level research and problem-solving skills are generic. This kind of learning involves teaching students to identify a problem, disaggregate the factors that give rise to the problem, analyze the causes of the problem, and finally, explore possible solutions. Whether the problem involves literature, history, the social sciences, or the sciences, students should have the intellectual tools to understand and interpret familiar and unfamiliar phenomena. For example, a favorite exercise in a college music-history class is "drop the needle." In this lesson, students hear a composition they have never heard before and are asked to analyze it—the form, the style, the performance, and the cultural context in which it was developed. The purpose of the exercise is not to guess the composer, but rather to demonstrate an ability to struggle with the problem of understanding the composition. Too often, students are expected to regurgitate the problem-solving techniques of those experts who came before them. This translates into an overreliance on textbooks or secondary sources to find the answer. College-level learning requires a student's engagement with the original or primary source, not a distilled version or a synthesis that emerges from someone else's research. While there are no easy ways to test whether a student is engaged in research and problem solving, there are several indirect ways of measuring whether the college emphasizes this practice. They include whether students use the library as more than a study center, whether faculty members include primary sources in their course syllabi, and whether students correspondingly use these original sources in their essays and papers.

A third practice that should characterize college-level learning is introducing students to subject matter that they would not ordinarily pursue given their educational or career goals. Using traditional definitions, this subject matter would form the basis of the student's general or liberal education while in college. It should not be geared toward the student's concentration, nor should it be simply a reflection of a state's mandated degree requirements. Instead, this subject matter should reflect the particular college's educational objectives. Too often, however, a community college designs a course of study requiring only those subjects that outside agencies (licensing associations, state-education departments) require. In other words, their curriculum represents the "least common denominator" course-credit approach to higher learning. For example, when a state mandates that an associate in arts degree must include 24–30 credits in liberal-arts fields, the college does not necessarily take that requirement and shape it into a coherent educational experience involving either a core curriculum or familiarity with a culture or language outside the student's experience. The practice of exposing students to alternative world views, other cultures, or simply new ways of looking at familiar issues should find expression in the curriculum of a college. The liberalizing benefits of this kind of educational practice are especially important in community colleges where faculty and administrators cannot assume that students are receiving this education on their own. While many urban community colleges serve diverse ethnic and racial populations, it would be a mistake to assume that these students are already familiar with each other's communities or the world beyond their neighborhoods.

The practice of exposing students to material outside their area of concentration is especially important for those students who are not pursuing degrees, but rather those who have chosen associate of science or associate of applied science vocational tracks. No other single practice separates community-college education from vocational training than the course of study students elect in this, the liberal component of their college curriculum. This theme has been most forcefully articulated by the Study Group on Conditions of Excellence in Higher Education:

> We thus conclude that the best preparation for the future is not narrow training for a specific job, but rather an education that will enable students to adapt to a changing world. . . . Adaption to change requires that one draw on history, and so on the experience of other nations, and that one apply the theories and methods of empirical investigation. . . . These requirements

are as relevant to the future of a medical technician in training at a community college as they are to the biology major at a university. To fulfill them is to achieve a liberal education. [National Institute of Education, 1984, p. 43]

By focusing on these three curricular practices, namely, placing an emphasis on writing assignments, research and problem-solving skills, and a broad liberal education for all students, we have not exhausted the characteristics of college-level learning that community colleges should exhibit. There are other equally valid ways of providing students with a collegiate education. Some researchers would urge community colleges to offer more opportunities for faculty–student dialogue outside class by structuring debating clubs, international studies efforts, and film societies. Others would focus on tightening grading practices to eliminate relying too heavily on incomplete grades. Still others might focus their attention on designing more sequential courses that demonstrate intellectual progress from introductory- to intermediate-level work. Many community-college courses lack prerequisities and therefore, do not appear to follow any educational pattern based on achievement. Clearly, there is room for improvement in each of these areas. But we must also begin to examine the practices that form the basis of college instruction. If they do not reinforce college-level learning, we run the risk of disappointing and short-changing millions of students. After all, they come to our institutions in search of a college education, not just an increasingly suspect credential.

References

ALBA, R. D., and LAVIN, D. E. "Community Colleges and Teaching in Higher Education." *Sociology of Education*, 1981, vol. 54.

Center for the Study of Community Colleges. *Transfer Education in American Community Colleges*, a report to the Ford Foundation, 1985.

COHEN, ARTHUR M., and BRAWER, FLORENCE. *The American Community College.* San Francisco: Jossey-Bass, 1982.

KARABEL, JEROME. "Community Colleges and Social Stratification in the

1980s." In Zwerling, L. S. (ed.), *The Community College and Its Critics.* San Francisco: Jossey-Bass, 1986.

NATIONAL INSTITUTE OF EDUCATION. *Involvement in Learning: Realizing the Potential of American Higher Education.* Washington, D.C.: U.S. Government Printing Office, 1984.

PINCUS, FRED L. "Vocational Education: More False Promises." In Zwerling, L. S. (ed.), *The Community College and Its Critics.* San Francisco: Jossey-Bass, 1986.

RICHARDSON, R. C., JR., and BENDER, LOUIS. *Helping Minorities Achieve Degrees: The Urban Connection,* a report to the Ford Foundation, March, 1986.

RICHARDSON, R. C., JR., FISK, E. C., and OKUN, M. A. *Literacy in the Open-Access College.* San Francisco: Jossey-Bass, 1983.

SHAUGHNESSY, MINA P. *Errors and Expectations.* New York: Oxford University Press, 1977.

SMITH, K. M. *Student Achievement and Open Admission: Do Student Outcomes Fulfill the Promise of the Open Door?* Los Angeles: ERIC Clearinghouse for Junior Colleges (JC 830 143), 1983.

3

Defining and Measuring Quality in Community College Education

CHARLENE R. NUNLEY
DAVID W. BRENEMAN

When the efficiency of community college baccalaureate preparation is viewed in the broader context of all possible post-high school choices available to those who desire a bachelor's degree, community college attendance has been found in the current research to be positively related to years of education achieved and to baccalaureate degree achievement.

National studies of elementary, secondary, and higher education that are critical of educational effectiveness have also contributed to emerging interest and concern about quality in the educational environment (e.g., National Endowment for the Humanities, 1984; Association of American Colleges, 1985; National Institute of Education, 1984). A special *Change* magazine report on "States and Quality" (1986) documents a variety of actions that states are undertaking to assure educational effectiveness. These include mandatory testing of college sophomores in order to qualify them for junior work and implementation of incentive funding for improving the quality of college education. Edgerton (1986) suggests that ". . . states have every right to demand higher performance from colleges and universities as well as better evidence about what's going on" (p. 11). Institutions too are demonstrating increased concern for quality as evidenced by examination of standards of academic progress in colleges throughout the country. The National Commission on Excellence in Education (1984) has defined quality as

> performing on the boundary of individual ability in ways that test and push back personal limits. . . . Excellence characterizes a school or college that sets high expectations . . . for all learners, then tries in every way possible to help students reach them. [p. 12]

For many four-year colleges, quality has been defined as taking those students with the most talent and highest educational potential and helping them to achieve their potential. As a result, quality of four-year colleges and universities has often been assessed by selectivity of admissions standards, ratings of quality of graduate schools, the number of students who make the *Law Review,* or the number of graduates who achieve outstanding professional accomplishments.

Such definitions have not proved to be particularly effective for community colleges. Community colleges were created from the outset as open-access colleges with a commitment to serving all those who can benefit from higher education. This creates a different context in which to evaluate educational effectiveness. As Breneman and Nelson (1981) point out

> the nature of community colleges virtually guarantees a continuing debate on what those institutions do for their students. Diversity may be a source of strength in the community

college sector, but it contributes to a proliferation of judgments on the outcomes from community college experiences. [p. 55]

Applying the same criteria in evaluating community colleges that have been used in evaluating four-year colleges certainly is not appropriate. On the other hand, the argument that has been advanced by some community-college educators that because of the nontraditional nature of their student bodies, whatever happens as a result of community-college attendance is a positive result, is equally inappropriate. This definition of effectiveness defines away failure and makes impossible the identification of evaluative standards and criteria.

Most community-college leaders do not accept this definition and recognize that research on educational results must be done. However, in conducting this research, measures must be constructed that are consistent with the unique community-college mission and the nature and objectives of their student bodies. The paragraphs that follow summarize the status and findings of research on community-college effectiveness and make a case for extending and improving the adequacy and comprehensiveness of this research. They also summarize a new national study of community-college effectiveness in baccalaureate-degree preparation with results that are considerably different from previous research efforts.

The Status of Research on Community-College Results

The difficulty of constructing appropriate measures of community colleges' effectiveness is increased by the fact that issues of institutional mission are being debated in many states and individual institutions. Community colleges have evolved as institutions serving multiple purposes including transfer preparation, vocational preparation, continuing education, and community services. Some policymakers are questioning whether this diversity enhances or impedes educational excellence in these institutions. Should community colleges continue their efforts to be comprehensive institutions offering transfer, vocational, and continuing education or should they narrow their focus and concentrate in one or two of these areas? How important is the collegiate function? How much attention should be given to the community-service role?

Questions about mission and inadequate mission definition have made comprehensive evaluation of results difficult. However, most community colleges do undertake efforts to assess and monitor performance in at least some areas. In several states, such as Texas and Maryland, statewide efforts to monitor effectiveness of career and transfer education are in effect. A few national studies have also investigated the effectiveness of elements of community-college education.

A variety of outcomes that relate directly or indirectly to community-college effectiveness have been measured in these studies. They have investigated associate-degree achievement, transfer rates, performance of community college transfers at four-year institutions, baccalaureate-degree achievement, employment of occupational-program graduates, employer satisfaction with community-college-graduate employees, earnings, reasons for attrition, student satisfaction with community-college preparation, and student attitudes toward the community college. A few have investigated occupational status, unemployment rates, and job satisfaction of community-college attenders.

The literature on results of community-college education is one that varies widely in quality, response rates, findings, and interpretations. Most of the local and many of the state studies have been descriptive in nature using no control groups, performance standards, norms or other measures that would improve their usefulness as evaluative tools. The state studies have been useful because they provide statewide data to which individual institutions can compare their performance. Generally, the state and local studies have been positive in their conclusions about the effectiveness of community-college education.

National studies, on the other hand, have been much less positive about community-college education particularly as it relates to the baccalaureate-preparation function of these institutions. Most well known of the national reviews are studies conducted by Astin (1977) and by Breneman and Nelson (1981). They have studied community-college outcomes for recent high-school graduates. These studies generally have used statistical methods to create "matched" comparison groups and have therefore lent themselves more readily to evaluative conclusions than have the local studies. The authors of these studies have found that even after controlling for socioeconomic status, high-school grades, educational aspirations, part- or full-time attendance, type of program, and type of college, the probability that a given recent high-school graduate would have earned a bachelor's degree was lower for one attending a community college than for one attending a four-year school. In examining several other possible results of attendance, Breneman and Nelson found no effect of community-college attendance on wages, a possible negative effect on occupational status, a positive effect on employment rate, no effect on job satisfaction, no effect on student ratings of their progress toward career goals, no effect on status of the occupation aspired to, and no effect on educational goals for community-college entrants. Again, these findings were noted after controlling for high-school grades, full- or part-time college attendance, type of program enrolled in, sex, and many other factors that have demonstrated a relationship to educational outcomes in prior research studies.

There are several concerns about the methods employed in the national studies, particularly as the findings relate to bachelor's degree achievement of community-college entrants. In virtually all of these studies, data were collected only four to five years after the student entered college. If, as is likely to be the case, community-college students take longer to achieve degrees because of less regular attendance patterns or other reasons, it is probable that differences in degree achievement rates will decline as the time between college entry and data collection increases. Also, both the Breneman and Nelson and Astin research compare only a limited set of available post high school choices for students who graduate from high school with baccalaureate-degree goals. They include analyses of only two-year and four-year college attendance ignoring the fact that many students with four-year degree goals choose or are forced to delay entry to college, or choose to attend a vocational–technical school or to attend some other type of postsecondary institution. As Leslie (1982) cogently points out, "comparing community college students' achievements to high school graduates' achievements may be more appropriate than comparing them to four-year college students' achievements" (p. 7). Such a comparison, in his opinion, more satisfactorily tests what community colleges are all about: "provision of opportunity for those who would not attend otherwise" (p. 7). Unquestionably, comparisons of results of all alternatives available to the high-school graduate with a bachelor's degree objective is necessary to assure a comprehensive evaluation of community-college effectiveness.

Because of the diversity of mission and programs in community colleges, national studies are likely to disguise rather wide variations in effectiveness among individual institutions. This is a reasonable concern with regard to vocational programs and continuing-education activities that vary widely from one college to another. On the other hand, it is probable that the transfer function bears some reasonable similarity from institution to institution. In their transfer programs, all community colleges are striving to produce graduates who will meet admission requirements of four-year colleges without undue loss of credit hours. The main differences among institutions are probably differences in the variety of transfer courses available and differences in the characteristics of their student bodies. While these differences are not unimportant, they are not nearly as significant as the differences in vocational programs and continuing education that exist among institutions. Differences in entering-student characteristics, for example, can be controlled through appropriate statistical techniques.

Finally, the national studies of community-college effectiveness have been limited by the fact that they have not investigated alternative benefits for those students who do not achieve bachelor-degree goals. For community-college students, the issue of alternative results is particularly important, since short-term career program alternatives that do not exist in four-year colleges are available to community-college entrants. Therefore, when community-college students change majors, they may select a program that is designed for direct career entry after two-years rather than for transfer to a four-year college.

The studies have several advantages, however, that make further consideration and exploration of their methods important. First, the research approaches are strongly founded in theory. The research of Breneman and Nelson, for example, has been derived through application of the concept of economic efficiency—a concept that provides a framework for evaluating the implications of the research findings. Certainly this is not the only theoretical framework that could be applied; however, it is a useful one. Much of the community-college-outcomes research that has been conducted to date has no theoretical base. Second, the national studies have employed statistical methodology that permits the creation of statistically matched comparison or control groups. This improves the evaluative usefulness of the research. Statistical matching, though imperfect, is probably the best that can be achieved in this kind of evaluative research since random assignment of students to educational institutions is not possible. Finally, in those areas where varying types of postsecondary institutions are performing the same or similar functions (such as lower-division baccalaureate preparation), it is useful to compare and contrast their effectiveness in order to support implementation of sound educational policy.

The Concept of Economic Efficiency as a Theoretical Base

Efficiency is defined by economists as maximizing net benefits. According to Breneman and Nelson, "an efficient allocation of resources is said to occur when the total benefits from the production of some good or service exceed by as much as possible the total cost of producing it" (1981, p. 41). Assessment of efficiency therefore requires measurement of costs and benefits as well as assessment of the net benefit (benefit minus cost) of producing the same result through similar or different methods. The existence of benefits to the individual is what produces individual investment in higher education. The existence of benefits for society is what justifies and results in public support of higher education. While there is some disagreement among economists about the ratio of individual to social benefits, most would certainly admit to some social benefit of higher education and to the fact that this benefit justifies some level of public support.

The economic efficiency of a public-finance system is assessed by determining whether the maximum amount of public service is being provided for the dollars expended. Because of increasing competition among alternative recipients of limited public resources, policymakers have become increasingly concerned with assuring an efficient allocation of resources among differing types of postsecondary education and between postsecondary education and other competitors for public resources. Two ways to judge the efficiency of allocation of resources to education are through application of the value-added approach to the evaluation of outcomes and through rate-of-return analysis. In both approaches, measurement of outcomes is exceedingly important. Breneman and Nelson explain that "in theory considerations of efficiency assume an understanding of outcome levels . . ." (1981, p. 40).

Astin is one of the chief proponents of use of the value-added approach in assessing educational effectiveness. In evaluation of the outcomes of higher education, the value-added approach asks how much the college experience has added to the student's intellectual, economic, and personal development over the level that would have been achieved if college had not been attended. The value-added approach, therefore, requires use of control groups of students who have not had an opportunity to attend college so that motivational and other effects can be disaggregated from the effects that are specifically attributed to college attendance itself. It also permits comparison among different types of educational institutions of the level of benefit achieved in similar programs offered by these institutions.

Rate of return is similar to value added but it adds "the cost of generating the benefits into the calculations" (Breneman and Nelson, 1981, p. 56). Generally, rate-of-return analysis has been applied to assessment of earnings of students who do and do not attend college. A substantial number of these "human-capital" studies have been undertaken, but few other than the research of Breneman and Nelson have attempted to sort out the value added by community-college education and contrast it to the value added by other types of educational experiences.

Key in assessment of value added is defining and contrasting suitable comparison groups. For example, in assessing the effectiveness of community-college education, it is possible to compare the results of community-college attendance to four-year college and university attendance, to attendance at proprietary schools, to attendance at other types of postsecondary institutions, and to no postsecondary attendance at all. Depending on the comparison group or groups used, different conclusions may be reached. Findings about community-college effectiveness may differ substantially depending on whether community-college-student achievements are contrasted to high-school-student achievements or to four-year-college-student achievements. Probably most appropriate in assessment of educational efficiency of community colleges is the inclusion of all possible comparison groups so that a comprehensive assessment can be obtained.

Why use comparison groups at all? Why not simply test students on entering and exiting skill levels? While this type of "value-added" research is certainly useful and should be considered by more than the handful of institutions that use it today, without comparison groups it is impossible to sort out the effects of maturation (Campbell and Stanley, 1963) from the effects of the educational experience itself. Over any given period of time, all people change. What they know changes, what they believe changes, goals change, attitudes change, earnings change. Value-added research without comparison groups will identify these changes and attribute them to the educational experience. Comparison groups permit one to determine more conclusively those outcomes that result from the educational experience itself. In addition, few institutions have undertaken the kind of pre- and posttesting that is necessary to assess value added if comparison groups are not used.

Analysis of outcomes is a useful tool when one is reviewing the economic efficiency of a public-finance system. The concept of economic efficiency provides a framework through which findings can be interpreted. However, value-added research has significance in and of itself, since it represents one of the few clear ways by which research results can be attributed to the effects of the educational experience itself.

Breneman and Nelson's Methodology for Measuring Efficiency: Comparative Analysis of Results Using a Value-Added Approach

In assessing the efficiency of community-college education, Breneman and Nelson (1981) examined labor-force, educational, and psychological outcomes of community-college attendance. Their research is important because it included one of the most comprehensive varieties of measures to be included in national studies of community-college effectiveness. Their analysis used two approaches. In the first, they attempted "to explain each of the three kinds of outcomes as functions of background characteristics, external factors and post-high-school experiences, focusing on initial postsecondary educational choices" (p. 70). In the second, they tested

> the proposition that the process of educational attainment is different at community colleges than at universities, and also tried to determine whether a given type of student would have been better or worse off following a different post-high school path than the one chosen. [p. 70]

In their first approach, they employed the statistical method of multiple regression. In the second, they used analysis of covariance. In their research they hypothesized that

> a person's standing four years after graduation from high school in terms of outcome measures is a function of (1) characteristics upon high school graduation; (2) experience after high school; (3) external conditions beyond the person's control; and (4) random factors. [p. 69]

They defined and included as many of these factors as possible in their analysis. Breneman and Nelson were interested in a national assessment of community-college effectiveness since they were undertaking their research as a part of a national study of community-college finance methods. They decided, therefore, that the National Longitudinal Study of the High School Class of 1972 was the most useful available data set for their research. This data set includes a nationally stratified sample of approximately 23,000 students who were high-school seniors in 1972. Follow-ups of this class were conducted in October 1973, October 1974, October 1976, and October 1979. The 1979 survey was not available at the time of their study. Response rates to the National Longitudinal Study are rather high; for example, 86 percent of the initial sample responded to the 1976 follow-up.

Breneman and Nelson employed the data base to assess: (1) years of postsecondary education achieved; (2) bachelor-degree achievement; (3) hourly earnings; (4) occupational status; (5) weeks worked as a fraction of weeks in the labor force; (6) job satisfaction; (7) change in occupational aspirations; (8) change in years of education desired; and (9) satisfaction with progress toward goals for age thirty.

Among Breneman and Nelson's findings regarding community-college results, the most negative relate to educational attainment. They found that

> attending a community college instead of a four-year institution does tend to reduce the probability of receiving a bachelor's degree and the number of years of education completed four and one-half years after high school, even controlling for the independent variables" such as ability, socioeconomic status, degree objective, high school program, college program, and so on. [1981, p. 71]

They found an 11 percent reduction in probability of earning a bachelor degree for a student who entered a two-year college as contrasted to a four-year college. They concluded,

> the strongest effect of the educational path chosen right after high school is on educational attainment; choosing a community college has a negative effect on the amount of education received within the first few years after high school graduation. [1981, p. 72]

In the educational-attainment part of their analysis, Breneman and Nelson contrasted only community-college attendance and four-year-college attendance. In all other aspects of their research they included post-high-school choices other than two-year- or four-year-college attendance, including vocational-school attendance and no college attendance.

Breneman and Nelson's negative findings with regard to educational attainment of community-college entrants caused a stir in the two-year-college community in part because the research was subject to several of the limitations of other national studies on community-college effectiveness as specified earlier. In particular, the Breneman and Nelson research measured results only four-and-one-half years after college entry; compared results of two-year-college attendance only to four-year-college attendance thereby ignoring other available choice alternatives; and did not assess the possibility of alternative benefits to bachelor's degree achievement for community-college entrants with degree objectives.

A Modified Approach to Evaluating Transfer Education Results

To further examine the results of community-college baccalaureate preparation, recent additional research has been completed using a 1979 follow-up of the High School Class of 1972 (Nunley, in press). This data set permitted assessment of outcomes seven-and-one-half years after high-school graduation, thereby addressing one of the major limitations of previous research. Seven-and-one-half years allows a more comprehensive assessment of community-college outcomes considering the nontraditional and sometimes erratic attendance patterns of community-college students.

In addition, the sample included in the study involved only those persons who indicated that their goal following high-school graduation was to achieve a bachelor's degree. Previous research in Maryland (McConochie, 1981; Tschechtelin, 1976; Tschechtelin and McLean, 1980) has identified a close relationship between students' educational objectives and actual educational attainment. Because of the availability of one- and two-year career programs and specific-skills courses at community colleges, many students who enroll in these colleges are not seeking four-year degrees. Most students who enter four-year colleges, on the other hand, are seeking at least a baccalaureate degree. Therefore, the student's entering objective is an important factor to be considered when assessing community-college effectiveness.

Also, a more comprehensive variety of the post-high-school options available to those students who have bachelor-degree objectives was included than in the Breneman and Nelson research. In light of the previously noted comments of Leslie (1982), a less than comprehensive analysis of the educational outcomes of community-college attendance results when educational attainment of community-college entrants is compared to attainment for only those students who attend four-year colleges and universities. An expanded perspective can be gained by undertaking analyses that contrast the effect of a broader set of post-high-school options. These options include attendance at a four-year college or university, attendance at a community college, attendance at a vocational–technical center, attendance at some other type of postsecondary institution, and delayed college entry.

Finally, a methodology has been developed for investigation of alternative outcomes and exploratory investigation of a few of the many alternative benefits that may accrue to students who enter community colleges with baccalaureate-degree objectives but who have not achieved those objectives seven years after entry to the college. In the alternative-benefits research the relationship of community-college attendance to earnings, job satisfaction, and job status was investigated for those students who entered community colleges with bachelor-degree objectives but did not ultimately achieve those objectives.

Findings

Using a direct replication of the Breneman and Nelson approach and a seven-year follow-up, a narrowing of the differential in years of education achieved by two-year- and four-year-college entrants was noted, but four-year-college entrants had still achieved higher educational levels than two-year entrants. Regression coefficients found by Breneman and Nelson suggest that attending a community college reduced years of education achieved by .28 years. With seven-year follow-up, this rate narrowed to .12 years (see Tables 3.1 and 3.2). This finding prevailed even when entrants were matched on important pretreatment variables.

TABLE 3.1 *Regression Coefficients for Bachelor-Degree Achievement*

Variable	Breneman and Nelson 1976 Follow-Up	1979 Follow-Up
Constant	NA	0.383 (4.765)**
CC72	−0.113 (−5.830)**	−0.114 (−6.847)**
SMCTYHS	0.051 (3.317)**	0.023 (1.534)
CMTYSIZE	—[a]	0.001 (.248)
HOMEWORK	0.006 (2.828)**	0.003 (1.572)
FRENPLAN	—	0.019 (1.034)
HSJOB	—	−0.007 (−2.287)*
COLDECSN	−0.037 (−5.477)**	0.021 (3.612)**
COLABIL	—	0.011 (1.081)
LIVARR72	−0.113 (−7.211)	−0.074 (−5.470)**
MARRY72	−0.190 (−5.292)**	−0.080 (−1.491)
KIDS76	−0.082 (−3.317)**	−0.202 (−8.496)**
ACAD72	−0.094 (−2.530)**	0.046 (1.821)
GRADES73	−0.063 (−10.91)**	−0.047 (−9.110)**
FTEN72	—	0.052 (1.603)
RACE Black	—	0.002 (.047)
White	—[a]	−0.002 (−.065)
SEX	0.042 (2.828)**	−0.026 −2.011)*
SES	0.003 (2.828)**	0.025 (2.506)**

TABLE 3.1 *(continued)*

Variable	Breneman and Nelson 1976 Follow-Up	1979 Follow-Up
EDASPMO	0.025	(0.015
	(2.236)*	(1.943)*
BAPLANHS	—	0.441
		(25.652)**
ENGLISH	—	0.015
		(.654)
HSGRADES	0.020	−0.017
	(6.245)**	(−6.384)**
HSACAD	—	−0.013
		(−.861)
REGION		
West	−0.234	−0.130
	(−10.583)**	(−6.472)**
South	−0.128	−0.087
	(−6.557)**	(−4.944)**
Northern	−0.129	−0.068
	(−6.557)**	(−3.834)**
PROGRAM	0.003	—[b]
	(7.071)**	
HRSWRK72	—	0.002
		(−3.350)*
R^2 (adj.)	.283[c]	.430
F	88**	105**
Number of Cases	3485	3732

Note: Breneman and Nelson included only significant regression coefficients in their final equation. They denote nonsignificant regression coefficients by dashes (p < .05). Breneman and Nelson report F-values rather than t-values. T-values have been estimated by taking the square root of F.

[a] Variable not included in the analysis.
[b] Variable not available in the 1979 data set.
[c] Breneman and Nelson reported raw rather than adjusted R^2.

* p < .05.   **p < .01.

TABLE 3.2 *Regression Coefficients for Years of Education Achieved*

VARIABLE	BRENEMAN AND NELSON 1976 FOLLOW-UP	1979 FOLLOW-UP
Constant	NA	2.472
		(12.482)**
CC72	−0.280	−0.120
	(−5.477)**	(−2.901)**
SMCTYHS	—[a]	0.016
		(.433)
CMTYSIZE	—[a]	−0.003
		(−.197)
HOMEWORK	—[a]	0.012
		(2.477)**
FRENPLAN	—[a]	0.067
		(1.519)
HSJOB	−0.004	−0.016
	(−2.000)*	(−2.255)*
COLDECSN	−0.106	0.037
	(−5.831)**	(2.537)**
COLABIL	—[a]	−0.012
		(−.448)
LIVARR72	−0.277	−0.180
	(−6.782)**	(−5.383)**
MARRY72	−0.675	−0.109
	(−6.708)**	(−.823)
KIDS76	−0.486	−0.688
	(−7.211)**	(−11.721)**
ACAD72	0.466	0.278
	(7.810)*	(4.482)**
GRADES73	−0.160	−0.140
	(−10.630)**	(−10.990)**
FTEN72	0.365	0.315
	(3.606)**	(3.958)**
RACE		
Black	—	−0.008
		(−.094)
White	—[a]	−0.011
		(−.172)
SEX	—[a]	−0.142
		(−4.396)**
SES	—[a]	0.066
		(2.690)**

TABLE 3.2 *(continued)*

VARIABLE	BRENEMAN AND NELSON 1976 FOLLOW-UP	1979 FOLLOW-UP
EDASPMO	0.108	0.063
	$(3.873)^{**}$	$(3.318)^{**}$
BAPLANHS	0.235	1.248
	$(4.690)^{**}$	$(29.442)^{**}$
ENGLISH	—[a]	0.005
		(.089)
HSGRADES	−0.048	−0.040
	$(-6.000)^{**}$	$(-5.925)^{**}$
HSACAD	0.107	−0.022
	$(2.449)^{**}$	(−.599)
REGION		
West	−0.270	−0.218
	$(-5.745)^{**}$	$(-4.382)^{**}$
South	—[a]	−0.167
		$(-3.834)^{**}$
Northern	—[a]	−0.153
		$(-3.522)^{**}$
PROGRAM	—[a]	—[b]
HRSWRK72	−0.005	−0.007
	$(-3.000)^{**}$	$(-4.834)^{**}$
R^2 (adj.)	.283[c]	.485
F	82^{**}	130^{**}
Number of Cases	3485	3731

Note: Breneman and Nelson included only significant regression coefficients in their final equation. They denote nonsignificant regression coefficients by dashes (p < .05). Breneman and Nelson reported F-values rather than t-values. T-values have been estimated by taking the square root of F.

[a] Variable not included in the analysis.
[b] Variable not available in the 1979 data set.
[c] Breneman and Nelson reported raw rather than adjusted R^2.

* p < .05 $-^{**}$ p < .01.

However, evaluating the effectiveness of community-college baccalaureate preparation in the context of all available posthigh-school options resulted in a quite different perspective on the effectiveness of community-college baccalaureate-degree preparation. With the modified approach, community-college attendance is found to have a significant and positive relationship both to bachelor's degree achievement and years of education achieved. Of all post-high-school options, university attendance demonstrated the highest positive relationship to educational attainment. However, community-college attendance is also a strong positive factor, particularly on years of education achieved and especially when compared to the alternative of delayed college entry for students who indicate that their objective is to obtain a bachelor's degree (see Table 3.3). If, as is likely to be the case, the choice for many students with bachelor's degree objectives who enter community colleges is attendance at the community college or no immediate college entry following high school, then the relationship in the analysis suggest that community-college enrollment is a strong, positive facilitator of educational attainment and should be encouraged.

With regard to assessment of alternative benefits, a regression methodology similar to that used by Breneman and Nelson in their analysis of employment, educational, and psychological outcomes was developed. The alternative-outcomes research was designed to pilot test this methodology and investigate whether outcomes in the area of earnings, job status, and job satisfaction vary with educational attainment and type of certification for those persons who have not achieved baccalaureate-degree goals.

In conducting the alternative-benefits investigation, the sample of persons who had not achieved baccalaureate degrees was subdivided into five categories:

1. Those who had never attended college.

2. Those who entered a community college in 1972 but had not achieved a degree by 1979;

3. Those who entered a community college in 1972 and had earned a community-college vocational degree or certificate by 1979 as the highest award achieved;

4. Those who entered a community college in 1972 and had earned a community-college transfer degree by 1979 as the highest award achieved;

5. Those who entered a university in 1972 and had earned no degree by 1979.

TABLE 3.3 *Regression Coefficients for Bachelor-Degree Achievement and Years of Education Obtained for Bachelor-Degree Seekers Only and Including All Post High School Options*

VARIABLE	BACHELOR DEGREE 1979 FOLLOW-UP	YEARS OF EDUCATION ACHIEVED 1979 FOLLOW-UP
Constant	0.407	2.431
	(4.606)**	(11.873)**
POSTSECONDARY OPTION		
CC72	0.160	0.880
	(4.846)**	(11.510)**
UNIV72	0.275	1.038
	(8.699)**	(14.195)**
VOTECH72	−0.153	0.002
	(−2.656)*	(.012)
OTHER72	0.239	0.959
	(3.681)**	(6.379)**
SMCTYHS	0.016	0.023
	(.889)	(.562)
CMTYSIZE	−0.002	−0.002
	(−0.312)	(−.144)
HOMEWORK	0.006	0.015
	(2.623)**	(3.051)**
FRENPLAN	0.043	0.176
	(1.998)*	(3.550)**
HSJOB	−0.010	−0.020
	(−2.863)**	(−2.534)**
COLDECSN	0.030	0.067
	(4.228)**	(4.086)**
COLABIL	−0.001	−0.035
	(−.103)	(−1.188)
LIVARR72	−0.065	−0.108
	(−4.124)**	(−2.956)**
MARRY72	−0.153	−0.328
	(−2.571)**	(−2.380)*
KIDS76	−0.272	−.682
	(−8.795)**	(−9.516)**
RACE		
Black	0.003	0.022
	(.067)	(.234)

Variable	Bachelor Degree 1979 Follow-up	Years of Education Achieved 1979 Follow-up
White	0.010 (.339)	0.050 (.698)
SEX	0.003 (.218)	−0.050 (−1.449)
SES	0.037 (3.273)**	0.118 (4.461)**
EDASPMO	0.016 (1.722)	0.049 (2.246)*
ENGLISH	0.019 (.717)	−0.022 (−.365)
HSGRADES	−0.028 (−9.510)**	−0.066 (−9.615)**
HSACAD	0.014 (.784)	0.073 (1.739)
REGION		
West	−0.149 (−6.380)**	−0.224 (−4.152)**
South	−0.099 (−4.975)**	−0.170 (−3.682)**
Northern	−0.065 (−3.259)**	−0.096 (−2.080)*
HRSWRK72	−0.002 (−3.612)**	−0.007 (−4.738)**
R^2 (adj.)	.264	.328
F	45**	61**
Number of Cases	3217	3215

* $p < .05$.   ** $p < .01$.

The outcomes investigated in the alternative-benefits research are admittedly a small set of the possible alternative outcomes that may result from community-college attendance. Other researchers need to extend this analysis to other measures such as unemployment rates, life satisfaction, value changes, voting rates, and many others.

Among those benefit measures included in the analysis, no positive relationship of community college attendance and/or certification was found to any measure (see Tables 3.4, 3.5, and 3.6). In

TABLE 3.4 *Regression Coefficients for Wages per Hour*[a]
(t-ratios in parentheses)

VARIABLE	REGRESSION COEFFICIENTS
Constant	8.181
	(5.652)**
EDUCATIONAL	
ATTAINMENT	
CCNODEG	−2.364
	(−2.227)*
CCVOCDEG	−2.142
	(−1.929)
CCTRANAA	−2.361*
	(−2.201)*
UNINODEG	−2.154
	(−2.063)*
RACE	
Black	0.067
	(.144)
	0.376
White	0.376
	(1.029)
SES	0.067
	(.460)
MARRY79	−0.119
	(−.563)
	(−.563)
SEX	−1.263
	(−5.960)**
HSGRADES	0.009
	(.239)
ENGLISH	−0.059
	(−.168)
HSJOB	0.055
	(1.388)
REGION	
West	0.793
	(2.447)*
South	−.108
	(−.379)
Northern	0.454
	(1.524)
YRSOUT	0.108
	(2.492)**

VARIABLE	REGRESSION COEFFICIENTS
JOBLENGT	0.143
	(3.121)**
SEI79JOB	0.000
	(.255)
FIRMSIZE	0.333
	(1.504)
OFFCSIZE	0.234
	(2.421)*
LIVARR79	−0.700
	(−2.315)*
HRSWRK79	−0.029
	(−2.840)**
HSACAD	0.203
	(.938)
R^2 (adj.)	.117
F	5.13 **
Number of Cases	715

[a] Among employed respondents only.
* P < .05.   ** p < .01.

TABLE 3.5 *Regression Coefficients for Job Satisfaction*[a]
(t-ratios in parentheses)

VARIABLE	REGRESSION COEFFICIENTS
Constant	2.198
	(11.431)**
EDUCATIONAL ATTAINMENT	
CCNODEG	0.259
	(3.013)**
CCVOCDEG	0.247
	(2.167)*
CCTRANAA	0.291
	(3.153)**
UNINODEG	0.288
	(3.919)**
RACE	
Black	0.128
	(1.393)
White	−0.032
	(−0.430)
SES	0.016
	(0.504)

TABLE 3.5 *(continued)*

VARIABLE	REGRESSION COEFFICIENTS
MARRY79	−0.114
	(−2.703)**
SEX	−0.025
	(−.529)
REGION	
West	−0.119
	(−1.756)
South	−0.102
	(−1.697)
Northern	−0.094
	(−1.448)
SEI79JOB	−0.001
	(−5.913)
WAGE/HR	−0.018
	(−2.147)*
FIRMSIZE	0.047
	(1.053)
HRSWRK79	−0.002
	(−1.010)
R^2 (adj.)	.062
F	5.07**
Number of Cases	990

[a] Among employed respondents only; ratings range from "1" for most positive rating to "4" for least positive rating.
* $p < .05$.   ** $p < .01$.

TABLE 3.6 *Regression Coefficients for Occupational Status[a] (t-ratios in parentheses)*

VARIABLE	REGRESSION COEFFICIENTS
Constant	493.727
	(7.815)**
EDUCATIONAL ATTAINMENT	
CCNODEG	54.821
	(1.666)
CCVOCDEG	58.810
	(1.392)
CCTRANAA	42.650
	(1.224)

VARIABLE	REGRESSION COEFFICIENTS
UNINODEG	53.097
	(1.857)
RACE	
Black	−71.691
	(−1.822)
White	−37.809
	(−1.347)
SEX	35.605
	(2.093)*
OCCSTAFF	0.064
	(1.915)
HSGRADES	−4.245
	(−1.423)
HSJOB	−7.801
	(−2.309)*
HSACAD	−15.224
	(−0.844)
FIRMSIZE	30.159
	(1.662)
OFFCSIZE	−23.492
	(−3.038)**
SUPERVIS	1.244
	(2.444)*
REGION	
West	−23.977
	(−.920)
South	−38.168
	(−1.629)
Northern	−39.772
	(−1.655)
LIVARR79	−36.481
	(−1.571)
R^2 (adj.)	.049
F	2.856**
Number of Cases	650

[a] Among employed respondents only.
* $p < .05$.   ** $p < .01$.

some cases, negative relationships were noted. Thus, for those students who entered community colleges and did not achieve entering bachelor-degree objectives, no advantage in earnings, job status, or job satisfaction was found over those students with bachelor-degree objectives who did not enter college at all. This finding held even for students who completed transfer or vocational-associate degrees.

While these findings are disconcerting and contrast rather sharply with previous research on the effects of education on employment-related benefits, no prior research has investigated a range of educational attainment as narrow as that included in the alternative-outcomes analysis. All members of the alternative-benefits sample had at least completed high school and at most completed a two-year associate degree. Even the four-year college dropouts had, on the average, completed less than two years of college. Also these outcomes have been measured on a relatively short-term basis. Whether these findings would persist throughout the sample's lifetime is unknown.

In reviewing these findings it should be remembered that in addition to the fact that it has examined a narrow set of alternative benefits, it also includes in its sample only those persons who noted that they had bachelor-degree objectives that had not been achieved in seven years after high-school graduation. There is, therefore, no way of knowing how the findings might differ if community-college attenders were compared to all high-school graduates who had not entered college within seven-and-one-half years of high-school graduation.

Policy Implications

The policy implications of this research differ from those suggested by Breneman and Nelson. In the conclusion of their research on *Financing Community Colleges*, Breneman and Nelson note,

> the demands of an era of limited growth or retrenchment in higher education will force state policymakers to consider institutional performance carefully in allocating limited resources

for higher education. One area within the community colleges that is likely to be examined critically is the educational performance of academic transfer programs. [pp. 208–209]

Based on the findings of their research they state that they

favor an educational division of labor among institutions in the 1980s that would result in community colleges enrolling fewer full-time academic transfer students of traditional college age and retaining a dominant position in those activities that four-year institutions have not undertaken traditionally and are likely to do less well. [pp. 211–212]

They encourage states to implement financial-aid programs that would equalize tuition and residential costs of four-year colleges to the tuition costs of two-year colleges.

Astin (1977) has reached similar conclusions. He states, based on his examination of degree achievement of two-year and four-year college entrants,

While community colleges provide important services to adults, part-time students and those pursuing technical courses that are not offered by four-year institutions, the results of this and other studies suggest that these colleges may not really serve the interests of students coming directly from high school to pursue careers requiring baccalaureate degrees. [p. 247]

These conclusions and policy recommendations may be overly negative because they are based on comparative analysis of two-year college entrants only. When the efficiency of community-college baccalaureate preparation is viewed in the broader context of all possible post-high-school choices available to those who desire a bachelor's degree, community-college attendance has been found in the current research to be positively related both to years of education achieved and to baccalaureate-degree achievement. This is not a surprising finding, but it is one that has been identified in prior national research on effectiveness of community-college transfer education. Its policies implications, in some cases, contrast sharply with those of prior research.

For example, the findings suggest that policies that encourage graduating high-school students with bachelor's degree objectives to enter college immediately, be it a two-year or a four-year college, can result in substantial gains in the educational level of the population. One can probably further extend this observation to conclude that the availability of accessible, low-tuition community colleges that have permitted entry to college for students who might not otherwise have been able to attend has already had this effect. Where it can be determined that a student with a degree objective is making a choice between immediate entry to a two-year college or delayed college entry, then efforts should be made to encourage immediate two-year-college entry. Where it can be determined that the choice for the student is between two-year- and four-year-college entry and financial considerations are a factor in the choice, then this study suggests support for financial-assistance programs to make the four-year-college choice more feasible.

In addition, community-college leaders and state policymakers should be concerned with assuring that community-college transfer programs achieve the highest possible quality and are well articulated with programs of four-year colleges and universities. A careful review of transfer programs should be undertaken to determine whether the differential in educational attainment of two-year- and four-year-college entrants can be reduced through improvement and modification to the programs. This recommendation is particularly important now when it appears likely that availability of federal financial-aid funds may decrease, which may result in increased choice of community colleges by students who desire bachelor's degrees.

The finding that community-college attendance and certification is not positively related to earnings or job status may relate to a lack of market differentiation by employers on the basis of associate-degree achievement. The lack of market differentiation could reflect a lack of economic value for the associate degree or could reflect lack of understanding on the part of the employment community of the kinds of skills that community-college associate-degree programs provide. The recent campaign by the American Association of Community and Junior Colleges (AACJC) to create market awareness of the value of the two-year degree suggests that community-college leaders believe that lack of employer understanding is the reason for nondifferentiation. As part of this campaign, AACJC is encouraging employers to advertise for positions with a statement, "associate-degree required" or "associate-degree preferred" in cases where such designation is appropriate. If the issue is one of employer education, then the AACJC campaign should result in improved economic recognition of the associate degree over time. If, on the other hand, the issue is one of lack of economic value of the two-year degree, then educational efforts will be ineffective in producing differentiation. The results of the AACJC campaign should be carefully monitored to determine what insights can be derived about the economic value of two-year degree preparation.

The current research found no alternative benefit of community-college attendance for the three measures included. While admittedly based on a limited set of outcome measures, these findings may imply that community colleges should do everything possible to encourage recent high-school graduate entrants with bachelor's degree objectives to achieve these objectives. Perhaps the ease of entrance, ease of exit and ease of alternating between part-time and full-time attendance that characterize the community college do not act to facilitate positive results among the recent high-school-graduate population that this study has reviewed. If this notion can be verified, community colleges need to introduce stronger counseling programs that discourage young students from "in" and "out" attendance patterns that are so popular among and so useful for adults. This possibility should be studied by community colleges as they evaluate the effectiveness of their baccalaureate-preparation efforts for the recent high-school-graduate population.

Future Research Needs

The agenda for future research on community-college results is a large and important one. Governors, state and federal legislators, local governments, taxpayers, students, and parents are asking questions about educational effectiveness and economic efficiency. Regional and specialized accrediting agencies are increasingly focusing their attention on outcomes. While progress has been made at the institutional, state, and national level in evaluating community-college education, much additional investigation is needed. On a national basis, for example, research needs to be undertaken using other longitudinal data bases than the High School Class of 1972 to determine the generality of the Breneman and Nelson and Nunley findings. Also, longitudinal data sets need to be created that will permit evaluation of outcomes longer than seven years after high-school graduation. Research designs should be carefully evaluated to assure that they are methodologically sound. Standards of performance should be established against which community-college effectiveness can be evaluated.

Also, research needs to be broadened to include groups other than recent high school graduates, the group that the available longitudinal data sets most often include. A significant and increasing part of the community-college population is adult students. The effectiveness of community colleges in assisting the achievement of positive results by adults needs to be investigated.

In addition, future studies should investigate whether variables that have not been included in the available national research may have contributed to the difference in educational attainment of persons who choose different college-attendance options. For example, detailed analysis of psychological characteristics of two-year- and four-year-college entrants may reveal differences that have not been noted in prior studies and that may explain the differences that have been found in educational attainment among the subgroups.

The issue of alternative benefits has not been systematically evaluated in prior studies; therefore, the Nunley research has been exploratory in nature. The alternative-benefits research needs to be extended to encompass other economic-, social-, and psychological-outcome measures. In addition, further research is needed with regard to those benefit measures included in the current study. Such research must be conducted before definitive conclusions about alternative outcomes can be drawn.

At the institutional and statewide level, studies need to be extended over longer periods to permit tracking of students' progress toward baccalaureate degrees and longer-term labor-market effects. Many of the existing state and local studies follow students only to the point of transfer to a four-year institution or to entry into immediate employment and do not collect data on ultimate degree achievement or longer-term employment, educational, and psychological effects. Longer-term research by institutions and/or states may permit identification of those community-college characteristics that are associated with higher levels of student success. These characteristics could then be emulated by institutions that are less successful in producing educational results for students. Potentially the most useful studies, in terms of ability to produce change, are those that are conducted at the local or state level. To enable this potential to be achieved, methodologically and theoretically sound local research must be increased and evaluative conclusions and interpretations must be drawn from the findings.

Finally, the effectiveness of community colleges in assisting students to achieve vocational or continuing-education objectives needs to be investigated using methods that permit evaluative conclusions. It is not enough to determine what percentage of vocational-program graduates get jobs, stay employed, and earn a given salary level. We need to ask questions about "value added" by the vocational-training experience and what positive results the student has achieved that would not have occurred without such preparation. We need to investigate why students enroll in continuing education and whether they achieve their purposes.

The agenda is a long and important one. Recent national studies on the status of higher education have led to efforts in some states to establish mandatory testing for participants in higher education. These studies suggest that the higher-education community needs to gain a better understanding of its results. Many have suggested that mandatory testing is not the answer. Policymakers and taxpayers have a right to seek information, however, about the efficiency with which their resources are being spent as well as information about educational effectiveness. It is not enough to respond to questions by stating that research that has been done is limited, not right, or inadequate. Community-college leaders need to work from inside to improve research on educational results, make it theoretically sound, and assure that it lends itself to evaluative interpretation. The outcome will be improved accountability, improved programs, and improved effectiveness for students.

References

ASSOCIATION OF AMERICAN COLLEGES. *Integrity in the College Curriculum: A Report to the Academic Community*. Washington, D.C.: Association of American Colleges, 1985.

ASTIN, A. W. *Four Critical Years: Effects of College on Beliefs, Attitudes and Knowledge*. San Francisco: Jossey-Bass, 1977.

BRENEMAN, D. W., and NELSON, S. C. *Financing Community Colleges: An Economic Perspective*. Washington, D.C.: Brookings Institution, 1981.

CAMPBELL, D. T., and STANLEY, J. C. *Experimental and Quasi-Experimental Designs for Research*. Chicago: Rand McNally, 1963.

EDGERTON, R. "Assessment Is Coming: Should We Retreat or Charge?" *Higher Education and National Affairs* 35(3)(1986):11.

LESLIE, L. L. *Financing Community Colleges: An Economic Perspective. Book Review*. Tucson: University of Arizona, Unpublished manuscript, 1982.

McCONOCHIE, D. D. *Four Years Later: Follow-up of 1976 Entrants to Maryland Community Colleges*. Annapolis: Maryland State Board for Community Colleges, 1981.

NATIONAL COMMISSION ON EXCELLENCE IN EDUCATION. *A Nation at Risk: The Imperative for Educational Reform*. Washington, D.C.: U.S. Government Printing Office, 1984.

NATIONAL ENDOWMENT FOR THE HUMANITIES. *To Reclaim a Legacy: A Report on the Humanities in Higher Education*. Washington, D.C.: National Endowment for the Humanities, 1984.

NATIONAL INSTITUTE OF EDUCATION. *Involvement in Learning: Realizing the Potential of American Higher Education*. Washington, D.C.: U.S. Government Printing Office, 1984.

NUNLEY, C. R. "Educational Attainment and Alternative Outcomes for Community College Entrants with Bachelor's Degree Goals" *Dissertation Abstracts International*, in press.

"States and Quality. A special *Change* Report." *Change* 17(6)(1986):11–45.

TSCHECHTELIN, J. D. *Maryland Community College Students Follow-up Study: First Time Students, Fall, 1972*. Annapolis: Maryland State Board for Community Colleges, 1976.

TSCHECHTELIN, J. D., and McLEAN, A. D. *Student Follow-up of Entrants and Graduates of Maryland Community Colleges*. Annapolis: Maryland State Board for Community Colleges, 1980.

4

The Educational Program of the American Community College: A Transition

ROBERT H. McCABE

The primary role of community colleges is to provide an education program to raise the quality of life of our communities.

Introduction

My father had gone to school only through the third grade. His great dream was for me to go to college, where, having had no direct contact with college, he believed that something magical would happen. My life would be transformed. I would be able to draw values from life experiences in a way that he had not, and new vistas would open, raising the quality of my life to a higher plane. Those of us who are involved with colleges know that the college curriculum is often not logically developed, that there are some classes that are required only because of a strong department chair or the special interests of a faculty member, and that the college faculty and administrators possess all of the human frailties of others. Thus, my father's concept seems idealistic and naive. But the truth is that he was right; my college experience transformed my life in ways that I have just now begun to appreciate.

Opportunities to attend college are so widely available today that many assume they may attend anytime they wish. The importance of the college experience in changing the lives of individuals is not understood or appreciated even by the staffs of the institutions. Students, faculty, and administrations tend to view the college program as career preparation. In curriculum design, little conscious effort is given to the development of students' skills and competencies for personal fulfillment. There is no doubt that productive employment is fundamental to life quality and must be an important curriculum determinant; however, it is not all that is important.

The primary role of community colleges is to provide an education program to raise the quality of life of our communities. I would hope that some of my father's naiveté and idealism as well as full appreciation of the value of our programs to our students would be represented in our educational planning.

Community colleges and those of us who work in them are blessed. Not only do we provide wondrous and undervalued opportunities, but we can provide it to many who would otherwise be excluded. If attending college meant so much to me, imagine what it means to an individual who has grown up in poverty, the immigrant in our country whose life has been one of hardship and who must learn our language and our culture, a single parent struggling in a minimum occupation to care for herself and several children, or the recently divorced woman in her forties trying to prepare for a new life and for entry into the work force.

Community colleges are not accorded the prestige of universities. Helping the underprepared, undermotivated, and problem-beset is difficult and unglamorous. But—community colleges are of immense and growing importance to our complex society. Faculty and staff can take pride in knowing that they are a part of the most important educational institutions in our nation.

One of the greatest strengths of American community colleges has been their adaptiveness. More often than not, these colleges have been at the right place, at the right time, with at least some of the right answers. In the expansion years, community colleges were primarily funded by enrollment-driven formulae that were sometimes poorly defined. They were growing rapidly—free to do almost anything. Who knew whether or not a program was within the mission? Enrollment brought additional funds and growth assured that new programs were additive and thus did not compete with existing programs or require reconfiguration of resources. In this rapid growth pattern, with enrollment-driven funding, each additional full-time equivalent (FTE) student produced more income than expense (stable support costs thus less cost per FTE, hiring of faculty at the lower end of salary schedules or hiring of part-time faculty, etc.). The funding approaches resulted in a wave of income that buried mistakes. What a wonderful environment for innovation!

While that innovative tradition remains in community colleges, many of the factors that encouraged bold behavior have become negatives. Our missions are more clearly defined; enrollment-driven funding does not recognize the increased cost per FTE when enrollment declines (stable support costs thus more cost per FTE, terminations of less-well-paid and part-time faculty). New programs compete with existing efforts. Innovation requires resource reallocation and establishment of clear priorities. Staffs are aging. Restrictive traditions have been established where none had existed.

It is certainly more difficult for community colleges to be adaptive and innovative in the late 1980s than in earlier years, but it is more important than ever. This is a period characterized by change in our communities, in the nation and in the world. Therefore, it is essential to understand the changing environment in which the colleges function as well as conditions within the colleges as a basis for evolving an appropriate educational program.

Society and Skills

Conditions of American society nearing the twenty-first century have important implications for the educational program of community colleges. Information technology has an impact on more jobs and many of the remaining unskilled–semiskilled jobs are leaving the country; there are a growing number of adults unprepared for employment because of lack of information and learning skills; there will be a growing number of adults experiencing difficulty in coping with life problems and unprepared to draw full value from life; there is increasing interaction with peoples and institutions from other nations.

Without doubt, this is a period of extraordinary and rapid change. Those that appear most important to community-college programs are the evolution of a world economy, the continued and escalating immigration to the United States primarily from the third-world countries, the decline in the information skills (academic skills) of Americans, the continued rise in the level of information skills that are required for basic employment, an apparent deterioration in social consciousness and ethical standards, the declining role (indeed, existence) of the family, and the persistent growth of a large underclass of individuals unable and in some cases apparently unwilling to participate in society.

Perhaps the greatest dilemma of paramount interest to community colleges is the growing gap between the requirements for employability and the competencies of our young people. Every indication is that the problem will become worse in the future:

> Over the next 10 to 15 years, the workforce will undergo a major change in composition. Most striking will be the growth of less well educated segments of the population that have typically been the least prepared to work. The number of minority youth will increase while the total number of youth of working age will decline. The number of high school dropouts will rise as will the number of teenage mothers. At the same time, entry

level jobs will increasingly require basic, analytical, and interpersonal skills. [NAB, 1986, p. 1]

The major conclusion of a recent study of the National Assessment of Education Progress (Irwin and Jungeblut, 1986) is that
literacy is a critical problem in our nation. The study indicates
that while large numbers of individuals are able to perform in the
middle ranges of literacy and thus cannot be classified as illiterate,
they are not really literate for a technologically advanced society.
The point is that the level of literacy that was sufficient for full
participation in the society in the past will no longer suffice. The
accessibility of data provided through the ever-expanding capabilities of technology is resulting in greater need for higher levels of
literacy in practically every occupation. Recently I visited a ship-
ping company in one of Miami's poorest districts. It was surprising
to learn that reading skills were a requirement for beginning loading dock employment. It was explained that the people working on
the loading docks now had to deal with loading sheets and that
each container had a mark-sense data-processing input card af-
fixed that had to be coded to provide data for a management-
information system that involved records, inventory, and cash-flow
management. This well illustrated the rising need for information
skills in virtually all occupations.

Another clear indication of the change in the needs for information skills is demonstrated by the College Board. Working with
colleges and high schools, the Board produced a book that sets
forth skills and competencies that are desirable to begin college. At
a later point, representatives of business and industries were asked
to review these skills and competencies and to indicate those that
they would prefer in a beginning employee. The surprising result
was that industries desired virtually all of the skills and competencies for a beginning employee colleges desired for entering
freshmen. This presents a profound message. All students, not only
those preparing for a professional career, must develop strong academic skills, and academic skills have become the most important occupational skills.

The growing dilemma in this country is apparent. At the same
time that jobs require even more information competence, the per-

centage of Americans who do not possess such competence is grow-ing. There are increasing numbers of less-well-prepared youngsters, especially minorities. There are greater numbers of young people coming from poor family situations, including the growing num-ber of children growing up in urban poverty pockets and rising numbers of immigrants, mostly with little educational background. Hodgkinson (1985) adds the sobering information that 40% of the children born in 1983 are living with single parents, 18 out of 100 children are being born illegitimate and poor, and every day in America 40 teenagers give birth to their third child. Hodgkinson puts it, who could be more at risk than a child of a child?

But appropriate skills for employability, while of exceptional importance, is not the only concern:

> . . . that we are beginning to accept less than wholeness for the growing individual. That the society suffers from a loss of skills for living, a loss of humanity and a growing lack of skills for dealing with a global society, a changing world, for manag-ing the new technology and deciding whether it will be master or slave. Further we risk a loss of sense of beauty, of credibility, of value and purpose and ultimately of control over our own destiny. We stand to lose our openness to new ideas, our appre-ciation of those who have gone on before us and therefore, our hope for the future. [Nelson, 1985, p. 8]

The educational program of a community college should con-cern itself with helping individuals toward full self-development and improvement of the quality of their lives. This includes devel-opment of learning skills for an ever changing world, information skills (finding, reading, interpreting, analyzing, formulating, and communicating information), reasoning–critical-thinking compe-tencies, appreciation and concern for those with different back-grounds and from different cultures, and developing values.

The Political Environment

It is clear that the public is dissatisfied with American education and frustrated by what appears to be declining achievement by students on all levels. The Southern Regional Education Board report, *Access to Quality Undergraduate Education,* summed up the attitude of legislators and the public:

> There is no question that the quality of undergraduate education is unacceptably low and needs to be raised. In the past six months, three independent national reports reached remarkably similar conclusions on the status of undergraduate education— all pointed to an incoherent curriculum, a lack of rigor in course and degree standards, inadequate methods of assessing student progress, and little consensus within higher education on what knowledge and skills should be emphasized. [1985, p. 2]

Some critics have stated that higher education needs to "get its act together" and have called on institutions for reform. However, in many cases, legislators have expressed their dissatisfaction through greater involvement in educational policy decisions and in a variety of punitive actions. In Florida, the legislature and the State Board of Education have gone so far as to mandate courses that students must take and the amount of writing that must occur in specific courses. They have instituted a "rising-junior" test for admission to upper-division status and required a standardized entry-placement program. In several states, selected courses have been eliminated from state funding. The imposition of standardized tests as a condition for students to progress to different levels is a growing trend. This is clearly an expression of lack of confidence: These tests are intended to "assure quality" that, it is believed, the colleges have not addressed themselves.

Because the greatest frustration is with education, teacher education has come in for particular review and regulation. It is one of the areas where standardized testing practices are most frequently being instituted. Most in education would agree that dependence on standardized testing is an oversimplified approach to assure quality and that such tests should not be used as independent criteria for making life judgments about individuals. However, there is considerable growth of interest within the profession in developing approaches for assessing program quality and results. There will be increased interest and application of program assessment and in the use of standardized tests, both by legislative fiat and institutional initiative.

The institution of oversimplified "quick fixes" to improve education is on the increase and presents a special peril for community colleges. In any state it is easy to rally support for improving the quality of the institutions of higher education. But that simply stated goal is inappropriate. It would be easy to improve the quality of the institutions of higher education by admitting only those who are well prepared and this might be best for some institutions within a state system. But that goal is misstated because the emphasis is on institutions rather than on students and society. It is imperative to the well-being of our society that we produce more, not fewer, well-educated individuals. A goal of improving educational quality must incorporate the requirement to increase the *number* of individuals completing programs with a high level of competence. Because community colleges are best suited by attitude and program to deal with those who begin underprepared, they are particularly vulnerable to simplistic actions to improve quality. Thus it is essential to community colleges that they continue to work toward public-policy understanding of the need for more better-prepared individuals.

It is also essential, regardless of admissions policies, that community colleges set high expectations for graduation and program or course completion. Access and quality must go hand in hand. The institutions should look at credits as their currency and indications of educational attainment. Both credits and grades should be dispensed with care. While it makes no sense to limit opportunity, it is equally unacceptable to graduate or grant credit to individuals who have not demonstrated the achievement that is certified. Certainly certification carelessness has been a practice for some community colleges and has contributed to an important credibility problem. Further, such practices are not in the best interest of students or society. Open-door policies, while more important than ever to our nation's well-being, are under attack. A quality program is both the best defense for the open door and best for students and society.

Much has been said of the superiority of other educational systems over that of the United States, but our system holds a precious and overwhelming advantage that must be protected. In other countries the educational system is a narrowing pyramid with individuals selected to proceed to the next step at stages in their education. Failure to be selected is irrevocable and the human talent of millions is wasted. In this country, we maintain our commitment to each individual. When one is ready to try there is opportunity and there are second and third chances. The human resources that are salvaged through this approach are worth the difficulties that such a system engenders.

The evidence of benefit abounds. Each of us knows individuals who succeeded after a poor early effort, and all of us have benefited from their contributions. In this human-salvage operation, the community colleges are in the front line and often without deserved support. But what a contribution they make! I am never more convinced of the merits of our programs than when individuals with apparently poor prospects succeed: Black women in their thirties and forties become registered nurses after years as cleaning women in hospitals; a young man from the streets of an intolerable ghetto neighborhood receives a degree; a 40-year-old divorced homemaker develops confidence and competencies to establish herself; a 25-year-old man who was not interested in his high-school education successfully attends evening classes while working and supporting a family. We should never make the mistake of believing that individuals do not have talent because they lack academic skills at a point in their lives.

Those who are opposed to maintaining access are misreading the position of the American public. No doubt the public has become disenchanted with many of the social programs that were born in the late 1950s and 1960s with such high aspirations and that seem not to have been able to deliver expected improvements. Open-door community colleges are social programs. But the commitment of the American public to opportunity for people to fully develop themselves remains intact. It is the programs, not the goals, which are in question.

The initial reaction of legislatures to a perception of poor performance or lack of quality is restriction and what might be described as punishment. The experience throughout the country appears to be one in which the community colleges are at various stages of moving through a period of external analysis resulting in restrictions and punishing actions to additional support to achieve the results that both the public and legislatures want. Much of the attention, both negative and positive, results from the public awareness of the critical importance of education at this period in our history. Recent actions of state government show both an interest in assessment and a concern for quality coupled with interest in relating funding to performance. There are discussions of value added, assessment of student outcomes, systemwide reviews, comprehensive studies of programs as the basis for state policy and incentive funding for undergraduate education. In Tennessee, the higher-education commission is currently setting performance criteria for a performance-based funding program. Incorporated will be the attention to value-added assessment, the weighing of variables, surveys of alumni, and evaluation of outcomes (Boyer and McGuinness, 1986).

The press to improve quality and tightening state budgets have also brought closer attention from legislatures. In a number of states, there have been state reviews of community-college mission, and in many more the elimination of programs from sponsorship and/or funding. The priorities of state legislatures have been more clearly expressed. The results in the states are remarkably similar in placing the highest priority on associate-degree programs and occupational programs, while placing many noncredit, personal-development courses in self-supporting or near self-supporting status.

A very worrisome development has been the increase in state control and regulation. The drive is to avoid "duplication" of programs and to assure compliance with state-policy decisions and to develop state systems. Increasingly, funds are allocated categorically with less opportunity for creative management at the institutions. State bureaucracies have evolved to manage the higher-education institutions with increased attention to "independent" institutions as elements in a single system filling a specified and clearly defined role. Often the expectation is that the institutions will operate in a specified way. I am convinced that this is an exceptionally undesirable trend, but that it is becoming well established. The cost of maintaining such systems far exceeds the cost of any duplication and the growth of routine tasks and overcontrol sucks the creative energies from the administrators and faculty in the institutions. Progress is made by creative individuals who have the freedom to try new ideas and approaches and who have ownership in the programs they implement. Standardization of practices may improve the unproductive but it lacks the fundamentals for creativity and locks in practices that should continue to evolve.

The political environment for community colleges for the near future will include more and more state regulation and control. Emphasis on assessment, continued vulnerabilty of open-door policies, less support for personal-development and community-service programs, most probably some form of performance-based funding, and mission more closely and narrowly defined are some features likely to be associated with these state efforts.

The Primary Mission

The quality issue has produced another dilemma for community colleges. Over a period of time we have expanded our programs to encompass service to a broad audience including learners of virtually all ages. Services have included occupational programs, college-parallel programs, developmental and remedial education and a dazzling array of community-service programs. In the late 1970s, there was a conviction among many community-college educators that our institutions should think of themselves as "educational filling stations" to which people "drop in" to get what they need and then leave. And many interesting and valuable services were developed in the drive to provide services to all. Some programs and individuals committed to this concept lost interest in the associate degree and even suggested that we should not consider ourselves collegiate—this clouded our true mission. In a significant number of institutions, the transfer function became of only minor importance. While we can firmly hold to the community-college goal of service to all individuals in our community, the continuing-education, short-program, workshop, outreach and noncredit operations must take a second priority. The associate-degree programs are primary. They are paramount for preparing people for the growing numbers of occupations that require postsecondary education, for providing easily accessible and low-cost programs for those who must work or live at home, and for access for the underprepared to transfer programs. There are no other institutions that can open opportunity for the large population of underprepared to gain the competencies that are necessary to complete a baccalaureate program.

The centerpiece of our mission must be the associate-degree-transfer and occupational programs and those services required for individuals to succeed in those programs. This is society's priority, and it is where the college's credibility is established. It is only possible to provide the wide array of other programs in which we believe and that are of benefit to our communities based on solid-degree programs. There is clear indication from the public and legislators that other programs and services are secondary and that institutions that emphasize those programs as their primary mission may well endanger public support.

Community colleges should focus their efforts on enhancing the associate-degree programs. They face difficult problems in developing an appropriate curriculum for the 1990s and the twenty-first century. Quite obviously, if someone is to participate fully in this society he or she must be employable. So many personal problems are irresolvable without a job and a reasonable income. Thus preparation for employment, with emphasis on information skills, must be a program priority. But substantial and growing percentages of students who come to community colleges begin with academic competence far below the minimum required to begin an effective college program. Large percentages of students enter community colleges undermotivated and with undeveloped study skills, having done little reading and virtually no writing in high school. The colleges must help those students develop the basic skills necessary either for employment or to begin a college program. Unfortunately, so many have so far to go that basic-skills programs have the prospect of dominating the curriculum. When more than half of the students require developmental courses and many for several terms, the scope of the program offering is severely limited. In many community colleges, second-level elective courses are endangered by lack of enrollment.

Community colleges struggling with waves of students with insufficient academic skills have often regressed in their programs—not only in the developmental courses—but in the expectations of the standard programs. Richardson, Fisk, and Okun (1983) have described a phenomenon they term "bitting"—helping students retain bits of information, rather than dealing with concepts, interpretation, and application. We cannot settle for this. It is critical for students to develop competencies that are variously called higher-order learning skills, critical thinking, or reasoning skills. These competencies are essential to functioning in the information age and to an individual's full development.

We certainly should be concerned with values and creativity, yet the overwhelming need to raise basic skills so dominates that it is squeezing the remainder of the curriculum. For deficient students, the combination or developmental courses and general education requirements leaves little opportunity for advanced courses. This both reduces the opportunity for students to enrich their curricula and, by reducing the number of students available to take such courses, endangers the institution's capability to offer them. Nevertheless, development of the basic academic skills must take first priority.

A Proposed Approach

Based on the overwhelming requirement to bring underprepared students' basic competencies up to reasonable standards and to establish an environment within which excellence can be expected, consider the following recommended fundamental approach:

1. Recognize and inform students at the beginning of the program that if they are starting with deficiencies, it is going to take longer to complete the program and their progress will be monitored and their program carefully controlled. Be sure that it is clear to everyone—administration, faculty, and students—that regardless of the starting place, the college has high expectations for all programs.

2. Provide entry testing and mandatory placement in needed developmental courses. Arrange the placement program in order that those operating the program make judgments in addition to reliance on standardized tests. For example, if students are assigned to a developmental writing course based on test performance and demonstrate early that their writing is acceptable, they should be moved from that course to a standard course. There should be standards for completing developmental courses as well as for placement. Development courses should absolutely not count towards graduation.

3. Students who test as deficient should be assigned restricted loads. Too often, students transfer from high school where they were attending 30 hours of class a week and think that each hour of college work will be comparable and thus 15 semester hours will be easy to handle. They do not realize the basic college assumption that two to three hours of work outside the class is expected for each one in class. All too often students who test deficient try to work full-time and carry 15 credits—a formula for failure. The design of the program should be the converse of the old openflow model that was concerned with "the right to fail," and let students take anything they wished, permitting experience to demonstrate readiness. Attention should be on opportunity to succeed. The student should be assigned to a program where there is good probability of success. The number of contact hours in developmental courses should be increased, even if some hours are minimally supervised work arrangements that might be compared to homework. As a group, underprepared students have the least concept of how to incorporate independent work as required by college courses. Thus, part of that external expectation should be brought into a controlled environment.

4. Students who begin with deficiencies should be provided orientation in the form of instruction in time management, study skills, and a group-guidance approach to career choice and development.

5. There should be a monitoring and feedback system so that students know at all times where they stand and where they stand and where they can get help when needed. The basic college environment for deficient students should be directive and supportive. The feedback system should have a college-organized approach for providing information concerning progress early in the term.

6. If possible, the deficient student's curriculum should be organized so that the student has a combination of developmental courses and regular coursework that has been selected as not needing competence in the area of the student's deficiency. For example, if the deficiency is in mathematics, there are many courses that a student could enroll in that do not require competence in that field. As early as possible, the student should have an opportunity to begin courses in the area of special interest. However, if a student is seriously deficient in all the basic skills, that approach is not possible, and an emergency program, perhaps of as much as five hours a day, five days a week, appears to have the best prospect of bringing the student's skills up to necessary levels.

7. The system should be designed to provide maximum flexibility for the student who begins without deficiencies or who has raised competence to an acceptable level. It is easy to develop a system designed to control and monitor the student who is experiencing difficulty and to create a situation that is too restrictive for the well-prepared student.

8. All students' progress should be monitored, and information fed back to the students every term. Establishing a directing and supportive system for dealing with basic skills and student-program monitoring should result in a situation in which faculty can hold high expectations and be successful in their work. If the program is properly designed, students in each course should have the minimum competencies and prior coursework for a good prospect for success. This is imperative if faculty are to hold high expectations for stu-

dents and experience the success that is so necessary to sustain their creative involvement. In colleges that permit open-flow enrollment, faculty are often faced with such a wide spectrum of abilities and so many students unprepared for the courses that they cannot provide a quality program. In these cases, faculty become disheartened and lose interest, they feel personally defeated by their work and the institutions lose their most essential resource.

Emphasis on Educational Program

This discussion has generally avoided the term curriculum in favor of educational program. Most discussion of the educational program concerns the curriculum that is thought of as a series of courses required or offered and the subject matter of each course. Unfortunately the program is most often administered from that perspective. In fact, the educational program is the sun of experiences that students are provided by the institution. This includes initial contact, intake, and orientation—and what has come to be described as student flow. The student-flow program guides, directs, supports, orders program elements, and informs students as they progress. It is integral to the educational program: It helps the student learn and succeed as well as controlling or guiding the course choice, volume, and order.

One of the most evident causes for low student retention and success is the failure of institutions to understand the importance of viewing the educational program as the full student experience and thus developing a planned and managed institutional educational system within which various components such as courses function. Random-access cafeteria approaches have little chance of success except with the most highly motivated and well-prepared students, yet they predominate.

The view of an educational program as a curriculum that is comprised of a compilation of courses each covering specified subject matter arouses an additional concern. The particular subject matter that students study is not the important part of the educational program. Rather, it is the development of generic competencies that students take with them from the college program that can be applied throughout their lives that is the essential. Why else is it that individuals who graduate from liberal-arts and business programs enter business enterprise and apparently perform equally well? Why is it that the myriad of curricula and course requirements in American colleges and universities have comparable results for students? There appears to be no special advantage of one curriculum over another. What is most important that students do take from the college years is a better understanding of our society and others, a capacity to deal effectively with other people, a value system as the basis for decisions, competence in learning and basic-information skills—the ability to find, read, analyze, interpret, communicate, and the ability to formulate new ideas and to make decisions.

All of these competencies are best developed in the context of substantial subject matter in which the student has interest. While there certainly is subject matter that is necessary as a part of professional preparation (for example, an individual preparing to be a biologist would need to develop knowledge bases in the sciences and in mathematics), the remainder of the curriculum could remain open. The challenge here is to develop a program that has as a key component a shadow curriculum. That is a curriculum that is always there but is not explicit as in a list of courses that are required for graduation. It is, however, a component of all courses. The subject matter of the courses would be taught and the subject matter's goals pursued but, additionally, in all courses, the subject matter would be utilized as a vehicle for helping students to develop values, information skills, and decision-making skills. Students would become skilled learners. They would leave the colleges with lifetime competencies especially applicable to our changing, information-packed, and complex society, rather than with mastery of certain "facts" that may or may not be true or useful some years in the future.

This program would require an extraordinary institutional commitment to faculty development in order to empower faculty to utilize their creative talents in the teaching of much more difficult competencies. It would also require institutional planning to insure that these generic skills were being addressed in all courses but with some order. There would be more choice of courses by students, so that they were more frequently enrolled in courses that dealt with subject matter of interest to them. Courses would be assigned freshman and sophomore levels (numbers) based on the degree to which higher-order learning skills were included. Prerequisites would be carefully observed and students would be required to take a specific number of sophomore courses for graduation. This would result in a progression for gaining the generic competencies from developmental to higher-order competencies by program completion.

Developing the curriculum in this way can help the excellent student and should improve retention for all. More students could choose courses that they have wished to take. Students would be interested and motivated in these courses and this would provide the best learning environment.

The focus of the educational program would be on the associate-degree programs. The program should address basic skills and provide a directive, controlled, and supportive environment for students. It should include a shadow curriculum of generic skills, freeing students to have a greater choice as their skills are improved. There needs to be a program for faculty development and support. Such a program would be difficult to develop and initiate, but would be eminently well suited for the needs of our society.

Realizing the Educational Program: Some Special Concerns

There are a number of areas of immediate concern to which community colleges should pay special attention during the remainder of the twentieth century.

Teaching and Learning

While some progress has been made to establish a true educational system and thus to improve students' chances for success, far too little attention has been paid to what happens in the classroom where the learning takes place. Since the 1960s, there has been considerable research about teaching and learning, and a great store of knowledge exists among community-college teaching faculty. Yet this knowledge is not part of the basic vocabulary of our teaching faculty. Integration of this knowledge into their work has not been encouraged by the colleges. Little is done to help faculty to learn how to get feedback about their work and to use that feedback in an ongoing process of improving teaching and learning. Efforts to support faculty development and systematically improve teaching and learning in the colleges should be a top goal.

Language and Culture

We live in a world economy. The United States is not isolated from events in other places in the world. Yet we are inadequate in language competence and in our knowledge of other cultures and other people. Unfortunately, foreign-language enrollment has been declining in our colleges and universities. Increasing our language and culturual-education programs both for full-time students and in service to our community is of special importance and deserves a development effort.

Business-Specific Programs

More individuals will be continuing their education over their lifetimes and more American businesses will require continued growth in the skills and competencies of their employees. Obviously, one goal of the community colleges is to help individuals to develop, but they should be concerned also with helping businesses to thrive. Colleges will need to find ways to remove the straight jackets of term boundaries and contract restrictions, in order that they can be responsive to industry by shaping courses and programs to their needs and their employees' needs, in content, methodology, location, and time.

Reaching Out to Four-Year Colleges and to High Schools

For an effective educational program, community colleges need to reach back to influence high schools in order to help more students develop basic skills before admission. High school counseling staffs often have not converted their thinking from that of many years ago with regard to the number of students who go on to postsecondary education. The result is that approximately one-third are in college preparatory programs and the remainder in other programs. In actuality, more than two-thirds will go on to some postsecondary experience within five years of high school graduation. Additionally, the academic competencies are necessary both to go on to postsecondary education, and in most cases, to be employable. Community-college leadership needs to reach back and work hand in hand with high schools in order to increase motivation and to bring more students into programs that will develop the skills they need both to be successful in our institutions and to be successful in life.

Community colleges have not done all they can to build the connection with four-year institutions. Community colleges should work aggressively to develop programs that assure students at the time they enter the community college of an arrangement with a four-year institution for continuation of their education. While many do not have their minds made up and will make choices later, it is important to many students, particularly those who need scholarship assistance, that they know when they enter the community college that if they are successful, there is a specific arrangement for completion of a four-year program. Those community colleges working on two-plus-two plans with universities are experiencing considerable success.

Improving Intake Services

Many community colleges are concerned about enrollment and retention. Yet, processes for bringing students into the institutions, including registration arrangements, are barbaric. We do not treat students as if we are interested in them. It is important for institutions to reorganize so that there is more personal attention to students as they enter. The registration process should be adjusted to demonstrate to individuals that the colleges are interested in them and students should be assisted in making sound program choices.

Communications Technology

We are essentially in a communications and interpersonal business. Yet we have made little progress in utilizing the capabilities of communications technology in teaching and learning. More has been done in the business areas of the college and in some cases student affairs. But we will not be able to continue to ignore the capabilities of communications technology. More students will become accustomed to dealing with the technology and will be prepared to use it. Colleges must work carefully in staff development to help faculty to introduce the use of technology in the teaching and learning programs.

Selection of Faculty

For many years there has been little employment of new full-time faculty in community colleges. After the growth in the 1960s and early 1970s, enrollments have stabilized and in some cases declined. With tight economics, the new full-time faculty positions that opened were often replaced with part-time faculty (a practice that has worked to the disadvantage of the educational program in many institutions). But now that large force of individuals who built the institutions are moving toward retirement. Indications from many community colleges are that over the next decade from one-fourth to one-half of their faculties will retire. Community colleges need to pay close attention to the processes employed in selecting new faculty and particularly in determining the characteristics and attitudes that the college hopes for. A close look at the best faculty could be a good beginning point. The institutions need to employ individuals who share the values and the vision of the institutions and who have good prospects of becoming excellent teachers. The number of faculty who will be hired in the next decade is so large as to become the dominant force in the colleges and to determine the future of the American community college.

References

Access to Quality Undergraduate Education. A Report to The Southern Regional Education Board by its Commission for Educational Quality, 1985.

ADELMAN, CLIFFORD, (ed.). *From Reports to Response: Proceedings of Regional Conference on the Quality of American Higher Education.* American Association for Higher Education. Washington, D.C.: U.S. Government Printing Office, 1986.

ALFRED, RICHARD L. "Critical Issues Facing Community Colleges." League for Innovation Colloquium. Los Angeles: February 9–10, 1986.

BOK, DEREK. "The President's Report 1984–85." Harvard University, 1985.

BOYER, CAROL M. *Five Reports: Summary of the Recommendations of Recent Commission Reports on Improving Undergraduate Education.* Denver: Education Commission of the States, December, 1985.

BOYER, CAROL M., AND McGUINNESS, A. C. Jr. "State Initiatives to Improve Undergraduate Education: ECS Survey Highlights." *American Association of Higher Education Bulletin,* February, 1986, pp. 3–7.

EATON, JUDITH. "The Challenge for Change at the Community College." *Educational Record* (Fall, 1985), pp. 4–11.

EWELL, PETER T. "Levers For Change: The Role of State Government in Improving the Quality of Postsecondary Education." Denver: Education Commission of the States, November, 1985.

General Education in a Changing Society: General Education Program, Basic Skills Requirements, Standards of Academic Progress at Miami-Dade Community College. Dubuque: Kendall/Hunt Publishing Company, 1978.

Getting Students Ready for College. A Report to the Southern Regional Education Board by its Commission for Educational Quality, Atlanta: 1986.

GILBERT, STEVEN W., and GREEN, KENNETH C. "New Computing in Higher Education." *Change* (May/June, 1986), pp. 33–50.

HODGKINSON, HAROLD L. *Teaching Tomorrow's Students: Celebrating Teaching Excellence.* Austin: University of Texas Press, 1985.

KIRSCH, IRWIN S., and JUNGEBLUT, ANN. *Literacy: Profiles of America's Young Adults.* The National Assessment of Education Progress, 1986.

MYERS, CHET. *Teaching Students to Think Critically.* San Francisco: Jossey-Bass, 1986.

National Alliance of Business. "Employment Policies: Looking to the Year 2000." Washington, D.C.: NAB, St. Louis, Mo: 1986.

NELSON, KATHRYN E. "Liberal Arts in a High-Tech World." St. Louis Community College at Forest Park, October 1985.

PUYEAR, DONALD E., and VAUGHAN, GEORGE B. (eds.). "Maintaining Institutional Integrity." *New Directions for Community Colleges.* 13 (52) (1985).

RICHARDSON, RICHARD C. JR., and BENDER, LOUIS W. "Students in Urban Settings: Achieving the Baccalaureate Degree." ASHE-ERIC Higher Education Reports 1985, Report 6.

RICHARDSON, RICHARD C., JR., FISK, E. C., and OKUN, M. A. *Literacy in the Open-Access College.* San Francisco: Jossey Bass, 1983.

5

Continuation of Community College Vigor: Strengthening the Liberal Arts, General Education, and Transfer Education

RICHARD K. GREENFIELD

. . . community colleges should not be blind to the strong likelihood that they may have erred in favor of mass equity at the expense of setting high expectations. . . .

It is difficult to generalize about the 1,200 American community colleges located in every part of the country. Some are central to large cities; others are in suburbs or rural areas. They range in size from tiny, that is, fewer than 100 students, to enormous, with more than 100,000 enrolled.

Currently, much attention is paid to the themes of actual or anticipated enrollment declines and retrenchment, wavering tax support, and public and legislative criticisms of the effectiveness of community colleges. Areas of special concern include minority access and retention, the transfer function, and academic standards. However, at least some community colleges and multicampus districts continue to experience enrollment increases and a healthy degree of public confidence and financial support.

Public access and equity in higher education have been the touchstones of the community-college movement for decades, especially as the number of these institutions and their enrollments burgeoned after 1946. For the present and near future, nationwide totals for enrollments appear to be stable at best, while some colleges are experiencing difficulties in maintaining minority enrollments. Since access and growth no longer seem to be the exclusive hallmark of the community-college movement, it is appropriate to discuss the future role of community colleges within the total framework of public and private higher education.

At the Crossroads

In discussing the fifteen years of dramatic growth and change since 1970, Deegan and Tillery (1985) refer to the growing confusion about the mission of community colleges, centered on the charges that traditional aspects of the missions, especially the collegiate or transfer function, were being neglected in favor of "community education" (pp. 16–17). They note that:

> As the colleges move farther into the next generation, there is still widespread ambiguity about the mission of the comprehensive community college. Perhaps more important are uncertainties about priorities and program balance within the mission. The issue is serious enough to cast doubt on the ac-

countability of some institutions. . . . Two major assumptions are central to criticism of the contemporary community colleges: (1) the preparation of students for transfer is being neglected; and (2) the colleges are doing things that should be left to other social agencies. [p. 21]

Richardson and Bender (1985) highlight the growing concern over the disparity between goals and outcomes and the elusive nature of the goal of equality of opportunity in urban areas where poverty, growng minority populations, and more recent immigrants combine to produce a college-age population where the odds are against the pursuit of higher education as compared with suburban counterparts. As they state so eloquently:

> The public policy undergirding American higher education is directed toward the ideal of equality and equity of educational opportunity. . . . An implicit assumption is that students who begin in an open access institution will, if successful, be able to move to other institutions providing different and more advanced opportunities. [p. iii]

Many leaders and staff in community colleges are defensive about reports on low transfer rates and spotty posttransfer performance as suggested in some studies. Cohen and Brawer (1982) have a useful reminder:

> If the purpose of the collegiate enterprise is to pass most students through to the baccalaureate degree, then the community college is a failure by design. Its place in the total scheme of higher education assures that a small number of its matriculants will transfer to universities and obtain the baccalaureate. It draws poorly prepared students and encourages part-time and commuter status. [p. 48]

There are varying definitions of "transfer students" preparing to go on to senior institutions. This has led to the lack of valid information and charges, perhaps to some extent unfounded, that community colleges are not performing well with regard to this function. It is true that the proportion of currently enrolled students who are in "transfer programs" and who actually transfer have declined over the past decade. The reasons include the shrinking in size of the traditional college-age pool, increasing competition from baccalaureate degree-granting institutions for students via easing of entrance requirements and greater availability of financial-aid packages, the emergence of an older, part-time student who has less concern for transfer education or continuity in program, the rise of the compensatory-education function with far more "high-risk" students enrolled in community colleges, and stress on the connection between higher education and economic development accompanied by a search for better jobs and higher income. This last has resulted in all types of postsecondary institutions providing for new or repackaged career programs and placing less stress on liberal-arts programs.

As a result of these factors, in at least some states, the transfer function for community colleges is now equaled or surpassed by the "reverse-transfer" phenomenon, with as many or more students coming to community colleges from the senior institutions as are being sent to them by community colleges. For observers who must have order and progression, the seemingly low transfer rates from community colleges to the senior institutions and the increasing reverse-transfer function have caused confusion and criticism. Much of this is aimed at the community colleges. Actually, this is a problem of articulation among all segments of higher education and the inability or unwillingness of institutions of all kinds to agree on a reasonable division of labor. This results from their reaction to tax support and appropriations ultimately resting on credit hour and enrollment totals. Particularly in urban areas where community-college systems, state colleges and/or branches of public universities coexist, the opportunity for genuine cooperation and the development of a truly integrated system of public higher education is often frittered away in open competition for all students and articulation difficulties.

In a recent article, Eaton (1985) raises some pertinent questions about the clash between traditional community-college values and changing societal needs including (1) the degree of commitment to general education in career programs; (2) the dilution of standards and "social promotion" for some students who do not develop basic work–life skills; (3) the stress on maintaining enrollment even if it is at the expense of educational substance; and (4) the relative rigidity of curriculum design, despite vast changes in the American economy and in society. These and other questions reflect both the achievement and the dilemma facing community colleges at the end of the twentieth century:

> The revolution in American education in which the two-year college played a leading role is almost over. Two years of postsecondary education is within reach—financially, geographically, practically—of virtually every American. . . . Open-admissions policies and programs for everyone ensure that no member of the community need miss the chance to attend. But the question remains "Access to what?" [Cohen and Brawer, 1982, p. 23]

The Road Ahead

The Theme of Excellence

As the focus shifts in most parts of the country from coping with expansion and accommodating dramatic enrollment growth to enrollment stabilization or even coping with decline, more emphasis is being placed on qualitative excellence. Until recently, the attention of educational reformers focused on the public schools. In the past few years, higher education, including the community colleges, has come under closer scrutiny in terms of relevance, focus, and efficiency.

As Alexander Astin (1985) and others have pointed out, colleges and universities have tended to be "rated" in terms of quality and prestige by input yardsticks and relative selectivity in the admissions process. The more an institution spends, the greater the cost to students, and the more difficult it is to get admitted, the "better" the college. The longer the list of impressive scholar/researcher/grant stars on the faculty, the "better" the teaching and learning opportunities for the lucky students. Consider Harvard, other Ivy League schools, and Stanford. But by these yardsticks, the open-door community colleges and most state colleges and universities fare poorly in public estimation, since the nonselective admissions process and comparatively low cost yields a heterogeneous student body with lower general-educational and socioeconomic status. It does not matter if the dedicated efforts of a high-quality, student-oriented teaching, student services, and other support staff result in documented impressive gains in student learning for so many.

John Gardner in *Excellence: Can We Be Equal and Excellent Too?* (1961) argued:

> We must develop a point of view that permits each kind of institution to achieve excellence in *terms of its own objectives* . . . in short, we reject the notion that excellence is something that can only be experienced in the most rarefied strata of higher education. . . . We must ask for excellence in every form which higher education takes. . . . We should assert that a stubborn striving for excellence is the price of admission to reputable educational circles. . . . We must make the same challenging demands of students . . . It is an appalling error to assume—as some of our institutions seem to have assumed—that young men and women incapable of the highest standards of intellectual excellence are incapable of any standards whatsoever, and can properly be subjected to shoddy, slovenly and trashy education fare. . . . It is no sin to let average as well as brilliant youngsters into college. It *is* a sin to let any substantial portion of them—average or brilliant—drift through college without effort, without growth and without a goal.

Community colleges throughout our land have sought to bridge the two ideals of equity and excellence in higher education. For many years, our role in making access a reality has been recognized. Indeed, comprehensive open-door community colleges are acknowledged to have been the major American invention in higher education in the twentieth century and a prime mover on the "equity" front. Our reputation for "excellence" is another matter—despite the unfairness of much of the criticism that is leveled at us in the name of academic standards, program quality, grade inflation, student attrition, and faculty prestige.

As Eaton (1982) summarized the situation:

> Data have been increasingly available which tend to confirm that

- Community college students lack basic skill levels compara-ble to lower division students in four-year colleges and uni-versities.

- Community colleges themselves impose lower academic stan-dards on students when compared with four-year colleges and universities.

- Community college faculty and administrators are not as credentialed or as well-trained academically as four-year col-lege or university faculty.

- Community college students are commuters, heavily em-ployed, and burdened with life responsibilities which consis-tently interfere with their academic progress. [p. 16]

In essence, community colleges fall short if they are measured solely on the traditional basis of student-transfer rates and acqui-sition of certificates or associate degrees or if measured by the rate of attainment of bachelor's degrees by former community-college students. Since so many community college students are part time and have specific short-term goals, this narrow critical focus is inappropriate. It is necessary to push vigorously for broader cri-teria against which to measure the effectiveness of community colleges such as student achievement in terms of their own objec-tives or achievement of viable skill levels. Moreover, it is time that community-college staff take the offensive in insisting upon ade-quate academic standards as distinct from being forced to act by various public and private agencies such as the U.S. Office of Ed-ucation. Community colleges need to clearly state the competency expectations the faculty have for their students.

While a good deal of faultfinding may be based upon pure snobbishness with a socioeconomic class status and racist tinge, community colleges should not be blind to the strong likelihood that they may have erred in favor of mass equity at the expense of setting high expectations and pushing all of their students to their natural limits, including those with better-than-average or superior intellectual capabilities. The pendulum is now swinging toward more rigor and more demands upon student motivation and performance. While it is necessary to guard against this "reform" movement if it becomes a cloak for a revival of exclusionary policies, community colleges should welcome this opportunity to take another look at themselves and their programs and services in terms of the eternal American ideal of equality of opportunity, that is, equity, *and* excellence. Community colleges have been in the forefront of the struggle for equity in higher education and they have made many unsung contributions to the search for excellence. It is time for them to take the *lead* in demanding more of themselves, their students, and their institutions, in order to come closer to that elusive ideal of pushing all of our citizens, regardless of differences in capacities, to the limit of their abilities to perform.

Career Education and Transfer Education: Two Separate Missions or One?

Dale Parnell (1985) in his "open letter" to high-school and community-college leaders, argues that: "There is nothing wrong with tough admissions standards as long as we do not allow college-entrance requirements to be viewed as the only key to excellence in a universal education system" (p. 5). He urges community-college leaders to continue to value the transfer function, but to remember that the vast majority of community-college students will never go on and earn a baccalaureate degree and that they, the "ordinary" student, deserve an excellent education, too.

What Parnell and others are concerned about is the changing nature of work and society that requires the development of more advanced, comprehensive knowledge and skills for the great "middle" of our population and work force. We need and will continue to need technicians in an information age who understand basic technological principles, have basic skills, and exhibit problem-solving capabilities, citizenship skills, and lifelong learning attitudes.

Truxal (1986) stresses that all students, including those majoring in liberal arts, need to understand technology's characteristics, capabilities, and limitations. He argues that:

Technology, after all, is simply the application of scientific knowledge to achieve a specified human purpose. As technology is directed toward a societal goal, every new technology involves questions of ethics and values, which must be judged from aesthetic, historical and philosophical viewpoints. Furthermore, technological change has economic, sociological and behavioral implications for both the country and those individuals directly involved. Clearly then, the teaching of technology must be interdisciplinary. [p. 12]

It is a matter of convenience or clarification to discuss career education and transfer education as if these missions continue to be clearly delineated. In reality, the changing needs and goals of community-college students have blurred these lines to the point where all programs other than short-term, noncredit ones need to be considered as both career and transfer oriented. Community colleges should stress as a core mission the goal of facilitating lifelong learning and career development instead of continuing to act as if transfer and career-oriented programs are distinct and apart from each other.

The General-Education Function

Most current statements of mission give a fairly clear idea of the transfer and career functions, but they tend to be vague or ambiguous in the areas of the general-education function. Many commentators concerned with curricular reform, including Cohen and Brawer (1982), conclude that ". . . a good part of the difficulty with general education rests with its definition" (p. 316). Gaff (1983) comments that ". . . despite its apparent simplicity and common currency, the phrase "general education" remains ambiguous; and its various interpreters propose different standards of practice and directions for reform" (p. 3). Perhaps as good a definition as any is that ". . . general education is a mediating influence that, through institution-wide requirements, ensures that all students obtain, from the many courses and programs an institution may make available, some knowledge of the ideas and culture that were once themes of the total liberal arts college" (Carnegie Foundation, 1977, pp. 164–65).

In discussing the three curriculum components of general education, the major, and electives, the Carnegie Report stated the obvious fact that general education is "general" in the limited sense of its being required of most or all degree-seeking students. General education as defined in this report includes one, two, or all three of the components of (1) advanced learning skills courses; (2) "breadth" or discipline distribution courses; and (3) integrative, that is, "synoptic" courses. The first is a universal component. All community colleges seek to impart sufficient language and mathematical skills necessary for any further learning above and beyond the huge volume of remedial or compensatory basic-skills courses they have to provide in the face of the severe handicaps of poor basic-skills performance levels exhibited by a majority of their students. Also universal for certificate or degree students is the typical distribution requirement ("six credits of this, three of that, etc.") aimed at giving vocational-program students a limited sampling of the major streams of thoughts in the social sciences, the sciences, and the humanities. Truly integrative courses for career or transfer students are relatively rare, even though interdisciplinary courses seem to be growing in popularity. This results in few students having the opportunity to comprehend our changing environment and the place of the individual within it or to grapple with issues or problems beyond those that may be addressed in elective courses. In brief, for many valid reasons, community colleges do not come close if ". . . the purpose is 'understanding,' as Whitehead (1938) designated it" (Gaff, 1983, p. 10).

It is difficult not to agree with the Carnegie Foundation's assessment that "general education is now a disaster area" and that "it represents the accretions of history more than a thoughtful concern for specialized current needs." Few of us would not share the Foundation's concerns over the neglect of advanced learning skills in English, language, and mathematics and the widespread use of introductory courses intended for transfer, or a smorgasbord of area electives, to meet the "breadth" or distribution requirements. We should also be concerned over the paucity of truly effective integrative, interdisciplinary courses or requirements.

Contributing to much of the frustration over the seeming lack of focus or coherence in the general-education function in community colleges is the attempt to do everything well. As Brawer and Friedlander (1977) state in their tropical paper on *Science and Social Science in the Two-Year College:*

By proclaiming that they have something to offer to all people according to their needs and abilities, community colleges are obliged to provide adequate and meaningful instructional offerings to their constitutents. These colleges must do several things and adopt a number of approaches in order to fulfill the objectives and promises of the open-door policy . . . non-transfer students . . . should be afforded the opportunity of taking a science or social science course suitable for their abilities and interests . . . many non-transfer students are neither willing nor capable of successfully completing a traditional transfer course and will either avoid it or, if forced by requirements to enroll, will fail or drop out.

General-education efforts are also affected by the stress on "bread and butter" career and vocational-degree programs. This leaves little room for courses or credit hours in general education beyond the bare minimum required either by state law or regulation or from accreditation purposes. Typically, 25 to 30 percent of the total credit hours in a vocational-degree program may be devoted to English composition (or report writing), an elective course or two in the social sciences, a mathematics course or courses (including "technical math"), and a science course or courses. On rarer occasions, an elective humanities course may be thrown in. This, then, is a common pattern of "distribution requirements" that passes as general education, with few, if any, courses designed specifically for nontransfer or nonmajor students. Given the growing preponderance of part-time students with their one or two course "stop-in and stop-out" pattern, the impact of the general-education degree requirements is even less in fact than it is on paper.

Myron Marty, in his paper that was included in the 1979 *National Assembly Report on Strengthening Humanities in Community Colleges*, stressed the need to upset the current imbalance in the curricula and the real difficulties in translating the theory of general education into practice, but urged such reform efforts as being essential to the fulfillment of the community-college mission. In referring to the report of the National Institute for Education's study group on excellence in American higher education, Frank T. Rhodes (1985) commented on the difficulty of agreeing on what some meaningful exposure to a "liberal education" means. In his view, a liberal education should be described in terms not only of content, but of the attitudes and spirit that should underlie the basic skills of reading and listening with comprehension, writing and speaking with precision and clarity, having a contextual sense of our place (physical, biological, social, historical), having an appreciation and insight into a time and culture other than our own, being able to reflect on beliefs, values, and experience, being able to respond to nonverbal symbols (art, performing arts, etc.), and being able to work effectively within a chosen discipline.

While it may be true that the "three C's" dominate community colleges today (career, compensatory, and community education), both the university-parallel (transfer) and general-education functions are not dead. What is needed to breathe more life into the general-education function in both transfer and vocational–career programs is recognition of the "new realities" of community-college clientele. These are the rapid obsolescence of specific job knowledge and skills and the need for a larger share of the curriculum pie to be remodeled to accommodate integrated general-education courses that are enticing and intellectually challenging. Needed above all are educational leaders and faculty who are willing to take what may be risks and who are willing to invest the tremendous time and energy necessary to allow them to go beyond lip service to general education and to come closer to that ideal of excellence and equity in mass higher education.

Conclusion

The continuation of community-college vigor in the late 1980s and in the 1990s will depend upon the willingness of faculty, administrators, and trustees to tackle two of the fundamental elements of community-college mission that have tended to be shortchanged by many institutions over the past few decades while other aspects of the mission increased in importance. Both the liberal arts–transfer function and the general-education function suffered in the 1960s and 1970s through a period of relatively benign neglect as the community colleges responded with alacrity and enthusiasm to the greater emphasis upon vocational–technical programs for job entry and upgrading. Compensatory education for the growing and alarming proportion of underprepared "new" students has continued to grow in importance, as have short-term, community-service programs for adult credit and noncredit learners, community development, and related activities.

While the vocational–technical component and compensatory education will continue to flourish, various aspects of community-service programs have been reduced in some colleges due to lack of public and financial support and concern over "image." The liberal arts have suffered because of enrollment declines in various areas outside the basic skills. As a result, the scope and breadth of liberal-arts offerings has tended to be reduced to the introductory-level courses essential for a barebones transfer program, even in good-sized institutions. Indeed, if it were not for the increasing presence of part-time adult learners, few courses beyond the skeletal program could be offered due to course-enrollment problems in an era of financial stringency.

The question facing many community colleges, especially those in areas where relatively low-cost, public, four-year institutions exist within the same commuting range, is whether or not the transfer function can survive in credible form. In its present form, it may not be viable—at least where reasonably convenient baccalaureate-degree alternatives exist. Admittedly, this still leaves the transfer function as an important element in many other locations in the country. But aside from the function of providing compensatory education for those underprepared students who might seek to pursue a baccalaureate degree, the community college will find it difficult to compete in a more cutthroat era when most public baccalaureate-degree institutions have become open-door colleges in fact, despite the fiction contained in their catalogs and brochures. Indeed, short of a deliberate plan to distribute initial enrollment opportunities based upon previous academic achievement similar to California's, or short of a division of labor giving community colleges the major responsibility for lower-division instruction and an upper-division and graduate-school role for the urban public university (an old idea that seems stillborn), demographics and competition have led to what is still a fairly civilized war for traditional college-age students. Community colleges have had to battle upstream to maintain their share of a shrinking pie, mainly through career programs and services to the underprepared.

Given the fact that community-college enrollments have shifted heavily toward the part-time, less-well-prepared, more immediate career-oriented students, it is reasonable to assume that the rate of transfers from community colleges, now in the 10% of enrollment range, will hardly increase and indeed may decrease in the next decade unless a major effort is made to stress this function. The liberal arts will continue to be an important segment of total offerings, but not because of large numbers of full-time transfer students right out of high school. Rather, the focus has to be more on quality courses offered to older, intermittent students who stop in and stop out, and who are not particularly interested in a sequential program, in obtaining a degree, or in transferring to a four-year institution (especially since an increasing number may already have the bachelor's degree).

For the liberal arts to revive and flourish in community colleges, there will have to be a fusion of the fuzzy and artificial concepts of transfer and career programs, since students have ignored these institutional definitions. Given technological, economic, demographic, and societal trends, community-college curricula must be realigned to reflect the need for more generic career–growth skills that include a greater proportion of general education, the core of which are the liberal arts and sciences.

Excellence in future community-college efforts calls for concentration on improving student persistence to associate-degree achievement and on enhancing the transfer rates of that part of their student body that has the potential and genuine interest in such goals. It also calls for development of adequate measures and acceptable goals in relation to developmental and short-term career and personal needs for the majority of the enrollees who realistically do not have degree or transfer goals for the short-term or mid-term future. Continuation of the encouraging of the development of appropriate academic standards for all courses and insistence upon adequate student achievement in relation to these standards is essential as well.

The transfer-education responsibility requires redefining the career and transfer functions as being an inseparable web spun around the mission of encouraging all citizens to maximize their personal intellectual growth and development involving lifelong learning for both career enhancement and more effective living in a democratic–pluralistic society. This means providing more staff resources and management structure for the liberal arts and science programs and encouraging persistence and transfer of qualified students.

Community-college general education needs a workable definition or definitions that serve to guide faculty and staff in course and curriculum modifications. This means recognition that general, liberal education is more than specific course content. Additional emphasis needs to be placed upon integrated interdisciplinary courses and cocurricular activities, blending the social sciences, humanities, and science and technologies.

Community colleges do have an exciting opportunity to respond to new challenges above and beyond access and growth. These include more stress on relevant measures of quality and a renewed emphasis on the general education–transfer function for lifelong learning. Given the enthusiasm, adaptability, and success of community colleges to date, there is every reason to believe that these dynamic institutions will respond positively and effectively to changes in demography, technology, and culture. They will continue to play a major role in higher education and in their communities in the year 2000 and beyond.

References

ASTIN, ALEXANDER W. *Achieving Educational Excellence.* San Francisco: Jossey-Bass, 1985.

BRAWER, FLORENCE, and FRIEDLANDER, JACK. *Science and Social Science in the Two-Year College.* University of California: ERIC Clearinghouse, 1977.

Carnegie Foundation Report. *Missions of the College Curriculum."* San Francisco: Jossey-Bass, 1977.

COHEN, ARTHUR M., and BRAWER, FLORENCE. *The American Community College.* San Francisco: Jossey-Bass, 1982.

DEEGAN, WILLIAM L., and TILLERY, DALE, eds. *Renewing the American Community College.* San Francisco: Jossey-Bass, 1985.

EATON, JUDITH S. "The Challenge for Change in the Community College." *Educational Record* 66 (4) (Fall, 1985): 4–11.

————. "Judging Community Colleges: Looking at Student Success." *Community and Junior College Journal* 53 (1) (September, 1982): 16–21 and 45.

GAFF, JERRY G. *General Education Today.* San Francisco: Jossey-Bass, 1983.

GARDNER, JOHN. *Excellence: Can We Be Equal and Excellent Too?* New York: Harper, 1961.

MARTY, MYRON. *National Assembly on Strengthening Humanities in Community Colleges.* American Association of Community and Junior Colleges. Washington, D.C.: Harley House, 1979.

PARNELL, DALE. *The Neglected Majority.* Washington, D.C.: Community College Press, 1985.

RHODES, FRANK T. "Reforming Higher Education Will Take More than Curricula." *The Chronicle of Higher Education* 35 (May 22, 1985): 80.

RICHARDSON, R. C., JR., and BENDER, LOUIS W. *Students in Urban Settings: Achieving the Baccalaureate Degree.* ASHE-ERIC Higher Education Report No. 6, Jonathan Fise, Series Editor, 1985.

TRUXAL, JOHN G. "Learning to Think Like an Engineer: Why, What, and How?" *Change* 3(2) (March/April, 1986): 10–19.

PART
TWO

Context-Defined Leadership

"That so few dare to be eccentric marks the chief danger of the times."

John Stuart Mill

"I have come to believe that the art of executive leadership is above all a taste for paradox, a talent for ambiguity, the capacity to hold contradictory propositions comfortably in a mind that relishes complexity."

Harlan Cleveland

"Democracy . . . is a charming form of government, full of variety and disorder, and dispensing a sort of equality to equals and unequals alike."

Plato

". . . leaders are people who perceive what is needed and what is right and know how to mobilize people and resources to accomplish mutual goals."

Thomas E. Cronin

6

The Reality and Illusion of Community-College Leadership

ROBERT BIRNBAUM

Leaders, then, are people believed by followers to have caused events.

Much has been written about leadership in general; little is known about it. The paucity of useful theories and good data traditionally leads discussions of leadership to be exercises in rhetoric, platitudes, and wishful thinking. Nonetheless, there is value in discussing some conventional ideas about leadership and their relevance to community colleges, as well as in considering the implications of some newer ideas that may give a somewhat different perspective. Some data from a recent study of college presidents provide modest support for these newer ideas.

Both the traditional and nontraditional views of leadership can provide useful insights. Although they are in many ways diametrically opposed, there is no need to choose between them. Accepting conflicting views may help to illuminate different aspects of reality and may give us a more complicated (and therefore probably a more accurate) understanding of our campuses. It also suggests some things leaders should be aware of, or can do, that seem reasonable under most leadership theories.

Models of Leadership

Four basic approaches to studying organizational leadership are found in the literature.* The first is trait theory, often referred to in the past as the Great Man Theory, which posits that leaders are persons endowed with specific physical, personality, or ability traits to a greater extent than are nonleaders. Examples in the higher-education literature are legion, the most recent being seen in George Vaughan's *The Community College Presidency* (1986). The presidents Vaughan surveyed identified 17 traits as being important to leadership, the highest ranking of which were integrity, judgment, courage, concern, and flexibility. These are all admirable traits, but a moment of thought about this representative list should indicate why trait theory in general has been abandoned by researchers as not useful. After all, who *would* follow a person of questionable moral soundness who exhibited poor judgment, cowardice, lack of concern, and rigidity? And is there really anyone who either can—or indeed should—exhibit all of the presumably positive traits all the time and in all situations?

*There are a number of summaries of the traditional literature of organizational leadership, including a readable synthesis and interpretation by Yukl (1981), and an exhaustive summary of research findings by Bass (1981).

The second approach considers not what leaders *are* but what leaders actually *do*. Among the most influential studies in this tradition are those that have identified two aspects of leadership behavior. One of these is an orientation to the task, when leaders give great emphasis to such activities as directing, coordinating, planning, and problem solving. The other is an emphasis upon group relationships, seen when leaders behave in a friendly, considerate, supportive, consultative, and open manner. Under some circumstances, to be effective, leaders should emphasize task accomplishment; under others, group maintenance and development should be stressed. It would not be startling to find that we can all agree that a president trying to get the task done regardless of the cost to people would probably be no more effective than one who did everything to keep people happy even at the cost of getting the job done. The problem is the right combination of the two, and there the literature on the effect of leader behavior on group performance or satisfaction is contradictory. Even the presumed causality of the relationships is questionable. For example, if it were found that presidential delegation was associated with institutional effectiveness, does it mean that delegation causes effectiveness, or that effectiveness makes it possible to delegate?

A third research tradition has focused upon how effective leaders use power. It has been suggested (French and Raven, 1959) that there are five bases of social power available to leaders through their office or through their personalities. Leaders can influence others through their offices because of the legitimacy provided by our social and legal systems (legitimate power), and through their ability to provide rewards (reward power) and to threaten punishments (coercive power). Legitimate power and reward power seem to have an inconsistent effect on organizational performance and the punishments of coercive power have a negative effect. A person who influences others *solely* through these powers of office can be termed an official (Etzioni, 1964).

Leaders can also influence others through their own personalities in two ways—their perceived expertise (expert power) and the extent to which others personally identify with and like them (referent power)—both of which have positive impacts on performance.

Persons who influence others *solely* by virtue of their personalities are called informal leaders. The greatest power, of course, is exercised by persons who influence others *both* through their offices *and* their personalities, and these are the people we refer to as formal leaders.

A major strand in this orientation to power and one particularly suited to helping think about leadership in colleges, is known as social-exchange theory. It considers the reciprocal relationships between leaders who provide needed services to a group in exchange for the group's approval and their compliance with the leader's demands. In essence, the group agrees to collectively reduce its own autonomy and to accept the authority of the leader in exchange for the rewards and benefits (social approval, financial benefits, competitive advantage) the leader can bring them. This does not mean that followers agree to cede *all* their potential power and influence. Indeed, several models of exchange theory suggest that leaders can increase their own power by empowering their subordinates.

Leaders accumulate power through their offices and their own personalities to the extent that they produce the expected rewards and fairly distribute them and lose power to the extent they do not. Leadership, in other words, is *limited* by what followers will permit. This suggests that one's effectiveness as a leader depends upon either fulfilling the expectations of followers or upon changing those expectations.

The distinction between fulfilling expectations or changing them is at the heart of Burns' (1978) distinction between transactional and transforming leadership. The transactional leader meets the needs of followers and emphasizes means; the transformational leader emphasizes ends and taps the motivations of followers to lead them to new and better values in the support of intended change. Neither form, says Burns, should be confused with what commonly passes for leadership—"acts of oratory, manipulation, sheer self-advancement, brute coercion, . . . conspicuous position-taking without followers or follow through, posturing on various stages . . . authoritarianism" (p. 427). This caveat is important. It illuminates a common cognitive bias that leads us to make judgments about leaders based upon the extent to which they have characteristics that make them *look* like leaders. We can joke about college presidents who had the two major requirements for success, white hair for that look of experience, and hemorrhoids for that look of concern. But it is not a joking matter when judgments of competence and ability are still too often made based upon myths such as remaining distant from followers, or upon other clearly unrelated factors or characteristics such as sex.

Burns's distinction between transactional and transformation leadership is useful, but it can also be somewhat misdirecting. It appears to demean the skilled and able administrator who can keep a college functioning effectively in turbulent times, but who when weighed in the balance is found wanting when compared to the exemplar of the charismatic who alters visions and moves institutions. Given a choice, who would not rather engage the hearts and minds of others than try to deal with faculty unions, budget cuts, irate legislators, and the other everyday problems of running a complex social system? But the state of grace that charismatic leadership implies is always in short supply in every field; to hold it up as an expectation in college leadership is unrealistic and potentially damaging.

The fourth perspective on leadership suggests that different situations require different patterns of traits and behavior if a leader is to be effective. What is effective leader behavior? Well, it all depends . . . on the nature of the external environment, the type of task, the personal qualities of the leader, leader–follower relations, maturity of followers, followers expectations, presence or absence of a crisis, availability of reward systems, role clarity, or any one of dozens of other factors depending upon the specific theory. These so-called contingency theories essentially say that no single approach to leadership is the best, but at the same time that not all approaches are equally effective. Discovering that there is no philosopher's stone for effective leadership is a great step forward both for theory and for practice. Understanding that what worked *then* in *that* situation under *those* circumstances may not work *now* in *this* situation under *these* circumstances is the beginning of administrative wisdom, and may prevent the making an error of gargantuan proportions. But it may not prove helpful in informing what you *should* do now.

Models of Colleges

These four traditional ideas of leadership are all plausible and familiar. Even without being aware of the theories behind them we have integrated them into our perceptions of everyday organizational life. There are other systems of ideas that we have probably internalized as well—ideas about how colleges are governed and managed—that also have implications for what effective leaders are presumed to do and be. Three such models* in particular help to direct our attention and give meaning to institutional events.

In the first model the college is seen as a large, complex, hierarchical, and goal-directed organization exhibiting the characteristics that would permit organization theorists to identify it as a bureaucracy. The leader in such an organization sits at the apex of a pyramid of power, gathering information about effectiveness and efficiency that flows upward, identifying and resolving problems, and issuing directives down through the organization. The effective leader establishes goals, decides how they are to be achieved, scientifically organizes the work of subordinates, plans, and monitors organizational functioning. The single word to describe the system and its leader is "rational." This model does capture part of college organization, but misses other essential elements such as the power of informal influence networks, the influence of external environmental factors, and the fragmented and highly specialized nature of many academic subunits.

The second model is that of the collegium, the community of scholars. Power in this system is widely dispersed, and decisions are made after full deliberation by those affected by outcomes. Operationalized in systems of shared authority, the role of the leader is not to make decisions but rather by serving as first among equals to move the group towards its ultimate goal, that of consensus. The leader listens, proposes, mediates, persuades, and influences through information sharing and appeals to reason. Again, the model identifies an important part of the process of many institutions, but ignores the reality of conflict, external influence,

*A good summary of the organizational characteristics inherent in common governance models can be found in chapter 2 in Baldridge, et al., 1978.

and internal status differentials. It perhaps reflects more our desires, our processes, and outcomes devoutly to be wished for than the reality of what actually happens.

The third model is that of the college as political system. Here the organization is seen as composed of various special-interest groups and subgroups with differing goals and values. Organizational process is characterized by conflict over the allocation of resources. The influence of leaders is limited by the political pressures of these groups, and leaders must spend time building positions that are supported by coalitions that change over time from issue to issue. The role of the leader is to help manage the process of compromise, coalition, and mediation that leads to acceptance of policies consistent with the leader's own goals.

Taken collectively, these various organizational and higher-education leadership models suggest that leadership is at the core of institutional functioning. While they are all different, the theories and models do have several ideas in common. They picture leaders as heroic figures. They assume that participants in an organization know what they want and have the power to get it. They assume that values and ideas direct behavior, that cause and effect are discernible and, except for some of the contingency approaches, they focus upon what happens inside the organization and pay little if any attention to what happens outside. They presume that leaders exist in a world that is rational, linear, and essentially certain.

But while administrators usually act as if the world were sane, we also know that sometimes things seem crazy and that our theories do not seem to be consistent with reality. When models do not work, we commonly try to manipulate and adjust them. When we try to understand why a planning effort was unsuccessful, for example, we commonly decide that the time-line was too short, the instructions were unclear, or the people involved were not appropriate, and we vow to correct the deficiency next time. An alternative strategy, and one that leads to new and potentially more useful ways of learning, is to consider the possibility that the execution of the model is not the problem—the problem may be that *the model itself* is flawed and should be changed. Changing models is not a trivial or unimportant task, because our models—whether of organizations, of solar systems, or of atoms—define how we interpret reality.

New Ideas About Organizations and Leadership

Between 1975 and 1985, a new group of organization theories were developed that in fact do try to alter our perceptions of reality. They are not merely refinements or elaborations of previous ideas, and they do not share many of the commonalities of the older theories and models. These new ideas, which in their various forms have been referred to as symbolic, cognitive, or cultural theories,* view organizations as systems of belief and perception in which reality is invented, not discovered. Organizations represent the attempt by humans with limited rational capacities to collectively impose meaning upon an equivocal, fluid, and complex world. The importance of facts, descriptions of events, or cause and effect relationships is not their objective existence but their interpretation. Much of this interpretation is influenced by the organization's culture—that is, the dominant values, norms, philosophy, rules, and other unquestioned assumptions of an organization's life. Culture has been referred to as the "glue" that holds organizations together, and can be seen in the patterns of language, the distribution of power, and the myths and legends that give meaning to interpreted events. Some analysts believe that the role of leaders is to "manage" the organizational culture; others believe that culture cannot be managed and that the role of leaders is therefore more symbolic than real.

A major idea in these approaches is that leaders in most organizations have relatively little influence over outcomes when compared with other forces that affect organizational functioning. This is particularly true of college presidents and others in institutional leadership positions. Consider, for example, the constraints on leader behavior that might affect a community-college president. They would include internal forces such as the expectations of board members, faculty, community groups, students, and fellow

---

*A sample of works in this tradition with specific implications for leadership include Deal and Kennedy (1982), Cohen and March (1974), Schein (1985), Sergiovanni and Corbally (1984), and Weick (1979).

administrators; institutional rules and regulations that appear to take on a life of their own; labor contracts; and continuing budget obligations (such as tenured faculty), all of which significantly limit presidential discretion. External constraints include new laws, enrollment shifts, budget formulas, general economic and social trends—and the list goes on.

Vaughan (1986) says, "the success of a leader is ultimately judged on the success of the enterprise he or she leads" (p. 103). But how many good presidents have paid the ultimate administrative price for campus problems caused by financial, political, or demographic trends over which they had absolutely no control? And how many indifferent presidents have survived—or even been acclaimed—because of having been fortunate enough to be in office during good times? Even Clark Kerr, who strongly argues that presidents make a difference, starts and ends his list of 22 items of "sage advice" for presidents with the statement "Be Lucky!" (Kerr, 1984, pp. 94–95).

If presidents are so constrained, and if luck is such a vital element in their success or failure, why then do we continue to believe in the importance of leaders? The theories suggest that the reason in good part may be related to the cognitive processes of the human mind. We search for and must find rationality and causal relationships in order to impose meanings on otherwise random or inexplicable events. Take as an example a sudden enrollment change in a community college. Many forces are at work on campus, in the community, and in society at large that affect enrollments on a specific campus. Chance events also play a role. And on most campuses the president has also publicly indicated interest and concern.

A sudden change in enrollments calls for an explanation of cause and effect. The psychological process known as attribution makes it more likely that we will see such changes as a consequence of some human agency rather than the complex interaction of impersonal forces. We then look for a person who can be assigned as the cause.

A tradition of research on the cognitive process through which we assign such causes* suggests that we will see what we expect to

---

*Summaries and interpretations of this research can be found in Nisbett and Ross (1982) and in Kahneman, Slovic, and Tversky (1982).

see (that is, our values will filter our perceptions), and that we will assign causation based upon the prominence and salience of the potential causes. That is, people upon whom we are most likely to focus our attention are most likely to be identified as potential causes. Rather than look for *all* the evidence, we are likely to rely on the most *available* evidence.

The primary causal candidate is likely to be the president, and we are likely to identify the enrollment change as a consequence of the presence (or lack of) "presidental leadership." In this case presidential leadership may not be real but is rather a social attribution—a result of the tendency of campus constituents to assign to a president the responsibility for unusual institutional outcomes because the leader fills a role identified as a leader, because presidents are very visible and prominent, because presidents spend a great deal of time doing leader-like things (such as engaging in ceremonial and symbolic activities, or forming enrollment task forces), and because we all have the need to believe in the effectiveness of individual control.

Leaders, then, are people believed by followers to have caused events. "Successful leaders," says Pfeffer (1977), "are those who can separate themselves from organizational failures and associate themselves with organizational successes." This means that we may identify leaders not so much by what they do as by their ability to manipulate symbols.

The most well-known treatment of the college presidency from this perspective is by Cohen and March in their book *Leadership and Ambiguity* (1974). They view the college as an organized anarchy characterized by problematic goals, an unclear technology, and fluid participation. Problems seldom get resolved through rational processes, and instead get tied up with streams of solutions, participants, and choice points. Things become associated no more sensibly than if they were all thrown together and mixed up in a giant garbage can. We may mistakenly believe things to be rationally connected to each other merely because they occur at about the same time (for example, if enrollments went up right after the report of the president's enrollment task force) even though they may in fact be unrelated. In this view, planning is symbolic, the presidency is an illusion, and presidents are largely interchangeable.

In another work, March (1984) characterized presidents as light bulbs in a dark room. This metaphor recognizes that presidents are essential for the effective operation of a campus, but it also suggests that under most conditions it makes little difference whether you are a 100-watt or a 300-watt president. This need not be viewed as demeaning the presidential role. To put out even the *minimum* light required to prevent organizational participants from stumbling around in the dark requires experience and judgment of an uncommon kind.

Rather than viewing the president as the omnipotent captain at the helm of the ship, Cohen and March see the president as the driver of a skidding car. The president's skill in this situation may turn out to be important at the margins, but by and large the president has little control over direction and outcome.

This concept of the presidency has not been enthusiastically endorsed by administrators or boards because it seems to deny rationality and diminish our importance. At the same time, evidence of our inability to control events, to develop *meaningful* statements of missions and goals, to predict outcomes, to solve problems, and to improve education, is all around us. We tend to respond to these discrepancies by trying to refine the model rather than by considering new models.

We deny the discrepancy between our espoused theories and our theories-in-use even when the gap between what we *say* presidents do, and what we *see* them do, is obvious. Presidents interviewed by Vaughan (1986), for example, said there were four leadership roles of community-college presidents. The most important was establishing and interpreting the mission of the college, followed by the president as educational leader, the president setting the campus environment, and the president as external leader.

Vaughan's presidents then commented on the actual performance of these roles. They felt that presidents had been unsuccessful in interpreting and clarifying the mission. They said "we are not as involved in the instructional role as we think we are," and their views of setting the campus environment appeared to be a hodgepodge of vague generalities such as "creating a climate of love." So presidents themselves agree that at least three of the four stated roles appear to be more symbolic than real. Even the fourth, that of external representation, may turn out upon closer examination to be primarily symbolic; that is, it is symbolically important that a president do it in a manner that meets the expectations of those being contacted, but for the most part the effects on campus life will not be effected by differences in how it is done. Perhaps the most telling quotation was one by a trustee who said that the most important thing she wanted in a president was for "the president to look and behave like a president."

The idea that leadership is an illusion is difficult to conceive of, much less accept. It is contrary to our experiences through which we have *seen* our significant effects upon our institutions. But how trustworthy are our perceptions of these experiences? Is it possible that at least *some* of what we see in our institutions is ambiguous and subject to interpretation? If that is the case, may we be subject in making these assessments to the same cognitive traps and limitations that lead people in other settings to make erroneous judgments under conditions of uncertainty?

Data on Cognitive Bias

A questionnaire recently completed by over 250 college presidents (Birnbaum, in press) asked these presidents to rate on a 100-point scale their own effectiveness as *institutional* managers, as well as the effectiveness of an "average" president and of their predecessor. They gave the average president a 66, they scored themselves as 77, and they graded their predecessor as 52. In other words, there appears to be a rather consistent bias for college presidents to rate themselves as more effective than the average president and their predecessors as less effective.

These perceptions are unlikely to be accurate representations of reality. If they were, as each below-average president was succeeded by a higher-than-average one, the quality of higher education would be exponentially rising—a situation that, if true, has somehow escaped the notice of recent national task forces and panels.

In this same questionnaire, presidents were also asked to assess the quality of seven aspects of campus life at the time they took office, the extent to which those aspects had changed under their leadership, and how much more they would change by the time they left office. The answers again were uniform; things were not good at the time they took over, they were much better now than they had been, and they will be still better by the time they leave office. These responses were true for all seven items, including financial strength, faculty morale, campus facilities, quality of instruction, community service, quality of students, and research productivity. It was particularly true for the most ambiguous item of all—faculty morale. Three-quarters of the presidents characterized faculty morale as fair or poor at the time they took office, 84 percent thought it was much better now, and 71 percent said it would be better still by the time they left.

Another item asked one group of presidents to identify who had been responsible for the past year's most important campus episode, incident, or change that had a *positive* outcome; 74 percent said that they as president had caused it. Another group of presidents was asked to identify an incident with a *negative* outcome, and only 14 percent said that they as president had caused it. Although there are no data to provide evidence, it can be assumed that campus faculty asked these questions would probably not respond as their presidents did. Consider within this context Pfeffer's earlier comment: "Successful leaders are those who can separate themselves from organizational failures and associate themselves with organizational successes."

Many implications can be drawn from these data, but the major point is that when faced with ambiguity or equivocality (what *is* "managerial effectiveness," after all, and how *does* one define, much less assess, faculty morale?) there are predictable cognitive biases in our judgment. They may lead us to believe that we are more effective than average and much more effective than our predecessor, that we are the main cause of positive events on campus (but not responsible for events with negative outcomes), and that things have gotten much better under our leadership (even though objectively they really have probably remained much the same). It almost appears as if we *have* been able to take responsibility for our institutional successes, and somehow separate ourselves from its failures. The secret, of course, is in getting others to see things as we do!

The same types of errors of judgment can be induced even with concrete data. When presidents were shown two sets of five numbers with a low correlation and led to expect that it would be a high correlation, they *saw* it as high (Birnbaum, 1986). Another group of presidents were shown numbers with a high correlation and were led to expect it to be low. They saw it as low. Our expectations can indeed overwhelm our data.

Presidents were shown data from a campus that was said to practice strategic planning, and asked to indicate the extent to which the campus' belief in the effectiveness of strategic planning was supported by the data. Presidents were also asked about the degree to which they themselves believed in strategic planning. The more a president believed in the value of strategic planning, the more likely the president was to believe that the data shown supported the value of planning.

In both of these items, and others as well, our preconceptions affect what is seen, what is not seen, and what is invented. Our preconceptions affect how we select and weigh data, resulting in a greater likelihood of self-confirmation. Cohen and March, in commenting on the old phrase "I'll believe it when I see it" suggest that it should really be "I'll see it when I believe it." Can it be that these processes of selective attention, attribution, and interpretation come to reinforce our belief in the efficacy of leadership?

Comparing the earlier theories of leadership to those that come out of the symbolic or cognitive approach puts us in a rather difficult situation. On the one hand, leadership has been referred to as almost everything, and on the other it has been considered as almost nothing. Our first inclination is to believe the first set of theories, but further thought makes us less certain. There is little empirical evidence to suggest that, in general, leadership makes a difference in organizational outcomes (but some to indicate that organizational outcomes makes a difference in our assessment of leadership, which is quite a different thing). There is nothing that all leaders must do to be successful, nothing successful leaders do that is not also done by unsuccessful ones, and nothing that can be done to guarantee success. Probably everything ever written about leadership is correct some of the time, but nothing is correct all the time.

People who write about leadership in higher education tend to ignore the research and the theories in their hortatory pronouncements. But even their definitive statements look less certain and directive if you examine them carefully. They say plan—but not too much or too little. They say be visible, but not to the point of leading people to unrealistic expectations. Community colleges are told to strengthen concepts of open access, but at the same time not to make the mistake of trying to be all things to all people. We are told to emphasize our missions and move towards goal consensus, even though our goals are ambiguous and organizations can operate effectively without agreement on ends as long as there is agreement on means. If we choose not to take precipitant action when faced with a crisis we may either be praised for our patience and forbearance or criticized for our lack of assertiveness. If we *do* take action, we are as likely to be lauded for our decisiveness as we are to be condemned for our lack of patience and judgment. It all depends, not on our behavior, but upon the outcomes—outcomes over which we often have little control. Essentially what those who tell us to exert more leadership are really saying is "be successful."

Recommendations

Consider these five simple recommendations for community-college leaders. They are consistent with cognitive theories, but at the same time they are not inconsistent with the more traditional theories that have been mentioned. Ironically, the most radical conceptual ideas lead to the most conservative suggestions. They may not help, but at least they cannot hurt.

1. *Complicate yourself.* The world is complicated, and it is possible to interpret any situation from a number of perspectives *any or all of which* may provide useful administrative insights. Simple administrators have a narrow framework for understanding a problem; complex administrators can draw on numerous explanations and frameworks to find actions to suit particular situations. Cognitive complexity leads to better understanding as well as to

more effective action. One of the best ways to develop complicated understandings is to be aware of the various conceptual models of organization and of leadership so that you can generate both multiple descriptions of situations and multiple approaches to solutions. The only thing more useful than a good theory is a lot of good theories. Only complicated minds can see the many and conflicting realities of complicated situations.

2. *Know your followers.* Leaders are constrained by the limits imposed by their followers. Leaders who exceed these limits will suffer a reduction in their status and lose their claim to leadership. This means that the dramatic, authoritative, and decisive leader-like behavior we often call for may often be counterproductive in a college setting in which the faculty as well as administrative subordinates *expect* participation.

Leaders must do what followers want, even when the followers do not know that they want it! To know what followers want, it is important to encourage open communication and then to *listen.* Acting is easy; listening is hard, particularly for leaders who believe that they have to *tell* other people what to do. But listening and influencing are both reciprocal—the more I listen to you, the more you are likely to listen to me. We influence others by allowing ourselves to *be* influenced.

3. *Check your cognitive biases.* Leaders are likely to believe themselves to have more positive influence than they really do, to cognitively dissociate themselves from failures and, like everyone else, to make self-confirming errors of judgment about cause and effect. Subordinates who can help correct leader error are beyond price, but they may be afraid to be the bearer of bad news or they may, over time, come to share some of the biases of their leaders. To increase their effectiveness, leaders should encourage dissent among their staff, should find value in conflict, and should accept criticism nondefensively. They should also recognize that there are two ways to deal with error—to try to prevent it before it occurs, or to try and detect and correct it afterwards. We often spend too much time on prevention, and not enough on detection. Think of the significant differences in how leaders would act based upon their interest in setting up systems for prevention or for detection. Our recent experiences with our own advanced technology (which is relatively simple when compared to social systems) suggest that

complete prevention is impossible and counterproductive. Systems for detecting error not only have lower cost and are more effective, but they also enable us to take risks.

4. *Increase your power.* Power is the ability to influence others. Of the five types of social power, legitimate power is set by your organizational role and referent power is related to your personality (both comparatively difficult to change), reward power has variable effects, and coercive (punitive) power creates alienation. This leaves one power base subject to your manipulation—expert power. Expert power is partially symbolic (our graduate degrees, for example), but it is also related to perceptions of our technical competence. One school of thought says that leaders will be more effective as they develop a repertoire of management, personnel, educational, and public-relations skills. Another school says that effectiveness depends not upon the skills themselves but upon other's *perceptions* that one is skilled. But in either case, expertise gives followers a sense of confidence that increases their willingness to follow, and that may increase institutional prestige and support among important external constituencies.

5. *Be equally concerned with substance and with process.* As Henry Higgins said, the French do not particularly care what you do as long as you pronounce it properly. In the same way, in *most* colleges and universities the prevailing mood for most substantive matters is apathy—most people are not concerned about most issues most of the time. But one thing they are almost *certain* to be concerned about is *process*, because their right to participate and get involved is linked to their organizational status. The right way to do things is usually (but not always) the way people *expect* it will be done. In higher education, process *is* substance, and leaders who forget that are likely to generate opposition to even the best ideas. The effective leader will never (well, almost never) sacrifice expected process for the presumed rewards of a desired outcome.

Summing Up

All of the theories and models of leadership that have been discussed are helpful in illuminating different aspects of organizations and leaders. Symbolic and cognitive approaches give us subtle perspectives not otherwise available, and it is important to learn more about them. Leadership is probably both a science and an art. As a science it is directed by understandings of structure, schedules, systems, and power that can be learned. As an art is it informed by sensibilities, connoisseurship, and intuition that can, at least up to a certain level, be developed. Trying to lead without science is often ineffective; trying to lead without art is usually sterile.

Comments about "the leadership crisis" are as commonplace in higher education today as they have been for the past 100 years. But given how little we actually know about it, it is almost less interesting that leaders can sometimes be misguided, and more interesting that they usually are not. Our criticisms of leadership in community colleges as elsewhere may be based upon unrealistic expectations of heroic behavior. The performance of our institutions may in general be less dependent upon leadership than we are willing to believe. Most college presidents do the right things, and do most things right most of the time. It is in the nature of our institutions that doing the right thing usually goes unnoticed—it is when the wrong things are done that presidential actions have the most visible organizational consequences. It is possible that college leaders can be made marginally more effective, as can board members, state senators, and others who must make public policy in an environment of ambiguous and incomplete information, and conflicting yet legitimate interests. But those who seek major changes in how leaders behave, or believe that such changes will make major and positive differences in institutional effectiveness, are likely to be disappointed.

References

BALDRIDGE, J. V., CURTIS, D. V., ECKER, G., and RILEY, G. L. *Policy Making and Effective Leadership.* San Francisco: Jossey-Bass, 1978.

BASS, B. M. *Stogdill's Handbook of Leadership.* New York: Free Press, 1981.

BIRNBAUM, R. "When College Presidents Are Wrong: The Effects of Knowledge Structures and Judgmental Heuristics on Administrative Influences." Working Paper, Department of Higher and Adult Education, Teachers College, Columbia University, 1986.

BIRNBAUM, R. "Leadership and Learning: The College President as Intuitive Scientist." *Review of Higher Education,* in press.

BURNS, J. M. *Leadership.* New York: Harper and Row, 1978.

COHEN, M. D., and MARCH, J. D. *Leadership and Ambiguity: The American College President.* New York: McGraw-Hill, 1974.

DEAL, T. E., and KENNEDY, A. A. *Corporate Cultures.* Reading, MA: Addison-Wesley, 1982.

ETZIONI, A. *Modern Organizations.* Englewood Cliffs, NJ: Prentice-Hall, 1964.

FRENCH, J. R. P., and RAVEN, B. "The Bases of Social Power." In D. Cartwright (ed.), *Studies in Social Power.* Ann Arbor, MI: Institute for Social Research, 1959.

KAHNEMAN, D., SLOVIC, P., and TVERSKY, A. *Judgment Under Uncertainty: Heuristics and Biases.* Cambridge, England: Cambridge University Press, 1982.

KERR, C. *Presidents Make a Difference.* Washington, D.C.: Association of Governing Boards, 1984.

MARCH, J. G. "How We Talk and How We Act: Administrative Theory and Administrative Life." In Sergiovanni, T. J., and Corbally, J. E. (eds.), *Leadership and Organizational Culture.* Urbana: University of Illinois Press, 1984.

NISBETT, R., and ROSS, L. *Human Inference: Strategies and Shortcomings of Human Judgment.* Englewood Cliffs, NJ: Prentice-Hall, 1982.

PFEFFER, J. "The Ambiguity of Leadership." *Academy of Management Review* 2(1977):104–119.

SCHEIN, E. H. *Organizational Culture and Leadership.* San Francisco: Jossey-Bass, 1985.

SERGIOVANNI, T. J., and CORBALLY, J. E. (eds.) *Leadership and Organizational Culture.* Urbana: University of Illinois Press, 1984.

VAUGHAN, G. B. *The Community College Presidency.* New York: ACE/Macmillan, 1986.

WEICK, K. E. *The Social Psychology of Organizing, Second Edition.* Reading, MA: Addison-Wesley, 1979.

YUKL, G. A. *Leadership in Organizations.* Englewood Cliffs, N. J.: Prentice-Hall, 1981.

7

Leadership Needs and Effectiveness: Vision with Competence, Strength with Integrity

JAMES L. FISHER

> *. . . leadership boils down to consideration of the touchy but fundamental subject of power.*

Recent sources boldly and clearly articulate concerns regarding the general condition of leadership in American higher education and, indeed, of American society itself. Clark Kerr, President Emeritus of the University of California and principal author of two recent national studies on the subject, maintains that the presidency is higher education's main problem (Kerr, 1984; Kerr and Gade, 1986). He concludes that the most dispirited presidents are in the public sector. Fisher (1984) has concluded that, unless governing boards restore the legitimacy of the presidential office itself, strong, highly principled presidents (exactly what we need) will be most vulnerable to the axe of the established order. Sociologist David Riesman of Harvard calls the typical college president today "faceless"—a personification of compromise. Recently a national conference on leadership heard Kenneth Clark, a senior scientist with the Center for Creative Leadership in North Carolina, say that administrators and faculty members "are not fulfilling their responsibilities in teaching leadership to students or in emphasizing the importance of leadership in our society" (Clark, 1986). And John Gardner, perhaps the nation's most respected leadership seer, has begun a new series of papers and studies on leadership to help with this pervasive problem in Western societies (Gardner, 1986). Yes, we have a problem with leadership.

How Did We Get This Way?

How did we get to the place where scholars and commissions conclude that stronger leadership, in this case at colleges and universities, is the imperative of the late twentieth century?

Dramatic changes in the role of governing boards and the decline of strong presidents began in the 1960s. It is probably not coincidental that in 1963 America experienced the tragic loss of the charismatic John F. Kennedy and campus unrest began at Berkeley. This purifying but self-righteous movement eventually swept the country—from community colleges in Baltimore to rural liberal arts campuses in Illinois.

That movement ended in the early 1970s, leaving higher education and other American institutions both better and worse. We had embraced equal opportunity and affirmative action, but compromised our programs in the name of a new "honesty." And except in the rarest of circumstances, the leaders of the reform movement were not our college presidents or our governing boards. The people—students, staff, and community—were the new leaders, and they left in their wake a system without legitimate positions. Power was now shared, and it became all but impossible for even the most assertive presidents to do anything in the face of the egalitarian tide. Strong leaders could not prosper or, in time, even be appointed to college presidencies. Boards of trustees bear the larger share of responsibility for this latter condition. Indeed, most governing boards, particularly in the public sector, have yet to set about restoring effective presidential authority.

Students, faculty, and staff became members of trustee committees and governing boards. State legislatures and local assemblies enacted sunshine laws mandating public disclosure of board deliberations. Newly created faculty organizations obtained direct access to governing boards. Formally and informally, many trustees became closely associated with students, faculty, and staff. Presidential evaluations and assessments, based on "user group" opinions and other "modern" techniques, achieved widespread popularity and publicity. Today most public institutions use them.

The cleansing wave of the 1960s left behind practices that continue today and, in large measure, represent the most serious obstacle to effective presidential leadership. The 1960s and 1970s were characterized by the involvement of everyone in everything. While that idea is not bad in itself, when it is practiced without structure and reflection it can be damaging and dangerous. It is fundamentally naive.

This new egalitarianism placed so many vested interests in the presidential selection process that the end result almost guaranteed a compromise candidate. As Fred Ness (formerly of the Presidential Search and Assessment Service) points out, unless he or she was exceedingly clever during the interview process or the institution was in grave distress, the finally anointed president was all but bound to be without style, strength, and decisiveness. The product of this selection process produced a plant manager rather than a strong leader (Ness, 1981). With few exceptions, a strong leader simply could not get through a screening. Some wisely stayed silent and many simply stopped trying. The unintentional end result was the most dramatic erosion of presidential authority in the history of American higher education. During the 1960s and 1970s, continuing into the 1980s, the authority and legitimate power of campus presidents eroded to the point of today's all-time low.

Governing boards in public institutions reduced presidential power, student and faculty authority in campus governance grew, pay increases became automatic, unaccountable selection committees were appointed for virtually every position, and students were granted autonomy in academic course selection, grading procedures, self-government, and social life. All of this was done in the name of meaningful involvement, without considering the constraints being wound around the ability of presidents to lead. *We upset the entire system by bestowing on faculty and students rights that formerly had been privileges granted or denied by college presidents.*

In effect, we loosened the glue that held higher-education institutions together. Presidents continued to be responsible for everything, as they should be, but their authority became eroded so that most were powerless to channel conflicting campus currents. Egalitarianism cost them the power of position. In higher education, as we threw out hypocrisy, we also tossed out tradition, courtesy, respect, and authority. The new "honesty" as not honesty at all, but a fuzzy, selfish existentialism that left us with almost no form or structure. Presidents had little left about which they could be benevolent, for their discretionary power had been given away by well-intentioned boards of trustees. They had no platform from which to express their vision.

What Can Be Done?

How can we improve this condition? There should be only one prime conduit to a governing board: the president. Every governing board in America should review its structure and policies in terms of appropriate presidential authority. An acknowledged outside authority or consultant could review the situation carefully and make appropriate recommendations to the board. Or the trustees could do it themselves through a self-study, but consultant or not, this task must be done.

But it is hopeless idealism to assume that governing boards, particularly in the public sector, will initiate the inspiration needed to restore the legitimate presidency. The same people always lead: strong, bold, principled visionary presidents who are not afraid to put their jobs on the line. College presidents, albeit legitimized somewhat by outside authorities who will serve as consultants, will lead the restoration. But when push comes to shove, it will be a single college president who says, "Enough—it's time to put this institution on track." Without the power of position, the visionary college president might as well spend his or her time dreaming at the old fishing hole. And according to recent reports, increasing numbers are thinking of doing just that (Kerr and Gade, 1986).

The Characteristics of College Presidents

What are the characteristics of the men and women who occupy college presidencies today? And are the characteristics of "effective" presidents different from those of "typical" presidents? Although the profile is somewhat fuzzy, the typical president holds an earned doctorate, is 53 years old, has taught for 11 years, and moved through the "pipeline" to the presidency or by taking a serendipitous route. Most have been full professors with a strong liberal arts teaching background. They are articulate, tall, male, and look presidential. They are negotiators, collegial, and big on consensus building. They are internally oriented and want to stay in office indefinitely (Astin and Sherrei, 1980; Kaufmann, 1980; Kerr & Gade 1986; Peck, 1983, Vaughan, 1986; Pruitt, 1974; Fisher and Tack, in press).

And yes, the limited evidence we have on the effective president paints a rather different image. The effective president often does not have a doctorate and is 47 years old. Twenty-five percent have never taught and those who did, taught an average of four years. Few have been full professors. More come from the behavioral sciences and education than from the liberal arts. Most plan their presidential pathway early (they were not serendipitous). They believe that governance is a means to an end rather than an end to a means. They tend to be strong, more distant, and less collegial than the typical president. They are especially big on the external presidency and are highly mission-oriented risk takers. They are doggedly persistent and most believe in a finite time in office (Astin and Sherrei, 1980; Kaufmann, 1980; Kerr and Gade, 1986; Peck, 1983; Vaughan, 1986; Pruitt, 1974; Fisher and Tack, in press; Cohen and March, 1974; Gilley, Fulmer, and Reithlingshofer, 1986).

Obviously then, there may be significant, even dramatic, differences between the characteristics of the typical and the effective college president. Granting that no characteristics-type study is completely acceptable and that there is considerable overlapping in both categories, it nonetheless does seem clear that American colleges and university presidents generally have modest leadership ability, or they are so constrained by governing boards that they can only perform at a modest level. The extent to which this applies to community colleges is not fully known. But recent studies of community-college presidents indicate that their profiles are not far from those presented above. Vaughan (1986) and Fisher and Tack (in press) found that the main difference between community-college presidents and others were that more of them had doctorate degrees in education. They were somewhat more involved in community activities, and more of them became presidents in the same communities where they attended high school.

The Development of Leadership Skills

How then do you develop stronger leadership skills? I contend that leadership characteristics are immutable and that they apply in most situations. Therefore, while community colleges may be closer to the action of our society, the effective community-college president will have characteristics similar to effective college presidents in any area of higher education or, for that matter, in American society.

Leadership itself has been the subject of serious research activities for most of the twentieth century. At the moment, there are two schools of academic thought on leadership: situational and trait. Literally countless articles have been written and studies have been conducted on these two subjects and scholars will probably always be unclear on the distinctions between the two (Stogdill, 1974; Bass, 1981). I suggest that both the situation and the individual are important in leadership, and that, after 50 years, the debate is pointless. The degree to which one supersedes the other depends on the setting or the time in the life of the organization where the leadership takes place. *It is also my assumption that anyone can lead who is reasonably intelligent, well educated, and highly motivated.*

Assuming these things, then, leadership boils down to consideration of the touchy but fundamental subject of power. For our purposes, leadership is the ability to acquire and use the various forms of power in an effort to inspire desired action in others. And most simply defined, power represents A's ability to get B to do something that B might otherwise not do. The person who best understands the nature and use of power, in this case the college president, is the person who motivates people to action.

Let us quickly dispense with the so-called pernicious nature of power seekers. We are all interested in power, in getting the "B"s in our lives to do something; it is simply a matter of degree. The extent to which we are successful is the extent to which we are happy, well adjusted, and productive. The extent to which we are not represents the frustration, cynicism, and unhappiness in our lives. After our need for food and shelter is satisfied, the need for influence is as important to us as sex, and, pathenthetically, is very closely related to sex.

During recent years, David McClelland and David Burnham (1976) have been conducting research clearly indicating that the most effective leaders (that is, most effective in getting results) are people motivated by power rather than affiliation (the need to be liked or the need for achievement—the need for recognition). If one is more inclined toward impact than toward the acceptance of others or personal recognition, one has better prospects of becoming an effective leader.

For our purposes, there are five forms of power under which all attempts to influence the behavior of others fall: coercive, reward, legitimate, expert, and referent and charismatic (French and Raven, 1959). *Coercive power* uses threats and punishment to gain compliance and is the least effective form of power. If you are a president, use it sparingly, if at all. *Reward power*—the ability to bestow favors, recognition and rewards—is more effective than coercive power but not as effective as you might think. *Legitimate power*—the power of position—is your presidential platform. Get on it, but wear it warmly and believe in it. It will serve you handsomely. *Expert power*—knowledge—further legitimizes position. Being president calls for being an expert in higher education rather than in an academic discipline. Indeed, in a local power sphere, a president should be perceived as the primary authority on community colleges. Outside authorities are to be brought in only briefly as consultants and then sent on their way.

Referent or Charismatic power is the single most effective form of presidential power. It is based on the admiration and affection that people feel for their leader. This is the true power of the leader and a subject a president should quietly spend his or her time studying (Fisher, 1984). The key to charisma is threefold: *distance, style, and perceived self-confidence.* And the greatest of these is distance. If you want to be one of the boys or girls, go back to the faculty. Collegial leadership is an absolute contradiction in terms. As the president, you are there to absorb the stress of others and celebrate their successes. It is not always pleasant, but it can be exciting and perhaps worthwhile.

Remember that in difficult, stressful situations, strong, active, and aggressive leadership is generally most acceptable. So choose your situations carefully (Fodor, 1976; Torrance, 1956/57; Selekman, 1947; Janis and Mann, 1977). For instance, you will become a leader more quickly in a troubled college than in a healthy one. It is always wise to follow a person who was not considered effective on the job. In the broader context, current conditions set the moment and can help create favorable circumstances from which it is easier for leaders to emerge.

Leadership ability is *not* an innate characteristic of the privileged few. Inherit only a potential for nurturing and developing it. As with charisma, anyone who is reasonably intelligent and highly motivated can cultivate a successful leadership style (Bennis and Nanus, 1985). So, anyone can learn to use the various forms of power. Paradoxically, there is evidence that those of exceptionally high intelligence have more difficulty become effective leaders than the less endowed. This may be true because they have difficulty identifying with those they would lead.

You: Leading or Managing?

The more you are able to act like a leader rather than a manager, the more effective you will be. You must be a leader. Most college presidents are collegial managers, so you will be a leg up. While good management is important, it is not leadership. We do not need autocratic "experts," cynical jungle fighters, or super-conforming, uncreative organization types (Kotter, 1985). During a self-appraisal at the midpoint of his presidency, Jimmy Carter criticized himself for managing the government rather than the country. By that time it was too late.

What is the difference? Wherever there are problems, leaders arise to show the way, inspire, and persuade. They are the risk takers. Leaders speculate and make judgments. They make decisions. Managers carry out those decisions efficiently. You can be completely efficient and still go out of business. The very personalities of the two types are antithetical. The more you study management, particularly in our most distinguished graduate schools of business, the greater your risk of not becoming a leader. You become so mired in the techniques of matrix management, strategic planning, collegiality, technical rationality, the rational model, or whatever the current rage, that you compromise your leadership effectiveness and the ability to act. Study these techniques, know them, and use them, but know that a leader does not stay at that level.

Managers implement and solve problems. They use a rational premise or an established policy for decisions. They are analytical, fair minded, and have a strong sense of belonging to the organization. Managers concentrate primarily on process. While leaders are often analytical and always fair minded, they *are* the organization rather than only *of* it. Leaders take chances, are visionary, and often act out of intuition with a high tolerance for ambiguity and paradox. Managers are deliberate and careful; they equivocate. Leaders are dynamic and confident. When a crisis comes, they make a firm choice. Often, though, their decisions seem based on intuition rather than analysis. Managers work within existing variables; leaders tend to extrapolate. Leaders are speculative and inclined to make decisions based on intelligence, high hopes, and dreams.

You should be a strong, bold leader from your first days on the job. You can be different from the mainstream president—but do not be weird. Be assertive and strong, but never excessively so. Outstanding leaders are often described as "monumentally self-confident," "impulsively dynamic," often "dramatic," and "unpredictable" in style. A consistent and reliable productivity seems to balance this changeability. Create an atmosphere of change and excitement about yourself. You must appear obsessed by your vision. Be unrelenting about your ideas or dreams. Excite, stimulate, and inspire others to work harder and more creatively. You should be driven by slogans like: "more, better for less," and quickly show a profit, whatever your bottom line.

Expect to make mistakes—leaders do, you know. Why? Because they are leaders and see themselves as risk takers rather than managers. When you are acting out of both expertise and intuition, you are bound to make mistakes. Mistakes, however, can be invaluable if you analyze them and learn from them. To dwell on them is self-indulgent and destructive. You will be the better for these experiences and subordinates will see your humanness and often feel more warmth towards you. But continue on in your bold style.

The Leader Sets Limits, Establishes Formats and Rules, Is Directive, Dilutes Business with Humor, Has a High Energy Level But Does Not Stay Too Long, and Is Rarely a Genius

Let us look more closely at the research. Contrary to popular belief, directive leadership is more effective than nondirective (Burke,

1966; Thiagarajan and Deep, 1970; McClelland, 1969, 1975; McClelland and Burnham, 1976; Steers, 1981). The collegial concept does not work well, especially in institutions that need improvement or change, but if you feel it works for you, use it. People seek an astute, strong, assertive leader who involves them in the decision-making process. This person respects their ideas but makes the final decision and accepts responsibility for it.

Leaders who are highly visible and who do not get overly involved in the details of their organization, but who retain final authority, are more likely to be effective. They are also more likely to realize desired organizational structure and goals (Scott, 1956; McClelland, 1975). Other studies suggest that group members do not develop or accept group norms and expectations unless these are well defined by leaders. Studies also suggest that too much informal or familiar behavior on the part of leaders tends to reduce their perceived legitimacy (Clark, 1956; McClelland, 1975; Pfeffer, 1981). The overly folksy president may soon become one of the folks again. The ideal combination is familiarity but always from the presidential platform. Whatever your position, do not be overly familiar or invite excessive familiarity.

People expect their leaders to try to influence them (Torrance, 1959a, 1959b; Benezet, Katz, and Magnussen, 1981). A leader who simply tries to reflect the wishes of a constituency or who declares neutrality on many key issues is evading responsibility. This person is often destined for a short term. Over the long term, people are rarely satisfied with echoes. This is especially true during crises. Disruptive behavior, antagonism, tension, and absenteeism increase under poorly defined and nondirective presidents (Burke, 1966). People, including the educated, want and need structure. An informed leader knows that if a majority opposition coalition develops, it may undermine effectiveness. And the coalition itself may informally assume the leadership position (Caplow, 1968). What is more, people want and need credit for their accomplishments. The more effective leader invariably attributes competence to followers (Price and Garland, 1981).

Studies conducted before 1940 correlate only four of 79 traits with leadership in general: a sense of humor, above-average intelligence, extroversion, and boldness or willingness to take the initiative (Bird, 1940). Twenty years later, other characteristics joined the list: courage, fortitude (persistence), and sensitivity (Mann, 1959). A decade later, researchers found that years of experience in one leadership role apparently did not relate to the effectiveness of leadership as measured by productivity (Fiedler, 1970). There appears to be a point of diminishing returns for most leaders—a point in time after which they lose effectiveness.

In the 1970s, researchers found that physical characteristics were not as important as earlier studies had reported. The democratization movement of the period obviously affected the popular image of leaders. While being a tall, attractive, white, Protestant male is not a disadvantage in achieving a presidency, the characteristics, while they still help, no longer seem to give a distinct edge. More recent studies suggest that leaders have or appear to have inordinate reserves of energy and stamina and maintain unusually good physical condition. Even leaders handicapped by physical disability or poor health usually display great vigor (Stogdill, 1974; Bass, 1981). The effective leader always appears to have energy left over, and never complains of being tired, having a cold, or working too hard. The effective leader perseveres, is verbal and remarkably confident, and appears to cope well with stress (Mant, 1983). The leader's personal characteristics and values must seem to fit the needs and aspirations of his or her following (Katz, 1973). The effective leader pays attention to clues and senses through body expressions, questions or the lack of them, and restlessness (Bass, 1960).

Researchers once believed that socioeconomic background played a significant role in creating leaders (Mathews, 1954). While coming from a good family does not hurt, recent studies report proportionately more top executives from poorer and middle-income backgrounds than from the wealthier classes (Bass, 1981). This has certainly been true for college presidents. Religious and ethnic backgrounds apparently remain a significant influence on upward mobility within formal organizations. But the educational level or type of school attended seems to offset drawbacks caused by socioeconomic, gender, or racial factors.

Women executives who were once in middle management find it more difficult than men to rise further. Once they understand the use of power, they move more quickly. A number of studies suggest that problems of effective leadership are more a function of power than of sex. Furthermore, in leadership, individual differences are more striking than sex differences (White, DeSanctis, and Crino, 1981). Women executives often try to appear incompetent in order to gain favor with male executives. And some will foolishly grant sexual favors (Bass, 1981). As executives, women who fail often are too self-effacing and demanding of other female coworkers and subordinates. So if you are a woman, it may be wise for you to appear more confident and be more assertive than you are initially inclined to be and be more generous with your same-sex colleagues.

What about the relationship of intelligence to leadership? Early studies find that leaders who are much brighter than their followers are less successful (Stogdill, 1948). Later studies find that leaders whose intelligence is consistent with followers are more successful than leaders whose intelligence scores were either low or very high (Ghiselli, 1963). More recent studies find that leaders are only *somewhat* brighter than their followers (Fiedler, 1981). Intelligence, as measured by verbal-ability tests, appears to relate to first-level supervisory performance. But the higher you go in the management hierarchy, the less significant is this correlation. Intelligence does not appear to be a real predictor of success at top levels (Korman, 1968). Indeed, a survey of managers to identify those who were effective politically ranked high in intelligence and logic the last two of 13 related characteristics (Allen et al., 1979). There is evidence, however, that leaders usually have superior judgment, decisiveness, knowledge, and fluency of speech (Stogdill, 1974).

In sum, although the elements of chance and timing undoubtedly play a part in the rise of individuals, effective leaders today generally have these qualities: a strong drive for responsibility, vigor (or its appearance), persistence, willingness to take chances, originality, ability to delegate, humor, initiative in social situations, fairness, sensitivity, self-confidence, decisiveness, sense of identity, personal style, capacity to organize, willingness to act boldly, high energy (or its appearance), willingness to share the credit for successes and absorb most of the stress of failure, and tolerance of frustration and delay (a quality undoubtedly induced and fostered by the advent of bureaucracies).

And so the time is ripe. The need and opportunities for presidential leadership have never been greater. Even with the apparent uncertainty of governing boards and the higher-education status quo, the future belongs to the visionary community-college president who behaves as if he or she knows. The job of the leader is to lead.

References

ALLEN, R. W., MADISON, D. L., PORTER, L. W., RENWICK, P. S., and MAYER, B. T. "Organizational Politics: Tactics and Characteristics of its Actors." *California Management Review* 22(1979): 77–83.

ASTIN, A. W., and SHERREI, R. A., *Maximizing Leadership Effectiveness*. San Francisco: Jossey-Bass, 1980.

BASS, B. M. *Leadership, Psychology, and Organizational Behavior*. New York: Harper, 1960.

―――. *Stogdill's Handbook of Leadership: A Survey of Theory and Research*. New York: Free Press, 1981.

BENEZET, L. T., KATZ, J., and MAGNUSSEN, F. W. *Style and Substance: Leadership and the College Presidency*. Washington, D.C.: American Council on Education, 1981.

BENNIS, W., and NANUS, B. *Leaders*. New York: Harper & Row, 1985.

BIRD, C. *Social Psychology*. New York: Appleton-Century, 1940.

BURKE, P. J. "Authority Relations and Disruptive Behavior in the Small Group." *Dissertation Abstracts* 26(1966): 48–50.

―――. "Authority Relations and Disruptive Behavior in Small Discussion Groups." *Sociometry* 29(1966): 237–250.

CAPLOW, T. *Two Against One: Coalitions in Triads*. Englewood Cliffs, NJ: Prentice-Hall, 1968.

CLARK, B. R. "Organizational Adaption and Precarious Values: A Case Study." *American Sociological Review* 21(1956): 327–336.

CLARK, K. *The Chronicle of Higher Education*. Washington, D.C.: May 28, 1986, p. 19.

COHEN, M. D., and MARCH, J. G. *Leadership and Ambiguity*. New York: McGraw-Hill, 1974.

FIEDLER, F. E. "Leadership Experience and Leadership Performance: Another Hypothesis Shot to Hell." *Organizational Behavior and Human Performance* 5(1970): 1–14.

————. "Leadership Effectiveness." *American Behavioral Scientist* 24, no. 5(May/June 1981): 619–632.

FISHER, J. L. *Power of the Presidency.* New York: Macmillan/American Council on Education, 1984.

FISHER, J. L., and TACK, M. W. "Characteristics of the Effective College President." In Press.

FODOR, E. M. "Group Stress, Authoritarian Style of Control, and Use of Power." *Journal of Applied Psychology* 61(1976): 313–318.

FRENCH, J. R. P., and RAVEN, B. "The Bases of Social Power." In *Studies in Social Power,* edited by D. Cartwright, Ann Arbor: University of Michigan, Institute for Social Research, 1959.

GARDNER, J. W. *The Nature of Leadership.* Washington, D.C.: Independent Sector, 1986.

GHISELLI, E. E. "Intelligence and Managerial Success." *Psychological Reports* 12(1963): 898.

GILLEY, W., FULMER, K. A., and REITHLINGSHOEFER, S. *Searching for Academic Excellence.* New York: Macmillan, 1986.

JANIS, I. L., and MANN, L. *Decision Making.* New York: The Free Press, 1977.

KATZ, D. "Patterns of Leadership." In *Handbook of Political Psychology,* edited by J. N. Knutson, San Francisco: Jossey-Bass, 1973.

KAUFMANN, J. F. *At the Pleasure of the Board.* Washington, D.C.: American Council on Education, 1980.

KERR, C. *Presidents Make a Difference.* Washington, D.C.: Association of Governing Boards, 1984.

KERR, C., and GADE, M. L. *The Many Lives of Academic Presidents.* Washington, D.C.: Association of Governing Boards, 1986.

KORMAN, A. K. "The Prediction of Managerial Performance: A Review." *Personnel Psychology* 21(1968): 295–322.

KOTTER, J. P. *Power and Influence.* New York: The Free Press, 1985.

MANN, R. D. "A Review of the Relationships Between Personality and Performance in Small Groups." *Psychological Bulletin* 56(1959): 241–270.

MANT, A. *Leaders We Deserve.* Oxford, England: Martin Robertson & Co., Ltd., 1983.

MATHEWS, D. R. *The Social Background of Political Decision-Makers.* New York: Random House, 1954.

McCLELLAND, D. C. "The Two Faces of Power." *Journal of Internatinal Affairs* 24(1969): 141–154.

————. *Power: The Inner Experience.* New York: Irvington, 1975.

McCLELLAND, D.C., and Burnham, D. H. "Power Is the Great Motivator." *Harvard Business Review* 54(1976): 100–110.

NESS, F. Personal conversation, 1981.

PECK, R. *Future Focusing.* Washington, D.C.: Council of Independent Colleges, 1983.

PFEFFER, J. *Power in Organizations.* Marshfield: Putnam, 1981.

PRICE, K. H., and GARLAND, H. "Compliance with a Leader's Suggestions as a Function of Perceived Leader/Member Competence and Potential Reciprocity." *American Psychologist* (1981): 329–336.

PRUITT, G. A. "A Blueprint for Leadership: The American College Presidency." (Ph.D. dissertation, Union Graduate School, 1974.

SCOTT, E. L. *Leadership and Perceptions of Organization.* Columbus: Ohio State University Bureau of Business Research, 1956.

SELEKMAN, B. M. *Labor Relations and Human Relations.* New York: McGraw-Hill, 1947.

STEERS, R. M. *Introduction to Organizational Behavior.* Santa Monica: Goodyear, 1981.

STOGDILL, R. M. "Personal Factors Associated with Leadership: A Survey of the Literature." *Journal of Psychology* 24(1948): 35–71.

———. *Handbook of Leadership.* New York: Macmillan, 1974.

THIAGARAJAN, K. M., and Deep, S. D. "A Study of Supervisor-Subordinate Influence and Satisfaction in Four Cultures." *Journal of Social Psychology* 82(1970): 173–180.

TORRANCE, E. P. "Group Decision-Making and Disagreement." *Social Forces* 35(1956/57): 314–318.

———. "An Experimental Evaluation of 'No-Pressure' Influence." *Journal of Applied Psychology* 43(1959a): 109–113.

———. "The Influence of Experienced Members of Small Groups on the Behavior of the Inexperienced." *Journal of Social Psychology* 49(1959b): 249–257.

VAUGHAN, G. *The Community College Presidency.* New York: Macmillan/American Council on Education, 1986.

WHITE, M. C., DeSanctis, B., and Crino, M. I. "Achievement, Self-Confidence, Personality Traits, and Leadership Ability: A Review of the Literature on Sex Differences." *Psychological Reports* 48(1981): 547–569.

PART

THREE

A Future Orientation

"... *people who do not educate themselves—and keep re-educating themselves—to participate in the new knowledge environment will be the peasants of the information society.*
Harlan Cleveland

"There is no sin except stupidity."
Oscar Wilde

"We realize that mediocrity is generally easier to live with than excellence—if only because it is less demanding— and is accordingly more prevalent."

Diane Ravitch
Chester E. Finn
Robert T. Francher

"Some people spend their lives failing and never notice."

Judith Rossner

8

The World of Work Revisited

DAVID MACAROV

The transition period from an economy based, at least theoretically, on human labor to one in which technology makes most human labor unnecessary will probably be a very painful period.

Technology is rapidly reducing the amount of human labor needed to produce the goods and services required by society. It is changing the content of that labor which remains. These changes in the world of work will affect so many other areas of societal functioning that, in addition to the work-preparatory goal of the educational system, preparation for every other aspect of life must also take cognizance of these shifts. This may make entirely new concepts of education necessary (Fischer, 1985).

There are those who demand more emphasis on preparation for work by arguing that education is important only insofar as it leads to better jobs (Ginzberg, 1976), and that current education is stressing attributes not applicable to the workplace (Greve and Gladstone, 1983). More specifically, it is maintained that education is not developing the type of mental discipline needed in industry and commerce (Anthony, 1978). Where education is seen as related to jobs, it is argued that the emphasis is too closely geared to immediate, rather than future, employment needs (O'Toole, 1977).

On the other hand, there are those who complain that too much emphasis is laid on job preparation during educational efforts (Anthony, 1978; Berg, 1971; Caplow, 1954; Herzberg, 1966), and that the goal of education has come to be the production of labor power (Bowles and Gintis, 1976). As summarized by a U.S. presidential commission: "The market value of education has driven out its other values" (*Work in America*, 1973). There are also those who see education as irrelevant to getting and holding a job (Hall, 1984). More education is viewed as only guaranteeing better educated but unemployed people (Arnold and Rosenbaum, 1973). Others view education simply as a form of social control or as a political solution to other problems (Moos, 1983).

Despite these debates, preparation for life in a world in which work is the central focus requires relating to that fact. Holding a job is one of the few socially acceptable ways of acquiring an income and is the method used by the great majority of people in the Western industrialized world. Nor should work be viewed purely as an instrumental activity. Through the influence of Luther, Adam Smith, the philosophy of mercantilism, and Freud, work has become overlaid with values to the point that working—and especially working hard—is equated with being God-fearing, a good neighbor, patriotic, and mentally healthy (Macarov, 1982). Work has not only invaded the educational system; it influences social-welfare programs, religion, the family, leisure-time activities, politics, national defense, and therapeutic efforts (Macarov, 1980). As Anthony (1978) points out, "There is no theoretical challenge to the system of values which maintains and is supported by an ideology of work (because) . . . alternative systems of values have been virtually destroyed."

This chapter, therefore, will discuss some anticipated changes in the nature of work, possible changes in the composition of the workforce, and probable changes in the amount of human labor to be needed. But first, a word about predictions generally.

Changes in Work

On Predicting the Future

No one can say with certainty what the future will hold. Probabilities can be assessed, however, using tools such as trend analysis and extension, analogies, technology assessment, simulations, and consensus-deriving techniques such as the Delphi method (Cornish, 1977). The probabilities thus derived can then be weighed against the consequences anticipated. In this manner, an event that is almost certain to occur, but whose influence will be trivial, can almost be ignored. An event whose probability is relatively low and whose eventuality would be catastrophic, requires at least the provision of contingency plans.

Further, lest future prediction be dismissed as impossible or useless, it is worth pointing out that everyone is continuously engaged in predicting the future—what they will do next year, next week, tomorrow, or in five minutes time. Such plans require predictions about what the situation will be at that time. Thus, the real questions concern only the *event* we are predicting, the *methods* of prediction used, and the *time frame* being considered.

The predictive method used to explore the world of work is trend analysis. With regard to time frames, it is conventional today to use the year 2000 as a target date. However, that is only 14 years away; few major changes take place during periods this short. Given that we are focusing on education, it is reasonable to use the working life of students being graduated about now. Using age 20 to 25 as the age of entry into the labor force and age 60 to 65 as retirement age, it is clear that today's graduates will work—however that is defined—for about 40 years, or until 2025. Since the lag between identifying a social need and including the material in the formal educational structures may be as long as 50 years (Marland,

1974), it is not too soon to begin planning educational curricula—
or to begin at least thinking about them—for 40 years hence.

Do We Understand the Changing Content of Work?

One of the most prominent changes taking place in the world of
work today is the shift from an industrial to a service economy
(Gartner and Reissman, 1974; Gersuny and Rosengren, 1973). In
1929, only 40 percent of the jobs in the United States were in the
service sector (Gersuny and Rosengren, 1973); in 1950, 51 percent
of the jobs were in services (Gartner and Reissman, 1974); in 1967,
this was 55 percent; and by 1980 it was estimated at over 80 percent (Thurow, 1981). Of all new jobs created between 1973 and
1980, over 70 percent were in the services (Bolan, 1981), and almost 50 percent of total job growth in the 1970s came from the
white-collar and service sectors (Leon, 1982). In addition, two-
thirds of the self-employed in the United States produce services
(Newland, 1982). There are predictions that, by the end of this
century, service employment will constitute from 95 to 97 percent
of all employment (Best, 1981a; Stellman, 1982).

Neither research, the literature, nor job training has yet recognized the significance of this shift to the service economy. There is,
for example, not even a generally accepted definition of service
occupations. In Britain, one-half of the people who are said to be
engaged in services perform functions that are in direct support of
production activities (Gershuny, 1978); about one-third of the people who work in goods-producing activities have service jobs
(Newland, 1982). Despite many attempts to categorize jobs (Morris
and Murphy, 1959; Robinson 1969; Roe, 1956; Super, 1975), a Bureau of Labor Report says, "There are severe conceptual as well as
data problems" in grappling with this question (Mark, 1982; Ruch,
1983; Shelp, 1981).

In addition to the definitional problem, there is a neglect of the
service sector when it comes to research on working patterns, attitudes, satisfactions, incentives, and productivity. Locke located
over 3,000 published studies on work patterns in 1976 and estimated that at least an equal number of unpublished studies existed. Since then, there has been a proliferation of such studies.
However, almost all of them were done in industrial settings.

Consequently, almost all of the instruments used to examine various aspects of the world of work are drawn from and designed for use in industry. For example, the 400 sets of tests published in two compendia for the use of researchers (Cook et al., 1981; Stewart, Hetherington, and Smith, 1984) were prepared almost exclusively for use among industrial workers and did not take into account the service workers in industrial settings. At least one study done in the services indicates the distortions that this might cause: given the opportunity to respond to open-ended questions, social workers gave different sources of satisfaction than those found on the instruments used to test industrial workers (Meller and Macarov, 1985).

Part of the dearth of suitable research instruments arises from lack of research in the services as such. Only a handful of the empirical-research articles found in a survey of social-work journals deals with work patterns or motivations (Tripodi, 1984). Similarly, "Very little research on work attitudes in British professional nurses has been published" (Redfern and Spurgeon, 1980). Studies of public-service jobs, including teachers, has been found to be "overwhelmingly impressionistic—almost anecdotal—in nature" (Beaumont and Partridge, n.d.). Although there is some literature on faculty and staff development in education, there is little empirical research concerning patterns, attitudes, sources of satisfaction, strengths of various motivators, or testing of theories such as the valence-instrumentality-expectancy theorem. Consequently, as compared to industry, little is known about work in the service sector and more questions can be raised than answered. Still, the growing shift to service jobs requires that what is known be taken into account, and that education for the future attempt to grapple with both the known and the unknown.

Jobs, Personality Characteristics, and Attitudes

Service Work

One question that has been raised is the extent to which work in the services requires specific personality characteristics, and whether these differ from those useful in other sectors. Some commentators on this subject are clear, holding that "Any job in which a person tries to help other people by working intensively and intimately with them over an extended period of time involves special talents and abilities in relating to people" (Pines and Kafry, 1978). Similarly, some service jobs are held to require specific human qualities such as "emotions, feelings, responsibility, caring" (Albeda, 1983). Still others hold that people taking human-service jobs must need to be loved (Levinson et al., 1979). Then there are those who hold that, generally, women are more suited to the human-service occupations than are men. Flick (1983), for example, feels that women are naturally more "caring" than men. McGill (1985), too, holds that men are so conditioned that they cannot exhibit the intimacy that some situations require. Others hold that individuals who express the importance of self-development are more suited (or, at least, more willing) to work in the service sector (Zetterberg and Frankel, 1983). Shamir (1980) has called attention to the need for service workers to live with the constant role strain of being between "service and servility." Others discuss the ability to resist "burn out" as a result of constantly being in a "giving" situation. It is for such reasons that Pearson (1982) questions whether presently unemployed unskilled male workers are suitable recruits for the service sector.

It is as a consequence of this belief in the necessity for certain personality characteristics as an a priori requirement for work in the human services that some educational programs attempt to identify these qualities in applicants. They use individual and group interviews, references, autobiographies, and tests for specific traits. These last may include altruism, empathy, and inner locus of control, among other things.

Other schools accept all applicants or all who pass entrance examinations. They base their procedure on the fact that there is no empirical proof that the search for personality characteristics really identifies them or that applicants with the characteristics become better students or better practitioners. These schools recognize the roots of altruism as complex (Macaulay and Berkowitz, 1970) and the existence of empathy—in the sense of sharing another's feelings—as extremely doubtful, or at least as doubtful of proof (Macarov, 1970, 1978). This is not to say that these schools reject the need for certain attitudes. However, they do not see these attributes as, in Neff's terms, relatively stable elements of the personality developed through a lifetime of socialization (Macarov, 1982). These attributes are perceived as attitudes that can be taught, inculcated, or changed via the educational process itself (Benbenishty, personal communication)—an assumption that has been challenged (Bar-Gal, 1981).

Whether the attributes required for successful employment or practice in the service society are innate or acquired, there seems to be rather general agreement that they are different from those needed in industry or agriculture. Exactly what they are, however, has not been agreed or tested. One source holds that service employment requires more initiative than does industry and that conformity and discipline are dysfunctional for the service situation (Moos, 1983). Toffler (1980) says industrial employers want workers who are obedient, punctual, and willing to perform rote tasks—presumably the antithesis of the qualities needed for intellectual or human-service jobs. Caplow (1954) disparages the competitiveness that marks much of the educational system; he hints that cooperativeness is more desirable. In short, the services are said to require workers who are self-directed, imaginative, and self-critical. The human services demand caring, sharing, relating, "giving" people who are able to subordinate their own needs and feelings to those of their clients.

Sources and Influence of Job Satisfaction

Since the seminal Hawthorne studies it has been assumed in industry that satisfied workers are harder and more productive workers. Recently, however, there has been growing consensus that there is little relationship between satisfaction and work patterns (Brayfield and Crockett, 1955; Glickman and Brown, 1974; Lawler and Porter, 1971; Macarov, 1982; Parnes, 1978; Smith, Kendall, and Hulin, 1969; Strauss, 1980; Tausky, 1984). One may be dissatisfied and nevertheless work hard or be very satisfied and still not work hard. However, whether this lack of relationship also exists in the services is almost completely unresearched and therefore unknown. Can a teacher, nurse, or social worker who is dissatisfied with having to work, with the job, with work conditions, or with the work itself—or any combination of these—create the same kind of warm, supportive relationship with clients or pupils, as one who is happy and satisfied at work? Or do education and training succeed in overcoming personal feelings when dealing with another? The answers to such questions still lie in future research.

And what of workers' satisfactions for their own sake—that is, for the workers' personal happiness? As noted previously, there is evidence that the sources of satisfaction among human-service workers—or, in this case, social workers—are different from those of industrial workers. These include relationships with clients and their families, contact with multidisciplinary staffs, and the availability of resources to do a good job (Meller and Macarov, 1985). For workers to find satisfaction from these areas may require education and training that is in contrast with that intended for people dealing primarily with material objects. In short, the service society may require "new communication" (Fischer, 1985).

The Impact of Technology

From Service to Self-Service

The shift to a service economy outlined above has been made possible by technological advances that reduce the need for human labor in industry. The same kind of advances in technology that brought about the shift from industry to services is already presaging the next shift—from the service economy to self-service (Gershuny, 1978; Glazer, 1983). This is because the services are proving just as vulnerable to the inroads of automation as is industry (Monk and Wheelock, 1984). Technology will not only have a significant effect on the way services are performed—it will also change the liberal and artistic sectors (Rada, 1980).

The move to a postservice society will be spurred by the high cost of human labor as compared to technology (Jones, 1980). A robot costing $5 per hour to buy and operate can do work for which a human receives $15 (Casner-Lotto, 1981). By the turn of the century, the cost of robot labor may be down to only a few cents per hour. Even now, an office transaction that cost $1.25 in 1956 can be done for a small fraction of a cent by a computer (*World of Work Report,* December 1985).

Work and Polarization

In both industry and the services, technology will impact on the content of work. On the one hand, technology usually enters to do the dirty, disagreeable, and dangerous jobs (Glenn and Feldberg, 1979; Kraft, 1979; Zimbalist, 1979), thus making life better for workers. Having done so, however, it removes the interesting aspects of the remaining work, thereby contributing to worker alienation (Richardson, 1982). For example, a study of mechanization in a bank setting found that fully one-half of the workers wanted more enriching work after the change (Gable and Meers, 1982). There are suggestions that technology polarizes work between a few interesting, high-paid jobs, and many dull, low-paid tasks.

The Bureau of Labor Statistics reports that the majority of new jobs are low skilled and low paid. Technology seems to lead to deskilling in many cases (Immerwahr, 1982; Sparks, 1984). The challenge for education may be to prepare people for rote, repetitive jobs, while emphasizing ways in which such work can be made endurable, if not palatable. For example, technology will not only free workers for more leisure outside the job, it will increase the amount of free time at work. At present, many workers doing monotonous work have difficulty giving the work meaning or passing the time (Garson, 1975; Kanter and Stein, 1979; Terkel, 1980). Further, "It is only because *workers choose not to find fulfillment in their work* that they are able to function as healthy human beings. . . . By rejecting involvement in work which cannot be fulfilling, workers save their sanity" (Fein, 1976). The challenge to education is to provide such workers with the inner resources that will allow them to escape this kind of work mentally and emotionally unscathed and to exploit the growing amounts of free time on the job for satisfying, if not constructive, purposes.

On the other hand, preparation for the few interesting, high-paid jobs will require the use of the very latest technical equipment constantly changed to keep it up to date. Continual monitoring of the present and future job market and the content of the jobs will also be required. This is where many current training and retraining programs fail. They train for yesterday's jobs, jobs that do not exist, or jobs that will no longer exist by the time the training is over. Consequently, the drop-out rate in such courses is high and those who do graduate often find jobs in other areas (Goldstein, 1972). In one reported case, only 44 percent of the graduates got jobs in the area for which they were trained (*Rehabilitation* . . . , 1974). Many courses would consider this an excellent result. When these trainees do get jobs in the field for which they were trained, the job or the pay is usually not as good as in the previous position. It is not surprising that one of the main findings of a broad European study is that such training has only a small impact on the unemployed (Mitton and Willmott, 1983).

The failure of training courses is not the fault of the staffs. Some courses are not intended to succeed. Many countries use enrollment in training courses as a method of reducing the unemployment figures (Mitton et al., 1983). Once enrolled, participants are students on educational stipends and not the unemployed receiving compensation. Sweden, for example, has more people in training courses than unemployed (*World of Work Report*, April 1983). Thus the official unemployment rate of 3 percent in Sweden is estimated to represent a real rate of 17 percent (Yankelovich et al., 1983). Consequently, keeping people in training courses becomes more important than the content of courses or the success rate. It is for such reasons that Horne (1983) refers to "dole colleges."

Summary

Little research attention has been given to the implications of the shift to a service economy, although there is a general feeling that the services either require certain personality characteristics or certain attitudes. Whether the latter are inherent or can be inculcated is not yet known. However, it is clear that workers in the services obtain satisfaction and are afflicted with dissatisfaction from sources mostly different from those in industry. The extent to which this impacts on practice is also not known. The technology that brought about the shift will affect service jobs as well making some jobs easier, but probably polarizing the work force into the relative few who have interesting high-paid jobs and the majority who have dull, low-paid jobs. *The challenge to education in the future will be to inculcate some attitudes and neutralize others; to increase the capacity for satisfaction from some sources, and to innoculate against dissatisfaction from others; to prepare for some important and interesting jobs; and to prepare people to find meaning in their increased free time at work while coping with the essentially meaningless job activity itself.*

The Absence of Work

A Different Workforce

Two interrelated changes will take place in the composition of the workforce of the immediate future: the entrance of women in even greater numbers into the labor force, and the growth of part-time work. In virtually every industrial country the proportion of women in paid employment has risen dramatically, especially during the last quarter century. In the United States in 1960, 38 percent of women of working age held jobs; in 1985, 56 percent; and it is estimated that by 1995, over 60 percent of women will be working (*Working Woman*, 1983). The same increase is true of married as well as unmarried women. In 1890, only 4.5 percent of wives were in the labor force; by 1950 that figure had risen to 23.8 percent; in 1970 it was 40.8 percent; and in 1982 it had reached 51.2 percent (Davis, 1984). The number of working mothers has followed the same trend—in 1965, 20 percent of mothers with children under six worked, and in 1985 that number had reached 50 percent (*Working Woman*, 1983).

The growing number of women, including wives and mothers, entering the workforce will bring with it new situations and exacerbate existing ones. Dual-career families, containing both "dual-worker" and "dual-career" couples (Ladewig and White, 1980), will experience familial strain, guilt feelings, rearrangement of domestic schedules, role strain and other problems. Many of these should become the focus of prior educational efforts. Further, more work opportunities for women will include those that have traditionally been men's jobs. The distinction between male and female jobs will thus continue to weaken. In the service society, education for work may entail preparing more men for what have been female-dominated professions—nursing, teaching, and social work, among others (Best, 1981a). More people will be called upon to fulfill triple roles—spouse, parent, and worker—each of which requires preparation, and all of which create stress. It is also possible that the spread of flextime (i.e., the opportunity to work at or near home) might ease these strains somewhat.

The growth of part-time work is also related to the entry of women into the labor force. Many women prefer part-time work and can sustain it; many are supplementing the family income. On the other hand, part-time work pays less (Olmsted, 1985), includes fewer social benefits, and is harder to organize into labor unions. Consequently, it is attractive to those employers who prefer to use part-time help whenever possible. Indeed, part-time work may begin to oust full-time work. At present, so-called contingent workers make up 28 percent of the total work force (*World of Work Report*, October 1985). This includes free lancers, temporaries, part-timers, and others. This "buffer work force" is growing.

The growth of the service sector may reinforce the tendency to part-time work, since many services lend themselves to this system more easily than does industry. However, part-time work offers fewer career opportunities, less responsibility, and is generally less interesting. All of this has implications for education.

Decreasing Employment

The same technology that is changing the content of the job and the makeup of the work force is also operating to reduce the total number of work opportunities—and probably to reduce them drastically. Since the beginnings of technology the need for human labor has been decreasing. This becomes obvious as one looks at the constant shrinkage of work times and the concurrent growth of both overt and covert unemployment in the face of continually growing per-person productivity. In 1900, the average workweek in the United States was 53 hours; in 1979 it was 35.5 hours (*World of Work Report*, July/August 1980). Over the past half-century, labor hours per unit of output have been reduced about 3 percent per year, and average hours worked per year have been reduced by close to .5 percent per annum (Kendrick, 1979).

Simultaneously, the amount of unemployment has risen. At one time, 2% unemployment was seen as the irreducible minimum. In 1973, however, the Council of Economic Advisors spoke of 3.5 percent unemployment as the "natural" (read: unavoidable) rate (Reich, 1983). In 1979, the Humphrey–Hawkins Act called full employment at 4 percent unemployment rate (*World of Work Report*, April 1979). Now, the same Council of Economic Advisors speaks of a natural rate of 5–7 percent (Reich, 1983). These increases represent a "ratchet effect" by which irreducible unemployment is higher after recovery from each recession.

These official unemployment figures contain definitional and statistical artifacts that conceal real unemployment rates from 50 to 800 percent higher than those admitted (Field, 1977; Kogut and Aron, 1980; Levitan and Johnson, 1983). In addition, there is covert unemployment in the guise of featherbedding, which means the maintenance of unnecessary jobs such as the 630 people given *lifetime* contracts by the *New York Times* to do jobs requiring only 350 people (Zimbalist, 1979), and goldbricking (time wasted on the job) such as 49 percent of the time spent by building workers in one study (Cherrington, 1980). Both of these phenomena are increasing (Kendrick, 1979), as are various kinds of job-sharing schemes intended to spread the shrinking number of jobs over a larger number of people (Best, 1981b). Further, although there is a plethora of job-reaction schemes, few of them make much of a dent in the unemployment figures (Taggart, 1977).

Despite these Canute-like efforts to conceal the growth of real unemployment, the need for human labor continues to decrease while, conversely, productivity increases. Taken over a long range, the amount of per-person productivity throughout the West rises about 2.7 percent per year (*Yearbook of Labour Statistics*, 1956, 1966, 1976). This aggregates to about 35 percent every 10 years. In other words, 35 percent more goods and services are produced every 10 years despite the use of less human labor. The basic reason for this paradox is, of course, the use of technology (Wilson, 1980). Machines are much more efficient than human beings. Most people do not exert their full potential at work (Yankelovich, 1978; Macarov, 1982), and on the average, use only about 44% of their ability (Walbank, 1980). Thus, changes in human work patterns are responsible for only 10–25 percent of changes in productivity (Rosow, 1981), and 75 to 90 percent of productivity increases are due to changes in methods, machines, and materials—not manpower.

In addition, the rate of technology is increasing almost logarithmically. Technology is synergistic, each change making possible and calling forth further changes. Since there is little possibility that techr `ogy will suddenly cease or even that its rate of development will decrease, the amount of human labor needed will continue to be reduced. Nobel-Prize economist Wassily Leontief (Leontief and Duchin, 1984) predicts that in 20 years, the amount of human labor needed to produce all the goods and services required will be 10 percent less than today. Projecting that figure onto the 40-year time span being discussed here, that would mean an official unemployment figure for the United States of 26 + percent—and a real figure of 40 to 80 percent. Other observers are less conservative—Jenkins and Sherman (1981) foresee 23 percent unemployment by the year 2005. *Consequently, by the end of the working lives of today's students, it is possible that the number of nonworking people will be greater than that of workers. It is also possible—and even probable—that almost all goods and services will be produced through technological means, leaving only a small minority of humans at work.*

The Almost-Workless World

The transition period from an economy based, at least theoretically, on human labor to one in which technology makes most human labor unnecessary will probably be a very painful period. The search for employment on the part of individuals may become increasingly desperate—including national service schemes, the government as employer of last resort, widespread use of training programs, and reduction of existing jobs to minute periods of time. Eventually, however, the almost-workless world will arrive, and with it will come the need for a new set of values and a new structure for distributing the resources of the automated economy.

Our value system will need to be revised so that work will no longer be the means of identifying and evaluating people, of structuring time, and of achieving self-fulfillment. Other attributes—perhaps cooperativeness, altruism, neighborliness, creativity, honesty; and other activities, such as parenting, volunteering, performing, engaging in sports, hobbies, the arts, will be the mark of the full, healthy, valuable person. In short, work will have to be dethroned from its central place in the current pantheon of values.

This may not be as difficult as it sounds. Despite the belief that values are deep-rooted and of long standing, there is ample proof that values change relatively quickly. Americans gave up part of their cherished privacy when telephones made telephone directories necessary (Brody, Cornoni-Huntley, and Patrick, 1981). Penicillin and the pill changed sexual mores in less than one generation, leading Saint George (1970) to remark, "How shallow are our values!" Gordon (1969) is more specific: "Values change to fit the world that technology presents." Thus, the advent of the almost-workless world may lead to relatively quick and painless value changes.

Structural changes may be more difficult. Suggested methods of distributing the resources created by technology include massive increases in welfare programs, including converting family and children's allowances (or income-tax deductions in the United States) into individual allowances; a guaranteed income for everyone; redefining work and paying people to do what they enjoy; forming cooperatives; and establishing collectives (Macarov, 1984).

In any case, it is clear that people will continue to have ever-increasing amounts of leisure time during the transition period. This time, incidentally, will be further increased by the current lengthening of life expectancy. Whereas at the start of the twentieth century life expectancy throughout the world was 48 years, today it is 72 years, and a child born in 1982 can expect to live for 83 years. Thus, people retiring from work at current retirement ages will have many more years of leisure than did their predecessors. Consequently, helping people find satisfying and fulfilling activities during their ever-increasing leisure time is a present and growing challenge.

Education and a Workless World

Work as presently defined is so central to the human condition that changes in the nature and the amount of work that seem destined to take place in the future will require changes in both the value system and the structure of society as well as impinging on relatively remote areas of human activity. As a consequence, changes in the world of work will both influence the structure of the educational system as it relates to employers, corporations, and other institutions. It will also require massive changes in the content of educational programs.

In some cases, education will need to be preparatory in nature, to equip students to deal with future changes. In other cases, it will be required to be flexible enough to deal with those changes that have recently occurred and are still happening. In still other cases, education must be anticipatory by coming to grips with future changes and trying to influence their development. In every case, teaching how to identify signs of change and to adjust to them is an important necessary element. The inculcation of general skills and attitudes that can be adapted to new situations is essential.

Specifically, education must prepare more people for the service jobs of the future, including the skills and attitudes necessary as they become known. Worker satisfactions and dissatisfactions in various occupations should be identified and elucidated and methods should be sought by which people could be helped to find some satisfactions in what will be essentially dull, boring jobs as well as using free time on the job for meaningful activities. More women in the labor force and fading distinctions between male and female roles and jobs will require shifts in many occupationally oriented curricula. The strengths and limitations of part-time jobs will have to be taken into consideration.

More difficult for work-oriented institutions will be the phenomenon of growing unemployment—in many cases long term, if not permanent, unemployment. The challenge inherent in making unemployed time fulfilling, pleasant, and acceptable will be one of utmost importance for a relatively long period. The futility of most training courses and job-search instruction will be difficult to accept.

With the growth of life expectancy adding nonwork time to that of unemployment and/or retirement, satisfying uses of leisure time will become a central element in curricula. As new societal structures replace those based on work alone, new attitudes and skills will be needed. Instead of the discipline that most work requires, the workless society will need other qualities—creativity, cooperation, and concern, among others. Education may have a role to play in instilling or encouraging such attributes. Finally, the value changes and structural adjustments that loom in the future not only will have an impact on the educational system but also will require active participation by the education system in determining what the values and what the structures should be. These are serious and difficult responsibilities being laid on the educational system by future prospects. As the Talmud says: "It may not be given you to complete the task, but neither are you free to desist." And Hillel adds: "If not now, when?"

References

ALBEDA, W. "Reflections on the Future of Full Employment."*Labour and Society* 8(1983): 57–61.

ANTHONY, P. *The Ideology of Work.* London: Social Science Paperback, 1978.

ARNOLD, M. G., and ROSENBAUM, G. *The Crime of Poverty: A Basic Overview of the Welfare Problem.* Skokie: National Textbook, 1973.

BAR-GAL, D. "Social Values and Social Work: A Developmental Model." *Journal of Sociology and Social Welfare* S(1981): 45–61.

BEAUMONT, P. B., and PARTRIDGE, M. *The Reported Job Satisfactions of Teachers.* Glasgow: Department of Social and Economic Research, University of Glasgow, n.d.

BENBENISHTY, R., Paul Baerwald School of Social Work, Hebrew University, Jerusalem, personal communication.

BERG, I. *Education and Jobs: The Great Training Robbery.* Boston: Beacon, 1971.

BEST, F. *Work Sharing: Issues, Policy Options and Prospects.* Kalamazoo: Upjohn, 1981 (a).

———. "Changing Sex Role and Worklife Flexibility." *Psychology of Women Quarterly* 6(1981): 55–71 (b).

BOLAN, R. S. "Social Planning and Social Welfare in the 1980's." *The Urban and Social Change Review* 14(1981): 4–11.

BOWLES, S., and GINTIS, H. *Schooling in Capitalist America: Educational Reform and the Contradictions of Economic Life.* New York: Basic, 1976.

BRAYFIELD, A., and CROCKETT, W. "Employee Attitudes and Employee Performance." *Psychological Bulletin* 52(1955): 396–424.

BRODY, J. A., CORNONI-HUNTLEY, J., and PATRICK, C. H. "Research Epidemiology as a Growth Industry at the National Institute on Aging." *Public Health Reports* 96(1981): 269–273.

Bureau of Labor Statistics data, reported in *World of Work Report* 10(February, 1985): 7.

CAPLOW, T. *The Sociology of Work.* New York: McGraw-Hill, 1954.

CASNER-LOTTO, J. "Robots Expected to Boost Productivity." *World of Work Report* 5(March, 1981): 17.

CHERRINGTON, D. J. *The Work Ethic: Working Values and Values That Work.* New York: Amacon, 1980.

COOK, J. D., HEPWORTH, S. J., TOBY D., and WARR, P. B. *The Experience of Work.* New York: Academic, 1981.

CORNISH, E. *The Study of the Future.* Bethesda: World Future Society, 1977.

DAVIS, K. "Wives and Work: The Sex Role Revolution and Its Consequences." *Population and Development Review* 10(September, 1984): 397–417.

FEIN, M. "Motivation to Work," in R. Dubin (ed.), *Handbook of Work, Organization, and Society.* Chicago: Rand–McNally, 1976.

FIELD, F. *The Conscript Army: A Study of Britain's Unemployed.* London: Routledge & Kegan Paul, 1977.

FISCHER, B. *Daily Labor Report.* Birmingham, England, quoted in *World of Work Report* 10(February, 1985): 8.

FLICK, R. "The New Feminism and World of Work." *Public Interest* 71(Spring, 1983): 33–44.

GABLE, R., and MEERS, A. "Impact of Two Successive Mechanization Projects on Motivation and Work Organization in a Bank," in G.I. Mensch and R. J. Niehaus (eds.), *Work, Organization, and Technical Change.* New York: Plenum, 1982.

GARSON, B. *All the Livelong Day: The Meaning and Demeaning of Routine Work.* Harmondsworth: Penguin, 1975.

GARTNER, A., and RIESSMAN, F. *The Service Society and the Consumer Vanguard*. New York: Harper & Row, 1974.

GERSHUNY, J. *After Industrial Society: The Emerging Self-Service Economy*. London: Macmillan, 1978.

GERSUNY, C., and ROSENGREN, W. R. *The Service Society*. Cambridge, MA: Schenkman, 1973.

GINZBERG, E. *Jobs for Americans*. Englewood Cliffs, NJ: Prentice-Hall, 1976.

GLAZER, N. "Towards a Self-Service Society?" *Public Interest* 70(1983): 66–90.

GLENN, B. N., and FELDBERG, F. L. "Proleterianizing Clerical Work: Technology and Organizational Control in the Office," in A. Zimbalist (ed.), *Case Studies on the Labor Process*. New York: Monthly Review Press, 1979.

GLICKMAN, A. S., and BROWN, Z. H. *Changing Schedules of Work: Patterns and Implications*. Kalamazoo: Upjohn, 1974.

GOLDSTEIN, J. H. *The Effectiveness of Manpower Training Programs: A Review of Research on the Impact on the Poor*. Washington D.C.: Government Printing Office, 1972.

GORDON, T. J. "The Feedback Between Technology and Values," in K. Baier and N. Rescher (eds.), *Values and the Future: The Impact of Technological Change on American Values*. New York: Free Press, 1969.

GREVE, R. M., and GLADSTONE, A. "Framework Paper," in D. Gaudart, R. M. Greve, and A. Gladstone. *"Changing Perceptions of Work in Industrialized Countries: Their Effect on and Implications for Industrial Relations*. Geneva: International Institute of Labour Studies, 1983.

HALL, K. "How Shall We Ever Get Them Back to Work?" *International Journal of Manpower* 5(1984): 24–32.

HERZBERG, F. *Work and the Nature of Man*. Cleveland: World, 1966.

HORNE, J. "Youth Unemployment of Programmes: A Historical Account of the Development of Dole Colleges," in D. Gleeson, (ed.), *Youth Training and the Search for Work*. London: Routledge and Kegan Paul, 1983.

IMMERWAHR, F. "The Future of the Work Ethic" in D. Macarov (ed.), *People, Work, and Human Services in the Future*. Garden City: Adelphi University School of Social Work, 1982.

JACKSON, T. *Guerrilla Tactics in the Job Market*. New York: Bantam, 1978.

JENKINS, C., and SHERMAN, B. *The Collapse of Work*. London: Eyre Methuen, 1981.

JONES, T. E. *Options for the Future: A Comparative Analysis of Policy Oriented Forecasts*. New York: Praeger, 1980.

KANTER, R. M., and STEIN, B. A. (eds.). *Life in Organizations: Workplaces as People Experience Them*. New York: Basic, 1979.

Kendrick, J. W. "Productivity Trends and the Recent Slowdown," in W. E. Fellner (ed.), *Contemporary Economic Problems*. Washington, D.C.: American Enterprise Institute, 1979.

Kogut, A., and Aron, S. "Toward a Full Employment Policy: An Overview." *Journal of Sociology and Social Welfare* 7(1980): 85–99.

Kraft, P. "The Industrialization of Computer Programming: From Programming to Software Revolution," in A. Zimbalist (ed.), *Case Studies on the Labor Process*. New York: Monthly Labor Review Press, 1979.

Ladewig, B. H., and White, P. N. "Dual Earner Marriages." *Journal of Family Issues* 5(1980): 343–362.

Lawler, E. C. III., and Porter, L. W. "The Effect of Performance on Job Satisfaction," in G. A. Yukl and K. N. Wexley (eds.) *Readings in Organizational and Industrial Psychology*. New York: Oxford University Press, 1971.

Leon, C. B. "Occupational Winners and Losers: Who They Were During 1970–80." *Monthly Labor Review* 105(1982): 18–23.

Leontief, W. W., and Duchin, F. *The Impacts of Automation on Employment, 1963–2000*. New York Institute for Economic Analysis, New York University, 1984.

Levinson, H., Price, C. R., Munden, K. J., Mandl, H. J., and Solley, C. M. *Men, Management and Mental Health*. Cambridge: Harvard, 1962; quoted in Lefkowitz, B. *Breaktime: Living Without Work in a Nine-to-Five World*. New York: Penguin, 1979.

Levitan, S. A., and Johnson, C. M. "The Survival of Work," in *The Work Ethic: An Analytical View*. Madison: Industrial Relations Research Association, 1983.

Locke, E. A. "The Nature and Causes of Job Satisfaction," in M. D. Dunnette (ed.), *Handbook of Industrial and Organizational Psychology*. Chicago: Rand McNally, 1976.

Macarov, D. "The Concept of Empathy and the Educational Process." *Applied Social Studies* 11(May, 1970): 107–113.

———. "Empathy: The Charismatic Chimera." *Journal of Education for Social Work* 14(1978): 86–92.

———. *Work and Welfare: The Unholy Alliance*. Beverly Hills: Sage, 1980.

———. *Worker Productivity: Myths and Reality*. Beverly Hills: Sage, 1982.

———. "Overcoming Unemployment: Some Radical Proposals," in H. F. Didsbury, Jr. (ed.), *Creating a Global Agenda: Assessments, Solutions, and Action Plans*. Bethesda: World Future Society, 1984.

———. "The Concept of Employment in Social Welfare Programs: The Need for Change in Concept and Practice." *Journal of Sociology and Social Welfare* 11(1984): 1–24.

————. "Planning for a Probability: The Almost-Workless World." *International Labour Review*, in press.

MACAULAY, J., and BERKOWITZ, L. (eds.). *Altruism and Helping Behavior: Social Psychological Studies of Some Antecedents and Consequences*. New York: Academic Press, 1970.

McGILL, M. E. *Keeping It All Inside: Male Intimacy*. New York: Holt, Rinehart & Winston, 1985.

MARK, J. A. "Measuring Productivity in Service Industries." *Monthly Labor Review* 105(June, 1982): 3–8.

MARLAND, S. P. Jr. *Career Education: A Proposal for Reform*. New York: McGraw-Hill, 1974.

MELLER, Y., and MACAROV, D. "Studying Satisfactions in Human Service Organizations: An Exploration." *International Journal of Sociology and Social Policy* 5(1985): 1–15.

MITTON, R., and WILLMOTT, P. *Unemployment, Poverty and Social Policy in Europe*. London: Bedford Square, 1983.

MONK, P. J., and WHEELOCK, J. "Technological Change and Employment Policy," in H. F. Didsbury, Jr. (ed.), *Creating a Global Agenda: Assessments, Solutions and Action Plans*. Bethesda, Md.: World Future Society, 1984.

MOOS, M. "The Training Myth: A Critique of the Government's Response to Youth Unemployment and Its Impact on Further Education," in D. Gleeson (ed.), *Youth Training and the Search for Work*. London: Routledge & Kegan Paul, 1983.

MORRIS, R., and MURPHY, R. "The Situs Dimension in Occupational Literature." *American Sociological Review* 23(1959): 231–239.

National Insurance Institute, *Rehabilitation of the Work Injured*. Jerusalem: National Insurance Institute, 1974 (in Hebrew).

NEFF, W. W., *Work and Human Behavior*. New York: Atherton, 1968.

NEWLAND, K., *Productivity: The New Economic Context*. Washington, D.C.: Worldwatch Institute, 1982.

OLMSTED, B. " 'V-Time' Pleases Employees, Helps Employers Cut Costs." *World of Work Report* 10(October, 1985): 3–4.

O'TOOLE, J. *Work, Learning, and the American Future*. San Francisco: Jossey-Bass, 1977.

PARNES, S., and ROSOW, M. *Productivity and the Quality of Working Life*. Scarsdale, N.Y.: Work in America Institute, 1978.

PEARSON, R. "Personnel Planning: The Importance of the Labour Market," in G. Mensch and R. J. Niehaus (eds.), *Work, Organizations and Technological Change*. New York: Plenum, 1982.

PINES, A., and KAFRY, D. "Occupational Tedium in the Social Services." *Social Work* 23(1978): 499–507.

RADA, J. *The Impact of Micro-Electronics*. Geneva: ILO, 1980.

REDFERN, S. J., and P. SPURGEON, "Job Satisfaction and Withdrawal of Hospital Sisters in the United Kingdom," in K. D. Duncan, M. M. Gruneberg, and D. Wallis (eds.), *Changes in Working Life*. New York: Wiley, 1980.

REICH, R. B. "An Industrial Policy of the Right." *Public Interest* 73(1983): 3–17.

RICHARDSON, V. "Social Change in Perceptions of Work Relations." *Social Service Review* 56(1982): 138–148.

ROBINSON, J. P. "Occupational Norms and Differences in Job Satisfaction: A Summary of Survey Research Evidence," in J. P. Robinson, R. ATHANSASIOU, and K. B. Head, *Measures of Occupational Attitudes and Occupational Characteristics*. Ann Arbor: University of Michigan, 1969.

ROE, A. *The Psychology of Occupations*. New York: Wiley, 1956.

ROSOW, J. M. "Productivity and People," in J. M. Rosow (ed.), *Productivity: Prospects for Growth*. New York: Van Nostrand Reinhold, 1981.

RUCH, W. A. "The Measurement of White-Collar Productivity," in *Human Resources Productivity*. New York: Executive Enterprises, 1983.

SAINT GEORGE (Szent Gyorgyi), A. *The Crazy Ape*. New York: Philosophical Library, 1970.

SHAMIR, B. "Between Service and Servility: Role Conflict in Subordinate Service Roles." *Human Relations* 33(1980): 741–756.

SHELP, R. K. *Beyond Industrialization: Ascendency of the Global Service Economy*. New York: Praeger, 1981.

SMITH, P. C., KENDALL, L. M., and HULIN, C. L. *The Measurement of Satisfactions in Work and Retirement: A Strategy for the Study of Attitudes*. Chicago: Rand McNally, 1969.

SPARKS, L. "Retail Employment in the Current Recession." *International Journal of Manpower* 5(1984): 3–10.

STELLMAN, J. *Human and Public Health Aspects of Telecommunications*. Paper delivered at Fourth General Assembly, World Future Society, Washington, D.C., 1982.

STEWART, B., HETHERINGTON, G., and SMITH, M. *British Telecom Survey Item Bank*. Bradford: MCB Universities Press, 1984.

STRAUSS, G. "Book Review." *American Journal of Sociology* 85(1980): 1467–1469.

SUPER, D. *The Psychology of Careers*. New York: Harper, 1975.

TAGGART, R. *Job Creation: What Works?* Salt Lake City: Olyumpus, 1977.

TAUSKY, C. *Work and Society: An Introduction to Industrial Sociology*. Itasca: Peacock, 1984.

TERKEL, S. *American Dreams: Lost and Found*. New York: Ballantine, 1980.

THUROW, L. C. *The Zero-Sum Society: Distribution and the Possibilities for Economic Change.* Harmondsworth: Penguin, 1981.

TOFFLER, A. *The Third Wave.* New York: Bantam, 1980.

TRIPODI, T. "Trends in Research Publication: 1956–1980." *Social Work* 29(1984): 353–359.

United States Department of Health, Education and Welfare. *Work in America: Report of a Special Task Force to the Secretary of Health, Education and Welfare.* Cambridge, Mass.: MIT Press, 1973.

WALBANK, M. "Effort in Motivated Work Behavior," in K. D. Duncan, M. M. Gruneberg and D. Wallis (eds.), *Changes in Working Life.* Chichester: Wiley, 1980.

WILSON, J. O. *After Affluence: Economics to Meet Human Needs.* New York: Harper & Row, 1980.

Working Woman. September 1983, p. 48.

World of Work Report. April 1979; July/August 1980; April 1983; October 1985; December 1985.

YANKELOVICH, D. "The New Psychological Contracts at Work." *Psychology Today* 11(1978): 46–50.

YANKELOVICH, D., ZETTENBERG, H. STRUMPEL, B., and SHANKS, M. *Work and Human Values: An International Report on Jobs in the 1980s and 1990s.* New York: Aspen Institute, 1983.

Yearbook of Labour Statistics. Geneva: ILO, 1956; 1966; 1976.

ZETTERBERG, H., and FRANKEL, G. *The Changing Work Ethic in Sweden* (mimeo), quoted by Greve, R. M., and Gladstone, A., "Framework Paper," in D. Gaudart, R. M. Greve, and A. Gladstone, *Changing Perceptions of Work in Industrialized Countries: The Effect on and Implications for Industrial Relations.* Geneva: International Institute for Labour Studies, 1983.

ZIMBALIST, A. "Technology and the Labor Process in the Printing Industry," In A. Zimbalist (ed.), *Case Studies on the Labor Process.* New York: Monthly Labor Review Press, 1979.

9

Teaching Civic Values and Political Judgment in the Community College

LEONARD P. OLIVER

Education for jobs and education in the liberal arts need to be accompanied by deliberate efforts to educate for the exercise of intelligence and informed public judgment. . . .

As demand-driven institutions, the nation's community colleges have their hands full in providing technical and occupational education for their students. Some community colleges have even permitted local businesses and their community's economic needs for a balanced workforce to significantly influence the community college's curriculum. At the same time, the community-college collegiate or liberal-arts–humanities function appears to be healthy. Community colleges have found creative ways to present the humanities and organizations such as the Community College Humanities Association and the League for the Humanities demonstrate the importance of the humanities to the community-college student's education in the career programs and in the transfer function—even though it is often an uphill struggle.

Building civic arts with values and responsibilities for citizenship* into the community-college curriculum, however, is seldom a focus for community-college administrators, curriculum committees, or individual faculty. The concept tends to get lost in the debate between the proponents of viewing the community college as a higher-education remedial or industrial training institute and those who believe higher education's fundamental purpose, at all levels, is to produce educated individuals through exposure to the best there is to study in history, philosophy, literature, and other liberal-arts disciplines.

The purpose of this chapter is to inquire if community colleges can fulfill their missions as higher-education institutions by not only concentrating on equipping individuals with skills for economic survival or for personal growth but also focusing on these skills that will enable them to participate more intelligently and critically in self-government. Building concepts of civic values and the civic arts into the community-college curricula does not imply traditional "citizenship education" where students are encouraged to conform to preconceived notions and the existing order of political life while engaging in patriotic understanding of our founding documents and political institutions. Teaching civic values does imply encouraging the community-college student to understand the role of critical analysis and dissent, toleration for minority views, and the complex forces and efforts by which organizations, communities, and governments work out their destiny. As interstitial institutions between secondary schools that offer pap as

---

* *Civic arts* are the knowledge and skills necessary to function in community life; *civic values* relate to why we need these skills in a democratic society, the rationale for an active, vital public life.

"civics" and four-year colleges and universities that assume it is
the student's personal responsibility to gain the skills necessary for
effective participation in civic and public life, the community colleges may be our only educational institution with the mission,
resources, and interest to systematically and effectively infuse concepts of civic values and the civic arts into their educational programs.

If we recall Socrates' trial, he defended the principle that living
among good citizens was better than living among bad ones, so
education should be concerned with civic virtue. Our sense of public life, our responsibilities for living in the "polis," according to
Aristotle, are shaped by our commitment to shared values. Community colleges fail their students to the degree they fail to emphasize these shared values in the technical–occupational
programs that encourage individualistic, not community, gain and
in their liberal arts programs where professors lecture about concepts and abstractions as learning isolated from life outside the
campus. Education for jobs and education in the liberal arts need
to be accompanied by deliberate efforts to educate for the exercise
of intelligent and informed public judgment—for connecting our
civic actions with others. This has all too frequently been over-
looked in community-college educational programs.

Technical-Occupational Education: Does It Work
Against the Teaching of Civic Values?

One cannot fault adult students over 25 involved in worklife, family, and community responsibilities for having a high sense of
vocationalism as they return to education through their local community colleges. It is difficult to ask these adult students to consciously pursue a civic dimension—a concern for shared
community values—in their courses, when their pursuit of knowledge and skills in a specific technical–occupational subject so is
intensely personal. Technical learning emphasizes a student's in-
dividuality, personal interests, aptitude, and capabilities. Students
choose data processing, nursing, television broadcasting, accounting, or respiratory therapy because they know the skills they need.

They know that the learning will, in all likelihood, allow them to enter a field, change jobs, or upgrade themselves in their present employment. They usually learn just as much as they believe they need to learn to meet their personal goals.

Sharing of ideas and identification with larger organizational, community, and public issues is rare and almost always instrumental in these programs. Learning about public issues and being aware of community life is considered useful only to further the student's occupational–career goals such as an accountant learning tax law, a student in a broadcasting major learning the role of a television station, or a nursing student discussing health-care costs. The social utility of the technical–occupational curricula is job specific. And social utility carries enormous weight with both the career-minded student and with business leadership in the community—hospital directors and government officials who will be deciding what jobs the community college students get. Students and their current or prospective employers are concerned with tangible results. Civic virtues, citizen skills, exercising public judgments, and participation in community life and public decision making are considered less central to their education.

Admittedly, community-college technical–occupational programs further the knowledge explosion by enabling students to master a set of specific, predetermined skills. But this type of education can also perpetuate an "ignorance explosion" about public life. The result can be social fragmentation, alienation, loss of personal control—the mindlessness and apathy endemic in American public life.

Teaching specific technical–occupational skills may give a community-college student the means for economic survival, but job-specific teaching can reduce one's role and significance as a citizen by failing to prepare students for the shared decisions they will be called upon to make in their organizations and in community life. "Man's ingenuity has outrun his intelligence . . . ," said Joseph Wood Krutch in his classic *The Measure of Man* (1954), "(and) wisdom and understanding have not kept pace with the necessities for them."

Where do the career-oriented students in the community college learn that understanding public issues and responsibility for informed participation in public life is fraught with ambiguities and compromise, unlike the binomial theorem, the two-minute newscast, or the accounting balance sheet? Political life is not like a football game with well-marked good guys and bad guys, winners and losers, where "experts" make the decisions from the sidelines. Public life does not require the football coach's technical expertise. Citizens are the "experts" in spite of the planners, economists, and engineers. Shared citizen value systems determine our destiny, yet we tend to act in isolation from each other in a community. We exercise individual judgments when we enter the voting booth, respond to a public-opinion poll, or write a letter to our congressional representative. These public decisions affect others. Yet, we seem ill equipped for the role of citizen where shared values as distinct from personal values should dominate. And community-college technical programs are not the place to seek answers to what the student needs to fulfill the "office of citizen."

Teaching Civic Values in the Humanities: The "Trickle-Down" Theory of Academic Disciplines

One of those esoteric debates that occasionally engrosses the interest of the academic community but is often neglected by the public at large began in 1982 when William J. Bennett became chair of the National Endowment for the Humanities (NEH). During the 1970s, perhaps since the founding of NEH in 1965, NEH ploughed its meager yet not insignificant resources for education into interdisciplinary, innovative, problem-oriented courses in the humanities. Many community colleges received institutional grants and designed new curricula based upon the interdisciplinary approach. Many such programs are still in operation today. These courses and curricular reforms, by starting with social issues and problems, encouraged the teaching of shared values and understanding of public issues.

Bennett reorganized the Endowment to focus more on the humanities disciplines, the humanities version of "back to basics," concentrating on traditional courses and the reading of great texts, usually from Western literature. Some community colleges adapted admirably, with these federal funds dictating direction, yet a number held on to their interdisciplinary, problem-centered humanities offerings.

Humanities scholars from the disciplines generally applauded NEH's moves, reinforced by Bennett's 1984 report, "To Reclaim a Legacy." It meant a return to concentration on "the humanities-as-themselves," a focus on the distinct disciplines, rather than accommodation to broad issues and concepts touching on but not central to a single field. For many community colleges, the change meant closer articulation with the lower-division coursework of the four-year institutions.

It is not my place here to argue the "disciplinary" versus "the interdisciplinary" approach to humanities teaching. My argument concerns the teaching of civic values. The "back-to-the-disciplines" movement in the humanities, in my opinion, works against helping community-college students think about the interrelationships of knowledge and how this knowledge can help us to think critically about larger public issues. It works against reaching of civic values.

There is, after all, no such thing as a purely historical, philosophical, or ethical issue. Public issues by definition are multidimensional. It seems logical, therefore, that a multidisciplinary approach to the teaching of the civic arts in the community colleges is the most effective means to prepare students for the citizen's task of analyzing issues and making critical and informed judgments about these issues, using knowledge from various fields rather than from a single field.

Traditionalist, discipline-oriented humanities faculty will obviously argue that exposure to basic courses in law and government, the history of our political institutions, the development of moral values, and reading and interpretation of our basic documents such as the Constitution and the Bill of Rights will cause students at all levels to be more concerned with citizenship. "Citizenship" in this concept is usually equated with knowledge of laws and government. This type of "civic learning" will help to create "a highly conscious citizenry" as one historian recently told me, overcoming the growing civic illiteracy among students at all levels. This is a questionable assumption.

Much of what is taught in discipline-oriented courses on civic education in secondary and postsecondary classrooms is designed to foster citizen adjustment—a form of education that emphasizes objective examination of how our system works; how our institutions have evolved; patriotic teachings about America; and broad, value-free concepts of liberty, justice, and equality. It is a type of education that does not encourage criticism, analytical thinking, or independent judgment about public issues, nor does it foster an examination of civic values outside of the formal curriculum and classroom. The civic arts—how to participate effectively in public life—are usually ignored in these classes.

Thomas Jefferson (Battistoni, 1985) argued that the "ploughman" was a better judge of public morality than the philosopher: "State a moral case to a ploughman and a philosopher. The former will decide it as well, and often better than the latter, because he has not been led astray by artificial rules." Jefferson put his finger on a nagging concern of mine with the disciplinary approach to teaching about civic values—not only the artificial rules found in all disciplines, but the distinct methodologies and the fragmentation of knowledge that create the boundaries for a scholarly discipline.

The humanities scholar's obvious answer is that understanding historical forces, interpreting literature, grasping moral–ethical concepts, and helping individuals wrestle with the meaning of ideas such as political democracy, equality, and freedom and liberty are ideal preparation for participation in public life. They have an arguable point. If properly taught, literature and history can teach us something about public life.

Suppose one wished to ideally teach civic values in a community-college classroom. One could start with some standard works from Western civilization. Decision making is essential to full participation in public life, but it can have tragic implications as seen in Sophocles' *Antigone*. Being a citizen also means searching for individual conscience versus the state as outlined in Plato's *Creto* and *Apology* or Thoreau *On Civil Disobedience*. The attempt to define justice and power leads us to the lessons of the *Republic*, or the *Peloponnesian Wars*, or Machiavelli's *Prince*. Understanding labor, class systems, and property would be aided by reading Marx's and Engel's *Communist Manifesto* or Adolph Berle's *Economic Power and the Free Society.* Locke's *Civil Government* or Mill's *On Liberty* help us in our grasp for freedom and liberty, while a discussion of equality ranges wide over literature from Rousseau's *Origin of Inequality* to de Tocqueville's *Democracy in America* or Martin Luther King's *Letter from a Birmingham City Jail.* For leadership in a community one could read Duerrenmatt's *The Visit,* while Orwell's *1984* or Skinner's *Beyond Freedom and Dignity* would provide ideas about how to deal with the future of public policy. All of these suggested works are grist for the intellectual's mill; all are in the humanities; all have appeared in course catalogs on the humanities and social problems; all could be on any good reading list on civic education.

So what is wrong? Is this not what any humanities instructor who has given some thought to the issue would propose in contemplating an assignment to teach civic values? The problem is that humanities instructors tend to look upon the teaching of civic values as the presentation of literature, the reading of good books, usually from their own disciplines. Social problems and public issues thus become academic questions. And, because they are academic questions, students have little or no stake in them. In splendid intellectual isolation, we contemplate the world outside the campus untarnished by the necessity for compromise, conformity, or concession—the essence of community and public life.

What we have forgotten and what humanities instructors may want to consider in teaching civic values in the community college is the classical ideal of the unity of knowledge related to public life. Increasing specialization and fragmentation of knowledge in the disciplines, "self-trivialization" as W. Jackson Bate (1982) of Harvard called it, have created barriers between fields, the loss of the interrelationship of knowledge, and the divorce of the humanities from the everyday concerns and experiences of civic life. Teaching about civic values by starting with the literature and abstractions of the humanities will remain only an exercise for the campus classroom or a community great-books discussion unless we can return to the classical sense of the humanities—the Greek ideal—aimed at developing responsible citizens, civically moral persons with educational judgment that comes through the application of knowledge.

For the Greeks, "moral" and "political" were interchangeable.

They could not conceive of an educated citizen or political life without moral foundations: the "political" was the public side; the application was the "moral" dimension. "Morals" were what individual citizens brought to politics. And both morals and politics are honed by the cultivation of critical intelligence and the nurturing of the civic self. If we are serious about the teaching of civic values and the civic arts in the community college, and if the college is to play a role in encouraging responsible and informed judgments among the students, then we should think long and hard about this classical ideal, about revising the practice of teaching from the disciplines abstracted from reality, and about the interrelationship of knowledge as it can enhance individual understanding of public issues and public life. But where do we start? How do we relate ideas to practice as we seek to teach students about civic values and participation in public life?

Teaching Civic Values: Student Experience as a Point of Beginning

Instructors in the community-college technical–occupational programs teach practical skills; they are not expected to consciously include ideas about civic values in their courses. Similarly, instructors in the humanities, if they teach civic values at all, tend to approach such teaching obliquely and from the perspective of their disciplines. What seems to be lacking in both the career and humanities programs in teaching civic values and civic arts is an ability to capitalize on the experiences of the students, many of whom are citizens, voters, and community members as well as students. Rephrased, how do we get beyond the pursuit of individual skills in the technical–occupational program and beyond the individual interpretation ethos of the humanities?

Some community-college faculty in both the technical–occupational fields and the humanities are concerned about civic values and genuinely interested in exploring with their students the idea of civic virtues, civic responsibilities, and participation in public life. If we are failing the community-college student in the teaching of civic values and if the issue itself is important enough to raise, where do instructors interested in helping their students to identify with larger community concerns and responsibilities go for guidance?

One useful starting point may be David A. Kolb's "Experiential Learning Model," as described in Arthur W. Chickering's *The Modern American College* (1981). Kolb emphasizes the match-up between "personal learning styles" and the "learning demands of different and unique disciplines." Consider Figure 1.

FIGURE 1: The Experiential Learning Model

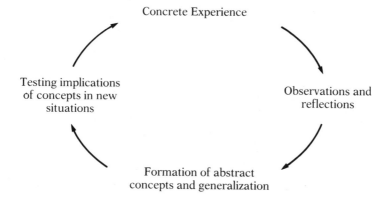

Kolb points out that in some disciplines, such as humanities subjects (history, philosophy, political science, or literature), and some of the social sciences (sociology, economics, or anthropology), effective teaching of adult students should start with their immediate, *concrete experiences.* These experiences can form the basis for student *observation and reflection,* using personal insights, texts, classroom discussion, and interaction with the teacher to build an idea, seek commonalities with others, generalize to other situations, and begin the process of the logical integration of social theory.

Kolb's next step in the model is to enable the student—informed by both the teacher and texts—to formulate *abstract concepts* emerging from the first two stages, seeking *generalization and theories* to explain the behavior. The final stage is the *application* of the learning—making decisions, solving problems, and creating new implications for action. In turn, such application can lead to new concrete experiences.*

There is nothing new about Kolb's model. It is based upon simple premises about adult learners, premises that have been presented in the literature and applied for years in educational programs for adults. These concepts include the idea of *adult self-concept* that provides adults with a sense of self-direction, *adult experiences* brought to the learning situation, *adult readiness to learn*, and *adults' problem-centered time perspective*.

By capitalizing on these characteristics of adult learners in their presentations on civic values, community-college instructors have an opportunity to develop coursework that respects an adult's experiences and needs, that encourages self-directed learning and avoids condescension, that is more problem centered than content centered, and that acknowledges the importance of adults learning rather than teachers teaching. Kolb's model of adult-education learning theory and similar concepts can be useful in all humanities and social-sciences courses, but may be most effective in teaching the civic values and civic arts. Why?

Civic values relate to life beyond the campus, to public issues, to ideas about how citizens function in a community and in a democracy. Civic values in the community-college curriculum are likely not to be taught best by an English instructor who offers "Romeo and Juliet and Juvenile Delinquency," or "Macbeth and Watergate," or "The Taming of the Shrew and Women's Lib." They will be taught best when both community-college instructors in the humanities and instructors in the career programs come to understand the public-issue dilemmas their students face daily in the real world—be it in the workplace, in the community, or in the media—and the types of learning experiences from their fields that can help their students to critically analyze and interpret their views on the issues. Teaching adult students about civic values pursued in this way can serve to inculcate in the students the type

---

* In one test of Kolb's theory at the University of Illinois, researchers found that certain disciplines and fields tended to fall within Kolb's quadrants; for example, history and literature were easier to teach starting with experiences, whereas math and physical sciences were more easily learned by starting with the theoretical aspects of the fields (Kolb, 1981, pp. 239–241).

of thoughtful criticism and thoughtful decision making upon which a democracy depends.

A Rationale for Teaching Civic Values in the Community-College Curriculum: A Return to a Shared Civic Life

We seem increasingly concerned with involvement and participation in our social institutions. Our largest private sector institutions such as corporations and labor unions are searching for ways to decentralize decision making and involve employees and members in the life of their organizations (AFL–CIO, 1985; Naisbitt, 1982; Peters and Waterman, 1982). This spirit of involvement has carried over in small ways to public life. Citizens want in. The town hall concept is alive and well in New England states: Over 200 community organizations are conducting annual public-issues forums and study circles under the aegis of the Domestic Policy Association's National Issues Forums (DPA/NIF). In spite of continuing widespread public indifference, more and more citizens are taking an interest in their schools, in neighborhoods, and local government, and in other issues they can control.

Still, we are influenced in large part and often overwhelmed by the complexity of public issues. This can mean leaving the policy field to planners, public-health officials, environmentalists, financial managers, and other experts, or to the bureaucratic technocrats who often have difficulty with public participation and decision making. As Seymour J. Mandelbaum pointed out in his *Community and Communications* (1972), those who plan and make decisions for local communities often, and in a misguided fashion, distrust the citizen, adding that "there is no practically feasible nor ethically appropriate way to expand the domain of expertise in the U.S. except by increasing the intellectual capabilities of the large public so that they may deal complexly with reality."

Social critic and pollster Daniel Yankelovich (1985) also speaks eloquently of a return to community and public life, overcoming the antagonisms and competition between our private lives and public life, and increasing relationships to other citizens through public dialogue and civic politics. The 100,000 citizens who participate annually in the DPA/NIF public-issues forums and study circles, for example, are not only voicing their informed opinions about policy issues, they are practicing the civic arts by engaging in spirited dialogue in community settings and motivating policymakers to listen.

David Mathews (1984) believes that such citizen engagement in public life can "make public citizens out of private individuals." Yankelovich underlines the interest in renewal of public life when he talks about citizens facing the reality of public issues together, dealing with hard questions, overcoming media (especially television) influence over public issues, and exercising "informed public judgments." Public judgment for Yankelovich arises from public dialogue and confrontation with issues, without deference to experts and policymakers, to opinion polls, or to the pervasive influence of the media on the way we perceive public issues.

Political theorists Hannah Pitkin and Sara Shumer (1982) underscore the importance of having educational institutions such as community colleges advocate teaching the civic values and civic arts to ordinary citizens:

> The idea that ordinary people are incompetent to deal intelligently with the issues affecting their lives rests now, as it always has, on an overly narrow idea of what constitutes politically relevant knowledge, and a confusion between knowledge and action.
>
> First off, stupidity knows no class. Maybe most people are foolish, but foolishness is found in all social strata. Education removes some kinds of ignorance, but may entrench or instill others. The cure is not to exclude some but to include as diverse a range of perspectives and experience as possible in political deliberation. Second, expertise cannot solve political problems. Contemporary politics is indeed full of technically complex issues, about which even the educated feel horribly ignorant. But on every politically significant issue of this kind, the "experts" are divided; that is part of why the issues are political. Though we may also feel at a loss to choose between them, leaving it to the experts is no solution at all.
>
> Finally, while various kinds of knowledge can be profoundly useful in political decisions, knowledge alone is never enough.

The political question is what we are to do; knowledge can only tell us how things are, how they work, while a political resolution always depends on what we, as a community, want and think right. And those questions have no technical answer; they require collective deliberation and decisions. The experts must become a part of, not an alternative to, the democratic political process. [pp. 54 and 55]

Be it Mathews's "public citizens," Yankelovich's "informed public judgments," or Pitkin and Shumer's concept of "citizen experts," being a responsible and active citizen, above all, implies "political judgment." Can one find a community-college course on political judgment? One of the best recent works on the subject is by Benjamin R. Barber. Barber (1985) addresses the role of individual political judgment in the revival of public life and criticizes the detached, rationalistic view of judgment in politics because it implies reason and the application of some universal standards to public life. Rational judgment in this sense can be taught in classrooms. It is a product of detached observation, of deriving ideas from texts, and in Barber's view, connotes spectating, not acting in public life. Citing Madison, de Tocqueville, James, and Dewey among others, Barber believes what actually happens in political practice is a frenzy of activity involving association, collaboration, discussion, and conflict with others. "Indeed," Barber writes, "common civic activity is constitutive of what we mean by political judgment" (p. 134).

Politics, for Barber, requires individual judgment in the face of *uncertainty*, not resting on philosophical or historical "reasoning." Political life also demands judgment in the face of *necessity*, or decision making that is not taught in classrooms. Politics generates *conflict*, arising from our value differences and opposing interests, which are often irreconcilable, except through exchange and compromise. These are the civic arts, and political judgment is at the core. But we do not teach civic arts in this manner.

Unlike philosophical argumentation where common ground can be sought in higher levels of abstraction, teaching civic values and civic arts implies a need for citizens who can exercise informed political judgment *beyond the application of abstract independent standards* learned in a classroom. It is the application of political judgment fitting for our uncertain political life that incessantly requires, according to Barber, some form of "dynamic, ongoing, deliberation and action . . . feasible only when individuals are transformed by social interaction into citizens" (p. 141). Teaching civic values and civic arts is teaching for social interaction.

A Role for Community Colleges

If there is a move toward decentralization of decision making, increased citizen activity in public life, and encouragement of informed public judgment, as Yankelovich and others point out, does the community college, as an educational institution with a defined geographic and political boundary, have a role in helping its students become informed, more responsible, participating citizens? Can the community-college curriculum, while maintaining its academic integrity, extend students' horizons and deepen their understanding of civic values, and enable them to apply the civic arts in the cause of justice in public life?

Community-college faculty have an opportunity in the teaching of civic values to prepare their students for citizenship, to create the link between knowledge and action in political life. Just as we learn to be accountants and data processors by applying our skills, we learn to be responsible citizens by having the opportunity to take civic responsibility, to exercise political judgment. What, then, can the community college do within the existing curriculum to further such civic learning? Is there another way to integrate concepts about civic values and civic arts into both the community-college technical–occupational programs and humanities programs? The concept of teaching civic values has been gaining advocates in the higher-education community. For example, some 100 higher-education institutional representatives gathered recently with Frank Newman of the Educational Commission of the States to examine how to introduce civic values into higher education. The 1986 American Association of Colleges (AAC) conference "Liberal Learning and the Work World" acknowledged increased recognition by higher education administration and faculty that "all undergraduate education should be informed by the commitment to prepare students to be responsible and active citizens as well as competent holders of a job" (Jacobson, 1986).

Community-college education can emphasize "we" thinking—participation with others in a community. It can be an education that enlarges the political experience of its students in a public life that demands judgments in the face of uncertainty and conflict. And teaching civic values can be integrated into existing community-college programs.

When it comes to teaching the civic values, therefore, community colleges can assist their students to think about the formation of informed political judgments by starting with the real-life issues students and their communities face. This does not mean an isolated course in civic education or a sequence of courses on government and politics. It means the encouragement of the kind of critical, analytical thinking that enables a student to build the capacity to exercise informed public judgment, to become a more responsible citizen. This is the core of teaching civic values and the civic arts—citizens bringing informed judgments to the decision-making process.

Not everyone can be an accountant, automobile mechanic, or lab technician, just as few of us can be well-known scholars, teachers, and writers in the humanities. Yet, we can all fulfill the office of citizen. We can all become citizen experts. The community college does not have a tradition or a mission in imparting the civic values, in teaching civic arts, but it has an opportunity with its students, especially its part-time, adult, working students, to encourage and stimulate their consideration of community and political life—and provide the tools and insights to enable them to play a more active, informed, and effective role in public life.

References

AFL–CIO. "The Changing Situations of Workers and Their Unions." Washington, D.C.: AFL–CIO, 1985.

Barber, Benjamin R. "The Politics of Judgment." *Raritan* 5 (Fall, 1985): 131–143.

Bate, W. Jackson. "The Crisis in English Studies." *Harvard Business Review* 85 (September–October, 1982):46–53.

CALLAHAN, DANIEL. "Applying the Humanities." Interviewed in *The Antaeus Report* (Winter, 1986):2.

JACOBSON, ROBERT L. "Academic Leaders Showing New Optimism About Reform of Undergraduate Education." *The Chronicle of Higher Education* 31 (January, 1986):1, 24.

JEFFERSON, THOMAS. "Letter to Peter Carr." Cited in Battistoni, Richard M. *Public Schooling and the Education of Democratic Citizens.* Jackson, Mississippi: University Press of Mississippi, 1985.

KOLB, DAVID A. "Learning Styles and Disciplinary Differences," in Chickering, Arthur W., ed., *The Modern American College.* San Francisco: Jossey-Bass, 1981.

KRUTCH, JOSEPH W. *The Measure of Man.* New York: Grosset and Dunlop, 1954.

MANDELBAUM, SEYMOUR J. *Community and Communications.* New York: Norton, 1972.

MATHEWS, DAVID. "Educating Communities." *Foundation News* 25 (4) (1984):68–69.

NAISBITT, JOHN. *Megatrends.* New York: Warner, 1982.

PETERS, THOMAS J., and WATERMAN, ROBERT H., JR. *In Search of Excellence.* New York: Harper & Row, 1982.

PITKIN, HANNAH, and SHUMER, SARA. "On Participation." *Democracy* II (Fall, 1982):43–54.

YANKELOVICH, DANIEL. "How the Public Learns the Public's Business." *Kettering Review* (Winter, 1985): 8–18.

10

Positioning Alternatives and New Partnerships

RICHARD L. ALFRED

> *. . . community colleges will need to develop compelling new definitions for "finished products" within the frame-work of a public service mission.*

The Carnegie Council for Policy Studies (1980), in an examination of enrollment prospects and organizational vitality for different sectors of postsecondary education, concluded with the observation that colleges and universities are remarkably resilient organizations. They have experienced wars, revolutions, depressions, and industrial transformations, and have emerged less changed than almost any other social institution in society.

This remarkable resilience on the part of postsecondary institutions supports the contention of Bennis (1964) that the organization and functions of colleges and universities are much more adaptive and restorative in relationship to changing societal conditions than are traditional bureaucracies and profit organizations. Community colleges afford perhaps the finest example of institutional capacity to adapt to social change as missions, programs, and staff have been modified to reflect changing constituency needs and priorities. These organizations are loosely coupled (Weick, 1976), fluid systems (Cohen and March, 1974) that have a great capacity to alter internal structures and functions to capitalize on environmental disruptions. They operate effectively in an environment marked by discord between public policy conditions that simultaneously support divergent themes and expectations. This capacity is most evident in the efforts of faculty and administrators to expand educational delivery systems to incorporate short-term job training and retraining programs into the traditional curriculum while at the same time altering general education requirements to facilitate academic reform.

On the other hand, community colleges today are facing perhaps the most serious challenge to organizational vitality in their brief history. Interest groups such as elected officials, K–12 administrators, parents of prospective students, and media representatives question the mission of the college and its efficiency in producing trained professionals with durable market skills at reasonable cost. Perspectives on the mission vary among writers and researchers. Richardson (1983), for example, has indicated that the battleground for community colleges in the future will be student performance, which is dependent on "completion" as distinct from "participation" in the educational experience. If success is interpreted as the percentage of the student population qualified for advanced study or employment as a result of completing a recognized educational sequence, problems will mount for community colleges. Cohen (1984) has questioned the vitality of institutions that blur public perception of their mission through random addition of programs and services without regard for their fit into a central or organizing scheme for the institution. Alfred (1985) has issued a call for faculty and administrators to consider variable institutional positioning possibilities through alignment of the mission and programs of the college with changing social conditions. He concluded that the community college that seeks to shape the course of public policy must function as a productive institution capable of eliciting the support of campus and extra-campus constituencies for new and continuing programs.

What these perspectives point out is that even with the capacity of resilience and adaptivity, community colleges operate in ways that do not take advantage of these capacities and subsequently may find themselves unable to adjust to environmental changes. When the unusual set of circumstances arises in the environment, some institutions discover that they have become incapable of maintaining resilience.

This chapter examines some of the reasons for this loss of resilience in community colleges and describes alternatives that can be implemented to improve organizational vitality through partnerships with public and private-sector organizations. In the section that follows, four Ps for the 1990s are identified—public policy, paradoxes, positioning, and partnerships. These four factors will dictate the capacity of community colleges to circumvent pressures to become rigid, inflexible, and conservative in the face of rapidly changing environmental conditions. The second section of the chapter discusses organizational transitions and positioning alternatives for community colleges with particular reference to paradoxes inherent in conflicting public expectations and policy conditions. The chapter concludes with a description of new partnerships that can be developed by community colleges interested in organizational renewal through linkages with public and private-sector organizations.

Four Ps for the 1990s

The predominant theme of the 1980s in community colleges has been qualitative growth or reordering of priorities to provide colleges with an opportunity to concentrate on selective growth and educational enrichment. The theme of the 1990s will be qualified change. This management of qualified change will involve the reconfiguration of educational programs and services based on their fit with emerging economic, social, and public-policy conditions. It will encourage the development of flexibility and provide an opportunity for colleges to concentrate on renewal through relationships with public and private-sector organizations. It will depend heavily on the capacity of community college faculty and administrators to undertake accurate assessment of four dimensions of change:

1. the future direction of *public policy;*

2. *paradoxes* stemming from policy issues that simultaneously encourage and retard institutional development;

3. *positioning alternatives* for future development that vary in accord with changing environmental and public policy conditions;

4. *partnerships* with public and private-sector organizations that yield selective benefits depending on the positioning alternative(s) chosen for institutional development.

Public policy in the 1990s will translate individual needs and expectations for postsecondary education into action dictates for community colleges. The general concern over quality among community college faculty and administrators will give way to a concern for developing public service initiatives to stimulate growth in enrollment and revenue. The burgeoning relationship between public policy and institutional behavior—a relationship not well documented in the literature or understood by administrators—will be complicated by multiple paradoxes facing community colleges inherent in conflicting demands. For example, institutional efforts to achieve a meaningful balance between "access" and "quality" will become a subject of debate among elected officials seeking to expand access through pricing policies and government agencies seeking to enhance quality through improvement in academic standards. Both groups maintain influence over the allocation of resources as well as vigilance over institutional performance and the degree to which such performance conforms to states expectations. Community colleges interested in pursuing a proactive approach to institutional development will face an impossible dilemma: they may open themselves to criticism and possible resource problems through neglect of the interests of either group yet they cannot afford a standstill strategy in the face of rapidly changing social conditions. The best course may be one of flexible policies that serve different groups at different points in time but fail to advance the institution along a discernible course of development.

Community colleges attempting to cope with paradoxes that simultaneously encourage and constrain development will need to constantly reexamine positioning alternatives in search of partnerships that yield maximum educational and financial benefits given changing environmental and public policy conditions. To accomplish this task, they will need to assume some of the characteristics of a public service organization in which success is determined by: (1) the capacity to alter programs and services to general new resources; and (2) the capacity to increase resilience through development of new partnerships with public and private-sector organizations. Two questions that will need to be answered if community colleges are to experience success in public service are: (1) How will "traditional" functions performed by the community college such as college transfer, occupational education, and remediation be integrated into the flexible programming mode characteristic of public service organizations? and (2) How can individual colleges build the resilience required to pursue new positioning alternatives and partnerships when many have developed characteristics that appear to be inhibiting rather than enhancing resilience? That is, during times of prosperity they have operated in ways that have made it difficult to respond effectively to conditions resulting from a changing environment. This second question serves as the focal point for analysis of community college positioning and partnerships in the 1990s.

Managing Organizational Transition

One reason for the vulnerability of community colleges to paradoxes inherent in the competing demands of external groups is the loss of resilience caused by mismanagement of transitions in the organizational life cycle. Transitions occur when there is a mismatch between environmental conditions, institutional strategic decisions, and positioning strategies pursued. These mismatches usually arise from changes in the external environment that alter constituency expectations and mandate new public policy initiatives or from self-generated changes in colleges.

Faculty and administrators spend a considerable amount of time managing "policy" and "process" in the academic organization. This attention to process may subvert attention to imperatives for institutional development implicit in changing external conditions. When opportunities for development are lost through inattention, neglect, or patterned responses to changing conditions, resilience will diminish. Environmental conditions such as demographic transition, changing federal spending priorities, tax reform, and advancing technology precipitate change in the postsecondary education needs and expectations of external constituencies. Through strategic decisions affecting programs and services, tuition, academic standards, and educational delivery systems, college faculty and administrators can either satisfy or fail to satisfy constituency needs. If institutions fail to respond to changing needs and expectations over an extended period of time, new public policy initiatives may reshape institutional decisions in accord with external needs. Resilience will diminish as external public policy initiatives shape both the context in which decisions are made and the outcome of the decision process.

To illustrate, community colleges choosing to respond to declining state revenues through across-the-board reductions in academic program budgets during a period of technological change and rising expectations for technical education could spawn state agency policy initiatives for quality assurance. In the absence of adequate internal controls, a transition in the organizational life cycle would occur as state agencies seeking to expand their influence over resource allocation decisions impose tightened accountability standards and formula approaches to bugdeting. A reexamination of positioning alternatives would be necessary to enable colleges to stabilize institutional resources in a changing public policy context.

The organizational transitions that community colleges will

need to manage in the future to avoid paradoxes implicit in public policy are the following:

1. *Public Cognition of the Social Adaptation Role Performed by Community Colleges.* National discussion of the ambiguous mission and role of community colleges focuses too simplistically on expansion of the mission without concomitant attention to the social factors underlying expansion. It is clear that community colleges have performed a social adaptation role by making postsecondary education available to learners who, if otherwise unserved, could become a source of social unrest. It is also clear that community colleges will continue to perform this role in the future as the pace of technological change quickens and as major changes occur in the structure of social institutions such as the family, government, and the economy; consequently, this role needs to be better understood and articulated. Further, the social adaptation role needs to be documented through examination of institutional capacity to reduce the gulf between individual aspirations and objective social circumstances. Administrators will need to quantify institutional performance in adapting individuals to change in American social institutions through attention to issues such as generational poverty, structural change in the labor market, advancing technology, changing government spending priorities, demographic transition, and vacillation in the performance of the economy.

2. *Redefinition of "Finished Products."* Concentration on the production of academic degrees as a measure of effectiveness in community colleges diverts attention from the public service mission of the institution. One of the major transitional challenges facing faculty and administrators in the 1990s will be how to document cost-benefits produced through the flexible delivery system characteristic of public service organizations in an era of burgeoning expectations for quality and academic reform—concepts best understood through assessment of institutional capacity to produce "finished products" through academic degrees. Nondegree programs and services are revenue generating and need-fulfilling forces. To resolve questions about productivity and quality, community colleges will need to develop compelling new definitions for "finished products" within the framework of a public service mission.

3. *Balance Between General Education and Technical Training in Academic Programs.* There is little flexibility in most academic programs for change in the distribution of course and credit requirements because community colleges have been adding faculty and courses since the late 1960s. The importance of flexibility in responding to changing labor market conditions and student preferences cannot be underestimated; consequently, major efforts will have to be made to renew program flexibility in the 1990s. Continuation of the status quo in the distribution of courses and credits will lead to the gradual deterioration of quality in academic programs as students experience excessive specialization in technical skills and underpreparation in general education. It will become imperative for academic administrators and faculty in community colleges to develop procedures and criteria for integration of general education and technical training to provide students with the broad range of skills necessary for both "access" and "success" in the labor market.

4. *Reconceptualization of Quality in the Context of Academic Renewal.* There will be a need for community college faculty and administrators to provide new conceptualization of quality as well as criteria for quality assessment. Institutional performance in preparing technically proficient graduates for the labor market or academically proficient students for four-year colleges is only one criterion for quality. A broadened notion of quality will be desirable in community colleges in which the concept achieves recognition as a reflection of institutional capacity to undertake periodic renewal through production of benefits that satisfy changing constituency needs given variable resource conditions.

5. *Velocity of Institutional Responsiveness to Changing Needs and Expectations.* Patterns of institutional response to changing constituency needs will undergo severe stress in a period of technological change. Top-down governance mechanisms in community colleges have been action-oriented rather than deliberative and are ill-equipped for enhancement of morale among faculty and staff. The internal politics of resources allocation are intense; multiple sources of information in the decision process are required to assess complex dimensions of social change and to determine appropriate targets for spending. For example, under a number of collective bargaining contracts, decisions guiding the allocation of

resources to programs and services in response to constituency needs is clearly a management prerogative. Yet faculty maintain up-to-date information on trends in the labor market, and, if permitted to contribute to planning and resource allocation decisions, could tailor the response of the institution to environmental conditions. Top-down governance procedures that determine institutional response to changing constituency needs are likely to prove futile in the absence of information provided by faculty that can be used to temper responsiveness in accord with emerging environmental conditions.

6. *Dualism in the Organizational Structure.* Existing divisions between faculty and administrators in governance and among faculty in the delivery of educational services will intensify as community colleges broaden their public service mission. There will be little opportunity to free administrators and faculty from the forces that divide them until efforts are made to involve faculty in strategic decisions that determine institutional priorities in resource allocation. Most administrators are not prepared for the consequences that will follow from expanded faculty involvement in decision making. Individual expectations for rapid decisions in the development of new partnerships with external organizations may need to be scaled down. On the other hand, faculty involved in decisions that affect the flow of students and resources to academic programs may prove surprisingly adept at achieving closure on decisions when the alternative is reduction or reallocation. Without substantial involvement of faculty in networking with public and private-sector organizations, administrators cannot expect to construct educational partnerships that will be the driving force for community college programming in the 1990s.

7. *Breadth and Depth of Institutional Relationships with Public and Private-Sector Organizations.* It will be difficult to overestimate the need for partnerships with external organizations that will increase institutional flexibility. Decisions to open new partnerships or to expand existing partnerships will only be one aspect of this strategy. Community colleges will also need to examine their budgetary, control, and planning procedures with the intent of increasing their organizational capacity to respond to new opportunities. Faculty and administrators will need to strive to develop a consistent philosophy regarding the depth and breadth of rela-

tionships with public and private-sector organizations. This philosophy should at once protect the integrity of the institution taking into account its history, culture, and operational procedures and provide realistic answers to the following questions:

- What are the short- and long-term benefits and liabilities of partnerships with public and private-sector organizations?

- What are the consequences for faculty of expanded or new partnerships?

- What is the impact of new partnerships with noneducational organizations on relationships with traditional revenue providers?

- What changes (positive or negative) will occur in the public perception of the mission and effectiveness of community colleges through new or expanded partnerships with private-sector organizations?

8. *Planning Strategies with Operational Meaning.* Within environmental constraints and a philosophy guiding relationships with external organizations, community colleges will need to develop planning strategies with operational meaning in the 1990s. If one can assume that there is a hierarchy of outcomes relative to planning, budgeting, marketing, enrollment, and revenue procurement, each institution will need to be specific enough to develop planning strategies that produce desired results in terms of specific goals developed by faculty and administrators. The adoption of precisely stated planning strategies will lead to the identification of value dimensions along which partnerships with external organizations can be developed and evaluated. Without such a synthesis, the institution will be solely a product of its environment, not the shaper of it.

Positioning Community Colleges for the Future

What are the implications of these transitions for community college positioning in the 1990s? It would seem that community colleges have not exercised the full range of positioning alternatives available to them with external organizations. This is particularly ironic since positioning strategies are one aspect of management that institutions can shape to a considerable extent. Problems related to positioning will not be fully resolved until community colleges assess the benefits, liabilities, and resource conditions associated with different alternatives.

A good start toward assessment of benefits and liabilities would be to pay careful attention to five critical questions:

1. Does the alternative contribute toward the effective management of transitions in the organizational life cycle?

2. Does the partnership alleviate resource problems facing the institution?

3. Does the institution receive the benefit of political leverage with funding sources as a result of new linkages?

4. Does the partnership lead to the formulation of new definitions of uniqueness which advantage the institution in resource decisions made by state and local agencies?

5. Does the institution receive direct and indirect benefits (e.g., enrollment and revenue gains) through cooperation with competitor organizations?

Based on the concepts of paradox, public policy, and organizational transition presented earlier, community colleges with a comprehensive program/service mix maintain three basic positioning alternatives that can be pursued with public- and private-sector organizations. They are the centrist approach, providing an unchanging core of traditional programs and services to a broadly defined population; the adaptive approach, providing a changing array of customized programs and services to narrowly defined constituencies; and the symbiotic approach, providing a carefully defined mix of programs and services in direct cooperation with regional public and private-sector organizations.

The centrist approach has the advantage of presenting a concise institutional image to the public based on commonly understood functions that are the hallmark of community college education. These functions include transfer preparation, occupational education, and remediation. As a positioning alternative, the organization employing a centrist approach probably functions best in a public policy context marked by relative stability in the labor market, steady economic growth, and constancy in the value of the associate degree. Influence for organizations employing this approach in resource acquisition is predicated on the ability of faculty and administrators to demonstrate efficient performance in the production of educational benefits (degrees and certificates), which are valued by general segments of the population because of historical prestige assigned to the benefits.

Community colleges selecting the adaptive approach are those that function best in a public policy context marked by dynamic change in economic conditions, demographic trends, technology, and social needs. This positioning alternative is predicated on organizational characteristics of flexibility in the decision system, discretionary income for program development, and visionary management focused on strategic planning. Administrators in colleges with these characteristics are able to obtain and manage information about public policy conditions that enable the institution to acquire resources through a quick response to emerging needs. Presidents and deans use their knowledge of emerging industry needs and labor market conditions, for example, to develop new courses and curricula, to allocate and reallocate resources, and to develop marketing literature and field contacts to shape the attitudes of key corporate decision makers. The adaptive organization is a constantly changing organization that will acquire resources on the basis of its ability to gauge accurately the direction and velocity of social change.

Institutions interested in the symbiotic approach draw power and resources through the relationships they build with public and private-sector organizations in the service region. Linkages established with business and industry in the development of technical programs, placement of graduates, design of facilities, training of faculty, and acquisition of equipment add to the stature of the institutions both in the resources they apply to instruction and the image they present to the community. As a positioning alternative, symbiosis can be applied successfully in a number of different public-policy contexts. Its benefits would be most clearly realized, however, in the context of resource scarcity when competitive programs and services offered by four-year colleges blur the image presented by community colleges. Using symbiosis to draw upon financial, technical, and political resources of community organizations, two-year colleges can: (1) enhance their appeal to student markets through provision of up-to-date technical programs reflecting a direct linkage of education and work; and (2) stabilize or improve the acquisition of revenue from funding sources through political leverage applied to elected officials. Symbiotic relationships help community colleges establish uniqueness and visibility for academic programs. They also provide the college with a channel of influence to policymakers and funding sources.

Emerging Partnerships

Colleges facing uncertain resource conditions, accelerating calls for accountability, obsolescence associated with advancing technology, and pressure for academic reform must concentrate on new dimensions of uniqueness through symbiosis with external organizations. Why should the symbiotic organization assume primacy among community colleges in the 1990s? What type(s) of partnerships should be developed as part of this alternative and with what organizations? Community colleges have historically maintained a strong tradition of public service with local groups and organizations. The very term "community" implies a public service orientation to educational programming and a willingness to alter delivery systems to meet local needs. This orientation and response flexibility comprise the foundation for development of a new power base for community colleges based on public service partnerships with public and private-sector organizations.

Some public service partnerships suggested for development in the 1990s are the following.

Business/Industry Partnerships

The emphasis here should be on program development and renewal through continuous exchange with business and industry. Community colleges would attempt to negate the need for industry-developed training programs through direct efforts to match curricula with identified training needs. Faculty would be injected into industry positions on a rotational basis while industry professionals would assume the teaching loads of faculty. Courses and curricula would be altered in accord with changing technology and labor market needs on the advice of industry professionals as would equipment inventories and instructional strategies. Academic governance as a process would broaden to encompass direct input from industry in turn for industry cooperation and support in marketing and recruiting, resource development, planning and research, curriculum development, student placement, financial aid, and professional development for faculty.

K–12 Partnerships

As the academic reform movement places pressure on educational institutions to improve student learning outcomes and as demographic data suggest a continuing decline in the number of high school graduates, K–12 school systems will be able to dictate actions that nonselective colleges will need to take to enroll students. Services heretofore considered for implementation only at the time students enroll in college will be extended to high school students in grades 10–12. Community colleges operating in a public service mode will need to provide leadership for this effort through determination of K–12 information needs. Based on periodic assessment, cooperative programs for aptitude testing, academic advisement, and career development could be developed by community college and K–12 staff and implemented with specific cohorts of K–12 students.

Service Organization Partnerships

Although research data are largely suspect, the increasing dependence of community colleges on state revenue and the growing

research, to governance, and to partnerships with external organizations that will result in new resources.

References

ALFRED, RICHARD L. "Emerging Issues in Public Policy and Financial Administration." In Campbell, Tole (ed.), *New Directions for Community Colleges: Strengthening Financial Management.* San Francisco: Jossey-Bass, June, 1985.

BENNIS, W. G. "Organizational Developments and the Fate of Bureaucracy." Address, American Psychological Association, September 1964.

Carnegie Council for Policy Studies. *Three Thousand Futures.* San Francisco: Jossey-Bass, 1980.

COHEN, ARTHUR M. Unpublished correspondence, October 1984.

COHEN, M. D., and MARCH, J. G. *Leadership and Ambiguity: The American College President.* New York: McGraw-Hill, 1974.

RICHARDSON, RICHARD C. "Open Access and Institutional Policy: Time for Re-examination." *Community College Review* 10(4) (Spring, 1983): 47–51.

WEICK, KARL E. "Education Organizations as Loosely Coupled Systems." *Administrative Science Quarterly*, No. 21, 1976.

11

Community Colleges, Local and Regional Development, and the Drift toward Communiversity

S.V. MARTORANA and EILEEN KUHNS

. . . we see a new dynamic developing between
postsecondary education and the society it serves.

Can institutions defined only by access and growth continue to
maintain themselves? The question calls attention to two distin-

230

guishing features of the "community college movement" which evolved during the first three-quarters of this century and came to climax with the "boom" of the 1960s. One was the commitment to *access* to higher education as explained by expressions commonly found in the literature. The other actually reflected the success achieved in the first. The people of America were ready for and needed the community college *service;* their response produced an unparalleled growth in numbers of institutions and attendance.

It was the appeal and quality of the service these institutions were providing that generated the positive response. The community colleges' commitment to access was a social service whose time had come. The result was a social occurrence of solid substance and not a fad or passing fancy or temporary phenomenon, as some decriers of the early emergence of the junior college and associate degree predicted. As long as open-access, comprehensive, multiple-service, postsecondary educational institutions provided a bona fide social function they found it easy to maintain themselves and to grow.

Is there a new function that community colleges can perform which, because of its substantive social service, will evoke continued public support and perhaps even acclaim? We believe that there is and that it will enhance community and regional development through a coordinated, as opposed to scattered, operation of the resources dedicated to education, training, and culture in the area. In the rest of this chapter we discuss this new coordinated level of social service and why we view it as one of high promise. We also indicate why it will generate new issues for leaders of community colleges to face and what those issues are.

A lengthy discourse could be written on the subject of "community or local/regional development" and its importance to the American social order of the twenty-first century. We will not pursue this undertaking here. For our purposes, "community development" refers to the advancement of the "good health" of a locality or region in all respects—economic, cultural, social, political—and the contribution to a better "quality of life" for the citizens who reside in it.

Current Strategic Place of Community Colleges in Local/Regional Development

At least four conditions give community colleges special advantages in serving as resources for local and regional development: (1) the number and geographic spread of locations of these institutions; (2) their dedication to community service and development; (3) the comprehensiveness of these programs; and (4) the grassroots nature of the constituencies who support them.

Number and Geographic Spread

There is an associate degree-granting college in every congressional district in the United States. Many are found clustered in large urban centers of population, but others serve relatively small cities, and a good number are considered "rural" community colleges. Viewed collectively, they constitute a network for action in public service that is not matched by any other similar aggregations of institutions or resources. This aggregation is not as large in number or as splintered in structure as the common schools (Grades K–12) when viewed as a network. It is at least as large and clearly covers more area of the nation than the four-year colleges and universities when viewed collectively. If common themes emerge for action across the nation to help local and regional development (and in the process, of course, help to strengthen the nation as a whole), the means for a systematic way to disseminate the concept nationwide and to formulate related programmatic action is at hand.

Two action programs developed in recent years by the American Association of Community and Junior Colleges (AACJC) serve to illustrate both the recognition and the use of the community colleges scattered over the nation as a network for action. One is the coordinated action of promoting local community forums on issues of national significance that Edmund J. Gleazer, Jr., then president of AACJC, set in motion in the early 1970s. The other is the recently established program, "Putting America Back to Work," inspired by Dale Parnell shortly after his assumption of the association's presidency.

Dedication to Community Development

From its beginning, the community college movement saw community improvement as one of its purposes. Early scholars analyzing the emergence of junior colleges and their gradual evolution to community colleges saw that commitment to community service was the distinguishing feature of the new institution. In his study of the emergence of the junior colleges, Koos documented the fact that these institutions saw as one of some twenty officially stated goals the "improvement of the community of location" (Koos, 1921, p. 17). It was not until the late 1940s, however, that the colleges' identification as broadly based resources for community development was sufficient to bring about the change of name to community colleges on a widespread basis.

The community service component of the community college has created problems as well. It has not always been easy to reconcile programs aimed at serving community groups and the community at large with others aimed at traditional collegiate services to individual students (Martorana and Piland, 1985).

Comprehensiveness of Program

Claims to be contributing effectively to all aspects of local/regional development would be hard to make if a college acted from a narrow base of programs and services. Community colleges typically attempt to provide for enhancement of social and cultural features of the locality as well as economic and political ones. In so doing, they gain a double perspective which strengthens their potential for effective community betterment. On the one hand, they can identify and appreciate the full range of consumer needs in each of these areas of human endeavor, that is, they can relate to individual students in terms of economic, social, cultural, and political development—a service to holistic human development. Thus, individual students wanting to grow in only one or a few but not all of these areas can be accommodated. On the other hand, community colleges can relate to other organizations and institutions in the locality (museums, theaters, concert halls, etc.) that also seek to serve the local constituencies through a more focused activity.

Strength of Grassroots Support

A wide range of evidence indicates that community colleges are much appreciated by the constituencies they serve. The strongest evidence, of course, is the fact that they are well attended. In the face of predicted declines, total enrollment in these institutions has held up longer than that in four-year colleges and universities. Moreover, enrollment of students who would be more attracted by open-access institutions is continuing to grow, even to predominate the student body.

Another indication of fundamental commitment is the consistent financial support provided to community colleges by their localities and the states. This support does not come automatically or even easily, but state and local commitment to finance community colleges keeps reasonably close pace with their needs (Wattenbarger and Mercer, 1985).

Not all of the evidence is in the form of enrollments and dollars. It is seen also in the pride expressed by localities, especially those where the institution is the only one in the area providing college-level programs. In such situations, there is usually an appreciation for the college that cuts across the whole community. In contrast, where other colleges exist along with a community college, the latter finds that its constituent base differs from that of the other colleges, and so some loss of contact with at least a part of the community results.

Current General Intent in Local/Regional Development

An interesting pattern of forces is producing both centralization and decentralization in American society. Often, the same causal development is generating social movement in both of those directions. For example, communications technology is making possible both a concentration of social attention and energy in an enterprise in a particular place (centralization) and dispersal of the individuals and groups involved in the enterprise (decentralization).

Futurists are not in complete agreement in this matter, but some claim that the wave of the future in society is toward more decentralization (Naisbitt, 1982). This prediction seems tenable in light of current trends in federal and state public policy and in the dynamics of local/regional action over the country.

Federal and State Governmental Policy Trends

Since the 1980 national election, federal public policy has been away from federal initiatives in social, economic, and cultural development and toward putting responsibility for such initiatives at state and local levels.

The result of these changes in public policy has been a spate of new programs among the states. Many of these have aimed at economic development and are designed to promote the shift in the American economic base from an older industrial/manufacturing economy to a "hi-tech" service economy. Pennsylvania has its "Ben Franklin Advanced Technology Center" program; Illinois has a program of "Economic Development Grants" and an "Advanced Technology Equipment Grant" program; New York and New Jersey have enacted legislation to promote special models or centers for "advanced technology"; and so on. The competition among the states for stimuli to new economic development using new technological knowledge can be described as the "war between the states" of the late twentieth century.

Critical Factors in Local/Regional Development

How localities and regions will fare in their development in the face of new conditions depends on many things beyond the influence of the broad public-policy directions described above. Some factors, while predictable in terms of their future presence, cannot be evaluated in terms of their future influence. One such factor is the changing demographic composition of the American population. While it is mathematically certain that in the next decades the American population will change drastically in the characteristics of race and age distribution, the effect of these changes on concepts of community and community living are hard to determine.

Aside from public policies aimed at economic development, federal and state policies having to do with taxation and local/home rule or control of government programs can also seriously affect local/regional development. Limitations on levels of tax authorized at local as opposed to state levels, for example, affect the capability of a locality to finance programs its wishes to promote. Home rule jurisdictions have the capability to use that condition in either way—to push local community development beyond or to keep it below what would be the case if the state had full jurisdiction.

Current State of Community Action in Local/Regional Development

The ability to face up to and conquer present-day problems and to move progressively to a better new time is characteristically American. Also characteristically American is the fact that conditions for such positive transition are being laid increasingly at the community and regional levels.

Documentation of the validity of this claim is found in the actions of leadership groups at local, regional, and state levels. No comprehensive summary, analysis, or description of the extent and nature of the local and regional development action programs is at hand. Were one available, it would need to cover the many actions aimed at economic development. It would need to recognize the many efforts at community betterment such as the "Neighborhood Watch," local antidrug campaigns, and organized concern for the homeless. It would also have to include a wide array of others focusing on improvement of educational and training programs such as are occurring in the Warren and Forest County Area of Northwest Pennsylvania and elsewhere.

Types of Connections

In the course of these actions in community and regional development, new coalitions and linkages among organizations and institutions are being created. Because the thrust in development is so often directed at economic improvement, the rapidly growing number of cases of business and industrial enterprises being joined with college programs and services is not surprising. Despite some concerns that these connections will be a two-edged sword and bring some negative as well as positive consequences (Martorana and Garland, 1983), coalitions of community colleges with business and industry are now widespread and growing.

Community colleges also are increasingly under pressure to join with other kinds of institutions and centers of education and training in their localities. This type of interorganizational action at first glance would appear to be a natural one. The expectation, however, is not found in practice. Connections even with lower school systems are often weak and in some cases virtually inconsequential in terms of outcomes. Functional associations of community colleges with other postsecondary institutions to achieve this goal are also rare. This condition exists because the historical stance expected of schools and colleges is for each system or institution to concentrate on its own defined mission and services.

But new forces are pushing community colleges and other educational institutions to plan and act more collectively and cooperatively to serve their purposes more effectively and, hence, to make the localities they serve better places in which to live. Concerns about efficient use of resources are causing state higher education agencies to put pressure on colleges to work together in local or regional configurations. In California the tripartite organizational system for providing postsecondary education by levels (community colleges, state university system, University of California system) is now being questioned as a proper base for determining need for programs, for gathering and analyzing data meaningfully, and for allocating resources. Against such purposes some voices are claiming that the concept of three segments (each with its component institutions viewed from common, *statewide* perspectives) is not feasible when regional needs in the state are the concern in planning. Rather, an examination of community and regional needs and data in terms of such configurations as urban, rural, or other bases is needed to differentiate among the several parts of the state.

Most states and multicampus university systems are considering such factors when information is being collected and operational issues resolved. Decisions about campus locations, opening new programs, and closing existing ones require looking to the larger area beyond particular institutions (Kuhns and Martorana, 1984). Regional planning is a functioning approach to decision making in higher education even though regionalism is not yet affecting the formal structure of higher education in several states in any significant way. This is true of both institutions located in urban areas and those in rural settings. The object of the collective approaches varies but the larger object is to enhance the local community or region—an objective that any community college sensitive to the full scope and meaning of its mission cannot ignore.

While regional planning and action have not generated significant change in the formal structure of postsecondary education in the states, it has generated considerable innovation in the informal or voluntary structure. As one correspondent said in reply to an inquiry about such development in her state, "We've got consortia all over the place!" Later in the chapter we will discuss the significance of this statement.

Defining the "Communiversity"

Given the complex of new forces operating in the society of the future, we see a new dynamic developing between postsecondary education and the society it serves. The dynamic, while preserving the need for the classically recognized services of instruction, research, and public service as the essentials to be provided by postsecondary education, will call for a stronger commitment to help improve the quality of social and economic life in the community and will enable the structure of institutions to be different from what now prevails. Gleazer sees the community college as "ideally suited to serving as the nexus" among agencies dedicated to community improvement (Gleazer, 1980, p. 10), but we see emergence of a new design by which the "nexus" function will be performed; this we suggest, will be the "communiversity."

The communiversity, while loosely structured, nonetheless will need to provide for linking together much more than universities, colleges, and schools; it must include clearly identified centers for education and training in organizations whose missions are not primarily educational. The communiversity will also serve to help community colleges and other postsecondary institutions to adopt a method of operation that will include other centers of learning.

The germ of this concept was first introduced by Martorana at a gathering of community college presidents in California in the mid-1960s (Martorana, 1965). The concept did not have a major impact at the time, but there was discussion of the idea. Since then, the concept has appeared in other places (Gould, 1970; Martorana and Kuhns, 1977) and is best expressed by Gould in his book, *Today's Academic Condition* (1970), in which he includes a section called "Enter the Communiversity." In it he says:

> The university of the future, as I envision it, will be a loose federation of all the educational and cultural forces of a community—at every age level. It will be a coordinated educational entity serving a single, fairly large community, or single, compact region if a group of communities is more appropriate. Whether it will have a single name or even be called a university any longer, it's hard to say. Parts of it will undoubtedly have names similar to those they do now. But what we think of today as the college or the university will constitute only a portion of the future whole [p. 90].

Although at present there are no fully developed complexes or collectives of community colleges, other postsecondary educational institutions, and other closely related institutions, beginning forms of implementation of the communiversity concept are easy to see. They are evident in such current developments as the community education councils advocated by the New York State Board of Regents to coordinate local and regional adult and continuing education; the Warren/Forest Higher Education Council, which links the offerings and related services of 14 colleges and universities, two vocational schools, local public libraries, and business/industry training programs in a two-county area of Northwestern Pennsylvania; and a growing array of similar voluntary consortia or official contractual arrangements.

Emergence of the communiversity will cause changes in how community colleges, as part of the new construct, will operate. It will affect more of their internal operations, such as planning and allocation of resources. Consequences of such a development are easy to envision. A community college will deal less often with local, state, and federal governmental interests and agencies on a one-on-one basis; these relations will more often be conducted in a collaborative manner with other educational and related community service organizations in the locality.

We see the emergence of the communiversity as a development whose time has come. It will not be a revolutionary development in terms of rapidity of change. Instead, it will be the result of gradual change, a kind of organizational drift, which, amoeba-like, will slowly but powerfully touch and change the structure and operations of most postsecondary educational institutions. But the end result will be quite revolutionary in terms of impact on postsecondary education as now generally perceived, particularly among its many practitioners.

Goals of Communiversity Action

Communiversity collaborative operations have five primary goals:

1. To enhance the quality of life in a locality through the development of collective and coordinated action programs involving all of the cultural, educational, and training resources of the community.

2. To improve the efficiency and effectiveness of resources in response to the needs of the locality, and thereby to help the accomplishment of Goal 1.

3. To raise the level of public awareness, appreciation, and use of the collective resources as a means for improving the quality of life in the locality.

4. To bring about a better balance of a locality's reliance on the community's collective resources, not only when used for economic development but also when used for the purposes of social and cultural development.

5. To provide a mechanism for matching the educational, training, and cultural *needs* of the local community or region with the *resources* available throughout the locality.

Manifestations of the Trend

Throughout this discussion we have alluded to the growing practice of postsecondary educational institutions to join with other organizations in carrying out their functions of public service more efficiently and effectively. The growth trend is evident in several ways, but the most readily observed in terms of operational development is the increasing number of consortia in postsecondary education, regional planning applied to postsecondary education, and linkages with business and industry. Of significance, too, is that the reality of these operational developments and their significant consequences are attracting increasing notice among both practitioners and scholar researchers in the field.

As the comment from a state official quoted above reflects, higher education consortia appear in many forms throughout the land. In a period of continued study of their emergence during the 1950s and 1960s, Patterson identified two types: "voluntary," that is, ones that spring entirely from actions among colleges and universities; and "mandated," interinstitutional arrangements stemming from policies such as statewide plans promulgated by official state agencies responsible for postsecondary education (Patterson, 1978). Over a hundred consortia have sought listing in the Higher Education Publication *1986 Higher Education Directory*. According to data compiled by the Council in Interinstitutional Consortia, there are some 300 formally organized consortia actually in operation.

Regional planning of postsecondary education is taking place under the auspices of various agencies at local, state, and interstate levels. An exhaustive baseline study of regionalism as a planning principle used in higher education by Martorana and Nespoli

(1980) reported a strong general acceptance of the concept in principle but a rather limited application of it in practice. Examination of the policy documents of state agencies such as those published in recent years by Florida, Minnesota, and Texas shows that the concept continues to be promoted steadily (Martorana and Kuhns, 1985).

Connections with business and industry usually involve more formal contractual arrangements between community colleges and corporations. Most are negotiated to assure production of a supply of trained workers needed by the corporate enterprise. Although using the formal, contracted approach more heavily than do the consortia and the structure for cooperation created in regional planning, these arrangements with business and industry make heavy use of business/industry/education advisory groups, affiliations with local Private Industry Councils (PIC), and structural tie-ins with local entities such as those required by agencies that administer the federal Job Training Partnership Act (JTPA).

These manifestations of the trend toward implementing the concept of communiversity are notable for several reasons. They are forcing greater attention to local area and regional needs. Simultaneously, they are generating examination of ways that education and training can be provided in less traditional ways. They tend to decentralize the educational enterprise, to stress outreach and diversity of programs, to encourage new uses of technology, and to extend involvement of other legitimate interests in policy decision making.

Yet these approaches also have some clear limitations. Chief among these is that they generally cover only a part of the total complex of resources available to serve a region. Even regional plans thus far promulgated show coverage usually of only college and university programs, leaving out secondary schools, proprietary institutions, libraries, hospitals, and museums. An even greater weakness of the manifestations of communiversity thus far developed is that they are usually controlled either totally (as in the case of the voluntary consortia) or at least partially (as in the others described above) by the colleges involved (Martorana and Kuhns, 1985, 1986). This fact begs the question we have raised in other places about the need for a stronger and more independent citizens' voice to be involved in determining the areas' needs and in coordinating the resources that can respond to them.

In order to counteract these deficiencies, we have elsewhere suggested a new model for regional planning in postsecondary education and for implementation of the communiversity concept. The two key elements in this model are (1) a citizens' council, independent of all "providers" of education, training, and cultural institutions and organizations in a region, that would act as facilitator of deployment of their programs; and (2) an advisory task force of personnel who represent each of the providers involved in the region (Martorana and Kuhns, 1984).

Role of the Community College

As one pursues an examination of the concept of communiversity and regional planning, one is impressed by the way that glimpses of recognition of the concept are emerging in the literature. We have already mentioned Gould's (1970) definition, as a sharpening of the concept suggested by Martorana in 1965, and we have noted Gleazer's (1980) notion of "nexus" as the role of the community development. Against this background we find the following observation and statement by Feldman to be particularly meaningful and an excellent transition to our discussion of issues that the concept of communiversity will likely raise for the leaders of community colleges. Referring to an idea raised by Pifer, Feldman (1985) writes:

> In his landmark speech to the convention of the American Association of Community and Junior Colleges in 1974, Alan Pifer introduced the concept of the hub, suggesting that community colleges should not think of themselves as a static sector of the educational establishment but rather as the hub of a network of institutions and community agencies—high schools, industry, the church, voluntary agencies, youth groups, even the prison system and the courts. Pifer proposed that community colleges begin to use what these other groups have to offer on the one hand and to serve and strengthen them on the other.

The hub metaphor is helpful, but it conveys a more static kind of role than a fifth generation may require. The educational system of the future may be less systematic—something of a non-system. The centers of initiative in education will continue to multiply—electronically equipped households, churches, museums, youth groups, factories, and offices, proprietary schools, apprenticeships, schools and colleges, and many more. And running in and around and through these entities like glue will be the presence of the community college—sometimes supplementing these other resources, sometimes strengthening them, sometimes moving boldly into a gap, sometimes withdrawing from a field in which alternatives are adequate, sometimes certifying the educational results achieved by other institutions of learning environments [p. 193].

Implications and Issues for Community Colleges

Our vision of the future, where community colleges are more than just the "hub," but indeed a catalytic force within the "communiversity," is fraught with implications and issues for the community college and its further evolution. We suggest that the most critical issues that these institutions must face are these:

1. *The issue of leadership.* Will persons in positions to "call the shots" for community colleges see a purpose and a promise in the role they can play in working with other community, educational, social, and cultural resources for community betterment? Will they exert their leadership and talents and energies to promote it? All of the other issues we can think of are related to this one and will be resolved depending on the way this one is dealt with. We agree with Feldman (1985) that "how and with whom community colleges form linkages will be major policy issues as community college administrators weigh alternative future programs and priorities."

2. *The issue of legitimacy.* Our research suggests that the major problem that confronts implementations of the concept of communiversity is its positive acceptance by the academic enterprise at large. Here is where the community college's special advantages

of location, commitment to community development, comprehensiveness of service, close relations to local leadership in all spheres, and tradition of innovation can make it the needed catalyst for action. Will current and future leaders of community colleges see this as a new opportunity for growth and development and, therefore, act to promote acceptance and implementation of the concept or will they ignore or oppose the possibility?

3. *The issue of control.* Implied in the two foregoing issues is the question of control of academic policies and programs. There is no doubt that entering into any kind of a cooperative arrangement with other organizations involves some yielding of unitary power in order to promote a larger collective good. That is, we believe, the thinking from which Gould drew the term "loose federation" in his definition of communiversity. Community colleges have special advantages that can help to make them effective catalysts for shaping communiversity action for community and regional development. They can be strong members of the federation. However, they cannot realistically expect to control it.

Earlier efforts to improve *vertical* articulation linking school systems, community colleges, and four-year colleges and universities provided ample evidence of the numbing effect of an institution's perceived threat to its own control of academic decisions. The perceived threat may cause refusal to enter into communiversity actions or to demand retention of an undue level of control. Both types of action would be a hindrance to implementation of the concept. This problem consistently confronts consortia and contributes to difficulty in their operations. Under the communiversity concept, with the increase in not only vertical but also horizontal linkages with organizations whose primary function is not education, those fearful about loss of control over academic matters will be further threatened.

4. *The issue of financial support.* Conventional methods of financing postsecondary education do not give positive support to interorganizational ventures. This is true even when all of the participants are colleges, universities, and school systems, that is, institutions designed for educational purposes. The lack of a suitable way to finance cooperative ventures becomes even more a problem when noneducational organizations are involved. Can new

ways to finance communiversity actions be found? Will community college leadership in all key constituent groups, such as trustees, administrators, and faculty, help to formulate them and to promote their funding?

Other questions concerning finances are also serious. Formative cooperative arrangements require special fiscal support. Who finances the preliminary prototype formulations of coordinating mechanisms, policies for cooperation, the initial area needs assessment, and so on? Will community colleges help to provide or help to find the finances needed? How can assurance be given that financial support will be concentrated in the coordination effort and not applied to support the takeover of academic operations that continue to belong properly to the several cooperating institutions?

5. *The issue of public interpretation.* Who is to promote a broader public understanding and acceptance of the communiversity concept? This question evokes related issues of responsibility and authority. Are there already particular centers in the local community or region where responsibility for this can be placed? Is the community college one of these? Is it alone, or one of several? Do any of these have an existing formal authority to act? How far does it extend, or can it be extended, to help to reach other organizations to involve them in communiversity actions and to help get public acceptance of them? Constructive resolution of the issue of public interpretation is especially important because of the newness of the concept both in the educational enterprise and in public policy.

End Note

Can institutions defined only by access and growth continue to maintain themselves? Our suggestion is that community colleges can do so by becoming the leading catalytic force for advancing the concept of communiversity and promote change toward enhanced community and regional development. In that evolution we see them continuing their commitment to access and continuing to be comprehensive postsecondary institutions in program offerings while simultaneously establishing a new justification for recognition and growth.

References

FELDMAN, M. J. "Establishing Linkages with Other Educational Providers." In Deegan, W. L. and Tillery, D., and Associates, *Renewing the American Community College*. San Francisco: Jossey-Bass, 1985.

GLEAZER, E. G., JR. *The Community College: Values, Vision, and Vitality*. Washington, D.C.: American Association of Community and Junior Colleges, 1980.

GOULD, S. B. *Today's Academic Condition*. New York: McGraw-Hill, 1970.

KOOS, L. V. *The Junior College*. Research Publications of the University of Minnesota, Education Series #5, Vol. I, 1921.

KUHNS, E., and MARTORANA, S. V. *Quality Beyond the Campus*. Washington, D.C.: Council on Postsecondary Education, 1984.

MARTORANA, S. V. "The Expanding Responsibilities of Community Colleges." Paper presented at the Kellogg Community College Leadership Conference, University of California at Berkeley, June 1965.

MARTORANA, S. V. and GARLAND, P. H. "Public Policy for Economic Development: The Two-Edged Sword." *Community and Junior College Journal* 55(3) (1984): 16–19.

MARTORANA, S. V. and KUHNS, E. "The Challenge of the Communiversity." *Change* 9(2) (1977): 54–55.

———. "Cooperative Regional Planning and Action to Enhance Postsecondary Education Across State Lines." A report to the Fund for the Improvement of Postsecondary Education (FIPSE), Pennsylvania State University, Center for the Study of Higher Education, and The Catholic University of America, School of Education, 1984.

———. "The Public Policy Framework for Institutional Research Pertaining to Interorganizational Cooperation and Regional Planning in Higher Education." Paper read at Association for Institutional Research, Portland, OR, April 1985.

———. "Citizens' Voice and Effectiveness in Strengthening Higher Education Through Interorganizational Cooperation." Association for the Study of Higher Education, Annual Meeting, San Antonio, February 1986.

———. "The Changing 'Citizens' Voice' in Linking Community Colleges with Other Community Organizations." American Association of Community and Junior Colleges, Annual Convention, Orlando, Florida, April 1986.

MARTORANA, S. V., and NESPOLI, L. A. *Regionalism in American Postsecondary Education: Concepts and Practices*. Pennsylvania State University, Center for the Study of Higher Education, 1980.

MARTORANA, S. V., and PILAND, W. (eds). *New Directions for Community Colleges: Designing Programs for Community Groups*. San Francisco: Jossey-Bass, 1984.

PATTERSON, L. *1975 Consortia Directory*. Washington, D.C.: American Association for Higher Education, 1978.

Conclusion: Observations and Recommendations

How do we further establish community colleges as colleges of choice? The contributors offer suggestions that provide direction for realization of the framework of values discussed in their writing. These suggestions are intended to assist in thinking differently about the community college experience. They are intended to encourage creative envisioning for the future.

Collegiate Identity

Two issues emerged as a result of the various considerations of renewed collegiate identity in community colleges. These were institutional effectiveness and institutional climate.

Institutional Effectiveness

The contributors to this volume see future institutional effectiveness as primarily determined by our willingness to rethink our approach to student achievement and to curricular substance and structure. They acknowledge the value of access and the pivotal role of community colleges in the expansion of higher education during the past 25 years. They point out that growth in student enrollment constituted the primary basis for assessment of community colleges as effective institutions in the past. However, they are advocates for alternative approaches to measuring community college effectiveness in the future.

In the area of curriculum, the authors affirm their commitment to community college curricula that meet the needs of students seeking to achieve career, transfer, or lifetime education objectives. Yet, they are constructively critical of the adequacy of present curricular assumptions, structure, and substance to meet these needs. They maintain that the generally held distinction between transfer and terminal education is not current and that lifetime education needs to be addressed in relation to those conceptual, generic, and information skills required to master other specific skills needed for multiple careers and likely changes in the social, political, and cultural environment in which we live.

The authors see institutional effectiveness enhanced by:

1. Development of community college strategic initiatives at the local, state, and national levels to take leadership in establishing more demanding institutional standards of achievement rather than allowing other agencies, organizations, and institutions to create a reactive community college environment in dealing with this issue. They are calling for institutional control of institutional change.

2. Movement beyond an institutional posture of defensive rhet-oric about access to serious institutional study of how com-munity colleges can provide access and quality—a shift from an access orientation to an access-achievement orientation. This needs to include identification of institutional success indicators based upon carefully developed student achieve-ment standards.

3. Acknowledgment that access broadly defined needs to in-clude the baccalaureate. This calls for strengthening tradi-tional transfer efforts, expansion of the transfer education to further incorporate transfer from career programs, increased cooperation between and among two- and four-year institu-tions (creative and more comprehensive approaches to ar-ticulation), encouragement of immediate college entry upon completion of high school for those with baccalaureate ob-jectives, and differential educational goals for two- and four-year college attendees to improve and modify transfer programs.

4. Consideration of actual student attendance patterns in the development of curricular structure. As students continue to insist upon part-time, intermittent, nondegree education, they need curricular coherence and generic skill education in appropriately sequenced programs with meaningful goals and institutional support. Pieces of coherent programs may not themselves be coherent.

5. Reconsideration of the need for general education in com-munity colleges in a context distinct from the ongoing university-derived debate about general education and on-going community college conflicts over distribution require-ments. General education calls for evaluation of the capacities of greatest potential value to students functioning in an environment likely to be significantly different from the environment in which debates about general education take place.

6. An approach to organizing student experience in a commu-nity college that reflects commitment to curriculum *and* to

competency development. An "educational program" approach stresses the associate degree, the curriculum as a vehicle for student achievement of institutionally sanctioned competencies, and appropriately integrated support services. It should include a "shadow curriculum," which provides assistance to students in developing values, information skills, and decision-making skills.

7. Movement toward "college level learning"—learning at least characterized by the expectation that students will comprehend material beyond the twelfth-grade reading level. Practices that can lead to college-level learning include

- frequent complex writing assignments to encourage dealing with ideas and not just facts.

- student engagement with original or primary sources to improve research and problem-solving skills in order to understand and interpret familiar and unfamiliar phenomena.

- introduction to subject material that forms the basis of general or liberal education.

Institutional Climate

While fully cognizant of the limits of the influence a commuter college can have on a nonresidential, part-time student population, the authors nonetheless point out that the climate of a community college does affect students. They call for:

1. clearly conveyed messages regarding the primacy of cognitive activity in the college commitment to mission and purpose;

2. acknowledgment of institutional responsibility for student intellectual and moral growth;

3. an institutional climate that values its commitment to support services and community services, yet makes clear that its intellectual mission is of greatest seriousness and the es-

sential element by which the worth of all other activities is assessed.

Context—Defined Leadership

The issue of leadership emerged again and again as various authors struggled with the challenge of change in community colleges. Addressed implicitly and explicitly, it is clear that strong-minded leadership is viewed as essential to the future well-being of community colleges. Energy may be profitably invested in:

1. Articulation of a new relationship between faculty and administration, a new dialogue whereby both devote themselves to the effectiveness of community college education as an important shared responsibility carried out from a basis of shared values. This can diminish institutional dissonance between faculty and administration brought about by bureaucracy and hierarchy.

2. Emphasis on the intellectual dimension of administrative leadership through working with faculty in the determination of institutional intellectual values and through periodic classroom instruction by qualified administrators.

3. Developing administrative emphasis on the general effectiveness of the learning environment as distinct from the tendency to concentrate on management and efficiency issues independent of academic concerns. This includes awareness that what appear to be purely management issues have serious instructional consequences.

4. Strenthening awareness of the potential liabilities and opportunities associated with leadership: leaders cannot avoid cognitive bias present in their judgments; they lose ground by assuming that the reality of an organization is presented—not invented. Leaders benefit from awareness that the consent of followers is required for leadership. Leaders increase

their ability to influence others through awareness of their constructive power.

5. Acknowledging leadership responsibility for preservation of process as well as focus on issues. Process in educational organizations is valued as a manifestation of individual prerogative—or the absence thereof. While there is little consensus regarding modes of effective leadership, leaders are usually perceived as heroic figures at the core of institutional functioning. They are "in charge" of process.

6. Realizing that higher education today needs strong, decisive leadership characterized by a risk-taking orientation, clear articulation of direction, a preference for individualism rather than affiliation. Leaders are to be strong, bold, directive, confident, and speculative. Leaders are to have vision and to be visible; they are to be persistent and energetic.

7. Reestablishment of the legitimacy of presidential authority in higher education. We need to reassert our support and sanction for the office of the president and demand that it be occupied by assertive, forceful individuals.

A Future Orientation

The attention of the authors focused on anticipated changes in the capacities and talents students will need in the future and anticipated differences in future environments (as compared to the present) in which students will be living. They also considered new relationships community colleges themselves will develop with their respective environments. Specifically, the authors have examined the changing balance of work and leisure, the conceptual and applied skills required for future work and life, and approaches community colleges might take to other educational organizations, governmental entities, public agencies, and the private sector. The author saw the following issues as setting the agenda for community colleges:

1. Emphasis on education for service work, for worker satisfaction, and for making unemployed time fulfilling and leisure time meaningful. This includes education for a society in which work ceases to be central to values.

2. Education to equip students to deal with change. Education for anticipation—coming to grips with future changes and attempting to influence their development—is increasingly important. This includes education to identify signs of change and education for general skills and attitudes needed to adapt to new situations.

3. Education for full participation in civic life. This can and should accompany career education and liberal arts education. This includes acknowledgment of other current efforts to strengthen civic values and civic education. It encourages a creative combination of traditional curricula and student experience as a point of departure essential to educational effectiveness.

4. New forms of relationships between colleges and their communities:

   a. The "communiversity"—a loosely structured inter-organizational grouping for collective and cooperative action. This new dynamic developing between postsecondary education and the society it serves will be dedicated to improvement of the quality of social and economic life in a community. Community and regional development efforts will be enhanced by this configuration of institutions and forces in creative, dynamic interaction.

   b. Employment of several positioning alternatives to preserve community college organizational vitality through partnerships. This can result in preservation of resilience and responsiveness as well as capacity for organizational renewal. A centrist approach to positioning calls for an unchanging core of traditional programs and services to a broadly defined population. An adaptive approach provides a variety of customized programs and services to more narrowly defined constituencies. A symbiotic approach offers a carefully defined set of programs and services in cooperation with other public and private organizations.

Index